Praise for *America's Best Colleges for B Students*

"This book contains practical information for any student searching for the right college 'fit' instead of simply trying to 'fit in' at the wrong college. From this small college's perspective, the 'solid B' student has the same chance as an A student to be successful in an environment where each is encouraged to develop his/her potential."
— *Sandy Speed*
Dean of Admission and Financial Aid
Schreiner University

"This book offers practical information and advice for students and parents alike. There is a great school out there for you — *America's Best Colleges for B Students* will help you find it!"
— *Mark Campbell*
Vice-President for Enrollment Management
McKendree College

"At last, a college resource book for real students and real families. We hear so much about how only over achievers get into good schools that we forget that college isn't just about grades and tests scores; it's about learning, living and moving forward. This is something that all students need, regardless of their high school performance. Tamra Orr has given families the tools to help their young adults find the perfect college for them. An invaluable resource!"
— *Teri Brown*
Author of Day Tripping: Your Guide to Educational Family Adventures

"Tamra Orr's refreshingly candid approach to the college search dispels the fear that B students and their families often face. An easy yet information-packed read!"
— *Bethany Bierman*
Assistant Director, Office of Undergraduate Admissions
Augsburg College

"Many hard-working kids (this book calls them B students) don't think they're college material because they don't have high college boards or the highest grades. In short order, this book dispels that myth! Tamra Orr has gathered helpful insights and suggestions that will, thankfully, elevate the expectations of such students to achieve college success."
— *Patrick J. O'Brien*
Retired high school counselor, former Marquette Northern California admissions representative and current ACT ambassador

"This excellent 'advice' book is a must read for those students and their parents who want to understand and navigate the process and find the right match toward that important degree."
— *Karen P. Condeni*
Vice President and Dean of Enrollment
Ohio Northern University

"This book will be a terrific introduction to the college search process. The format offers helpful suggestions in a non-intimidating approach. For many high school students the college process becomes a seemingly insurmountable task. *America's Best Colleges for B Students* is a terrific introductory tool that outlines the basic steps to begin the college search process."
— *Amanda (Mandy) Warhurst Webster*
Senior Associate Director of Admission
Salve Regina University

"Tamra Orr's book is just what the 'not so perfect' student needs. The advice is to the point and incredibly useful. You don't have to attend a huge Ivy League school to get a superior education. Orr's book should be required reading for individuals of all ages who are thinking of attending college."
— *Sandra Roy*
Educator and author

"What really makes a great student great? Is greatness limited to a letter grade on paper or a score on the SATs? There is so much more that factors into it like the sincere desire to not only succeed in the classroom, but succeed in life. There are some outstanding institutions of higher learning that understand that reality and offer programs from which B students will benefit the most as well as learning services that help them become better students. By offering an in-depth analysis of the best schools catering to the needs of real world students, this book will go far in helping families identify the best schools that suit individual needs. Education is not 'one size fits all,' and this book helps explain that — and will help anyone in search of higher education find the 'right fit.'"
— *Jennifer A. Fiorentino*
Director, Public Relations & Communications
Dean College

"With humor and insight, Tamra Orr sets the record straight about college admission, offering practical advice and hope to college-bound students. This book makes the important point that the college admission process doesn't need to be fraught with stress and anxiety. Many bright, interesting teens that underperformed in high school will recognize themselves in the pages of this book. Orr guides students in how to explore colleges where they can find themselves and achieve as never before."
— *Joan Casey*
College Planning Consultant
Educational Advocates

"Finally! A guide for motivated late bloomers — solid students who in the right environment will flourish. Tamra Orr has done her homework to provide you with the guidance and tips you need to find the college that's right for you — and help you succeed once you're there. Pack your suitcase for adventure and bring your drive, energy and personal commitment to achieve!"
— *Esther Goodcuff*
Associate Vice President for Enrollment Management and Student Affairs
Adelphi University

America's Best Colleges for B Students

2nd Edition

A College Guide
for Students
without
Straight A's

By Tamra B. Orr

**America's Best Colleges for B Students: A College Guide for Students without Straight A's
2nd Edition**

By Tamra B. Orr

Published by SuperCollege, LLC
3286 Oak Court
Belmont, CA 94002
www.supercollege.com

Credits: Cover design TLC Graphics, www.TLCGraphics.com. Design: Monica Thomas.

Trademarks: All brand names, product names and services used in this book are trademarks, registered trademarks or tradenames of their respective holders. SuperCollege is not associated with any college, university, product or vendor.

Disclaimers: The author and publisher have used their best efforts in preparing this book. It is intended to provide helpful and informative material on the subject matter. Some narratives and names have been modified for illustrative purposes. SuperCollege and the author make no representations or warranties with respect to the accuracy or completeness of the contents of the book and specifically disclaim any implied warranties or merchantability or fitness for a particular purpose. There are no warranties which extend beyond the descriptions contained in this paragraph. The accuracy and completeness of the information provided herein and the opinions stated herein are not guaranteed or warranted to produce any particular results. SuperCollege and the author specifically disclaim any responsibility for any liability, loss or risk, personal or otherwise, which is incurred as a consequence, directly or indirectly, of the use and application of any of the contents of this book.

ISBN: 1932662227

ISBN-13: 9781932662221

Manufactured in the United States of America

10 9 8 7 6 5 4 3 2 1

Cataloging-in-Publication Data
Tamra B. Orr
   America's Best Colleges for B Students: A College Guide for Students without Straight A's
   2nd Edition
      p. cm.
   Includes appendices and index.
   ISBN 1932662227
   1. College Admission I. Title
   2. Reference   3. Education

To my kids who brighten my life, my husband who enriches my life and my parents who gave me life.

Table of Contents

Foreword

If the prospect of receiving an A- in AP calculus keeps you up at night, this book is not for you. If, on the other hand, you are ecstatic about scoring that B in English, this book is exactly what you need!

One of the greatest myths about a college education is that you need to have straight A's or be the class valedictorian to get into an excellent college. The truth is that there are terrific colleges out there that want you — whether you are a B student or, gasp, even a C student. But don't assume that these colleges are looking for slackers. Quite the opposite: These schools know that good students don't always perform at their true potential in high school. For example:

- Maybe you didn't take high school seriously and only now have come to realize the importance of doing well academically.

- Maybe you managed your time poorly or were overcommitted with a job or activities.

- Maybe you were distracted by events in your life beyond your control.

- Maybe you were just bored with high school.

Whatever the reason, these schools know that your grades and test scores are not always reflective of who you are and how well you will do in college. So, if you are now committed to getting a college education and are willing to put in the time and effort to be a successful student, these colleges want you.

The key is: How do you find these colleges? What do you need to look for to make sure that you will excel? And how do you show the college that you are serious about getting a great education and will be an asset to their student body?

That's where this book will help. Here are just a few of the things that you will learn:

- How to identify colleges that accept students with less than perfect grades and test scores.

- What characteristics to look for in a college to ensure that you succeed academically as well as socially.

- How to best position yourself — both the positives and negatives — in the college application, essay and interview.

- Ways to pay for your education. (Scholarships are not just reserved for the A students. There are literally thousands also available for students based on non-academic skills and talents.)

- Tips for making that sometimes difficult transition from high school to college.

Tamra Orr has written this book just for you. She has been there, done that as a student like you without perfect grades or test scores. She knows there is no shame in being a B student. (In fact, Tamra knows how to present this as a huge positive to a college!) She also knows that just because you may not be in the "Ivy-League-Wannabe" crowd doesn't mean you are not motivated and committed to being successful.

Let her help you find that perfect college! We wish you the best in your journey!

— Gen and Kelly Tanabe
Authors of nine books on college planning including *Get into Any College* and *Get Free Cash for College*

Introduction

Once upon a time, long, long ago, almost anyone who wanted to go to college and could find a way to afford it went to college. SAT just meant the past tense of "sit" and GPA was an odd combination of letters that might have been a neat abbreviation for "Grandpa." After World War II, tests and test scores started to gain in importance, but it would be some time before they would become the determining factor behind going to college. Sure, if you had a great SAT score or a really high GPA, it was easier to get scholarships or get the really BIG colleges to give you more than a glance. But I remember applying to colleges without much thought at all about my numbers (I'm dating myself now, as that was back in the late 1970s). I was too busy scoping out the campus, checking the ratio of guys to girls and, oh yeah, seeing what majors were offered. (I must say, however, that 30 years later, I can STILL tell you my SAT scores.)

The picture is quite different today. Getting into college is not only more expensive but also much tougher. Colleges have become so selective that even valedictorians with a 4.0 average and perfect SAT scores are being turned away from some of the Ivy League institutions.

Because of this, many students are ready to throw their hands in the air and say, "Ok, I get it! I don't have good enough numbers, so I obviously can't go to college. I'll just forget it!" If you are among these, realize this: You, yes YOU, are the reason for this book. It is designed to give you two things: help with what it takes to get into many colleges (and an overview of what happens after you do) and leads on which colleges are eagerly awaiting your application.

For starters, get rid of the myths/assumptions you might have about choosing a college. If you believe any of the following, take them from the "The Earth is Round" list (truth) and put them in the "Santa Claus/ Tooth Fairy" list (fantasies). Here we go:

- You need a perfect GPA or SAT to get into a good college.

- The best way to pick a college is by reading the rankings in a magazine article/taking your best friend's recommendation/ choosing the names you recognize the most.

- Traditional four-year colleges are the only ones employers will accept.

- Only the large colleges are worth attending.

■ Your college should have more students than your high school does.

■ Small colleges offer inferior classes, faculty and degrees.

None of these above statements is true.

■ A perfect score or transcript is not required at most colleges, as you will see as you read this book.

■ The best way to select a college is to *not* accept someone else's opinion as absolute truth and to do your homework (yes, MORE homework) and find out which colleges best suit you and your preferences.

■ While four-year colleges are the norm, there are many two-year programs and other options that are just as appealing to future employers.

■ Small colleges often offer the conditions and student/teacher ratio that will ensure a high-quality, successful education. In no way are their classes, faculty or degrees inferior to those of the larger universities.

One of the biggest myths of all about college, of course, is that even if you find one that you like and will accept you, you will not be able to afford it. We will dispel that myth as well in Chapter Six.

You, standing right there in the middle of the library or bookstore (or at home scanning the intro because your parents told you, "READ THIS!"), you with the 2.9 or 3.1 GPA or the 1560 new SAT score or 19 composite ACT, *can* go to a college or university. You can find yourself at a wonderful institution where you will make friends, have fun, grow up and yeah, learn a lot of stuff and get a degree. These colleges are not runners-up to the "good" places; they are wonderful schools that are willing to look beyond the numbers to the person standing behind them. They have admissions departments that give your scores some thought, and then put them down and search for the human being on the other side of the digits. And really, isn't that what you would want them to do anyway? You are certainly more than any group of numbers could possibly represent.

This book was written to guide you to lots of helpful information about 100 colleges and universities that want you to be a part of their student population. It will also show you how to:

- Make the best use of the time you still have left in high school

- Make a great impression on the college admissions department through both the essay and interview

- Explain those less-than-stellar numbers and let your strengths shine through

- Survive in college once you get there

Belonging is one of the strongest natural drives inside each and every person. You want to find a college where you are happy, comfortable and accepted. The administrations of these colleges want students who feel like they have found a new home. Let this book be your guide to that relationship.

SECTION

CHOOSING

How to Choose the Right College for You

CHAPTER ONE

· · · · · · · · · ·

Where to Find Colleges That Welcome B Students

We Really Do Want You (Or, Why Colleges Love B Students...)

Why would a college want you, the B STUDENT instead of Ms. Straight A's or Mr. Perfect SAT Score? Easy! Colleges want diversity. They want all kinds of students and that means you too. You are so much more than your GPA or your ACT scores and most colleges realize that. They want you because you are curious, enthusiastic and interesting!

You want the chance to shine, and there are colleges that want to help you do it. Think about it for a moment. There are more than 3,400 four-year, accredited colleges and universities in this country. That's a lot of places to learn! You can be sure that there are many schools for everyone and there certainly are many choices for B students. Your statistics may make the search a little longer and a bit challenging but no less rewarding.

Nothing is as important to your educational success as finding a college where you feel comfortable. A key to success is being flexible and prepared to give the avenues open to you a fair chance. You have to be willing to look a little deeper and explore options, some of which you may not have thought of before. For instance, "Keep an open mind about going out of state," encourages Lynda McGee, college counselor at Downtown Magnets High School in Los Angeles. It is McGee's personal goal to find schools for all students. "Some students fear leaving the area, especially those in sunny California," she explains.

Judi Robinovitz, an educational consultant for more than 25 years, suggests that students be open to exploring colleges they may not already know about. "You have to dispel the notion that just because you have not heard of a college, it's a bad college," she says.

"There are no bad colleges," explains Patrick O'Brien, former admissions officer and consultant-ambassador for the ACT. "Remember, the 'best' school is the one that is best for you, not necessarily the ones that are highlighted in the books," says O'Brien.

But, why would a college be willing to take a chance on a student who doesn't have the kind of scores and grades thought to be required by a majority of colleges? It's simple: They have common sense.

First, a number of universities want a diverse student body roaming around their campuses. To achieve this, they have to broaden their ideas of what kind of student they will accept. Just as colleges accept people from all kinds of financial, ethnic, religious and racial backgrounds, they often will accept those with various levels of academic achievement.

Second, admissions officers often realize that while students may not have the most perfect numbers, they can still add greatly to the student body. They may be tremendous leaders, facilitators, speakers or organizers. They may exhibit strength in a variety of skills that can't be pinpointed with the average test score. For example, while a student may not perform well in math, he or she may excel in the humanities. These students can enrich the campus community in untold ways.

Last, colleges know that some students are genuinely working toward starting over, to changing their priorities and standards. Often this can be seen in school transcripts. Grades are improving with time; a new leaf has been turned over. Colleges recognize that some students really do go through difficult times such as the severe illness or death of a family member. Because of this, they are frequently willing to overlook some weak numbers and support that new dedication by accepting you into their college and giving you another way to continue your trend.

So the college that you assumed was out of reach because of your grades or test scores may actually be entirely possible if you can give them a reason for why you deserve to be there.

Looking Outside the Box

One secret to finding the right college is to look beyond the most popular schools that everyone you know is applying to and then to think outside of the box. Are there other colleges in your area? Before you start shaking your head because these "other" colleges aren't what you had in mind, at least do a little research. Look at their sites online, and check out the profiles at the end of this book. You can't say you don't like a place until you have enough information to know if you like it (otherwise known as innocent until proven guilty!).

Some schools that may be more open to B students include these:

- career-oriented colleges

- community colleges
- all men's colleges
- all women's colleges
- very small colleges

Don't Overlook Community College

For many students, one of the best options remains the local community college. Yeah, you still have to live in your hometown, and most likely, still at home with your family, but you benefit from a good education while saving some big bucks for the future or for transferring to a four-year college. Community colleges are more open to students with B or C averages than some four-year institutions, so they can be a great solution for you.

"Community colleges are stepping stones to four-year universities, and they cost less, build skills and develop maturity. Students in the community college system gradually get into the college culture but with the security of home and familiar circumstances."

— Patrick O'Brien, former admission officer and consultant-ambassador for the ACT

But hey, you've heard some rumors about community colleges, right? You've heard them called everything from "Only Chance College" to "Harvard on the Highway." Like everything else, community colleges have a few myths surrounding them, and — here's a real surprise — most of them just aren't true. For instance:

- *A degree from a community college is not as good as a university degree.*

That just doesn't make any sense. An apple is an apple. A degree is a degree. You did the work and earned the diploma. Is it the same thing as a degree from Harvard? Ok, maybe not, but most of the time it will still get you through the front door and into the job.

- *The people who go to community college couldn't get in anywhere else.*

Not true. Students go to community college for a variety of reasons. Maybe it is more convenient and less expensive for some people because it allows them to keep working, giving them a chance to save money while providing a quality education that sometimes may even serve as a stepping stone to a traditional college.

- *The faculty at community colleges is inferior to that of four-year institutions.*

The faculties and staff at community colleges and other colleges are quite comparable. They both have their degrees and years of experience to share with you.

■ *The credits from a community college will not transfer to other colleges.*

This is a myth. Credit hours from community colleges transfer in the same way that credit hours from four-year universities do.

■ *Since community colleges cost so much less, they can't be any good.*

Community College Facts

Here are some of the current stats on community colleges, thanks to the helpful people at the American Association of Community Colleges (www.aacc.nche.edu):

Public institutions	979
Private institutions	148
Tribal institutions	30
TOTAL	1,157

11.6 million students currently enrolled
6.6 million for credit and 5 million for non-credit
46% of all U.S. undergraduates
45% of first-time freshmen
58% women; 42% men
62% part time; 38% full time
47% of African-American undergrads
56% of Hispanic undergrads
48% of Asian/Pacific Islander undergrads
57% of Native American undergrads
Average tuition and fees: $2,076, and 37.8% of students receive some kind of financial aid.
More than 490,000 associate degrees
Almost 235,000 two-year certificates

Community colleges are fine institutions. The difference in tuition can be due to many reasons, but it is mainly because community colleges do not have the incredible overhead that residential colleges have.

In 2004, the American Association of Community Colleges conducted a survey to see what the hottest programs at these colleges were. The survey found that the top five fields to study were allied health (46.6 percent), skilled trades/industrial, public services, information technologies and business.

Go, Team, Go!

Remember that choosing a college is not usually an individual choice. Instead, it takes a team of people all working together, including your teachers, advisers, guidance counselors, principals, coaches and family members. You need help with a decision this big, because it is a complex one.

There are so many colleges that accept B students, that it is important for you to consider several different elements when you start your search. Ask yourself these questions:

■ What kind of student am I now, and what are my career plans for the future?

- What parts of school do I like the best and least now?

- What does the idea of success actually mean to me?

- Where do I see myself in two years? Five years? Ten years?

- What part of the country appeals most to me?

- Do I want a small, intimate college or a bustling, exciting university?

- What percentage of males and females would be ideal for me?

- What is the cost and how much financial aid does each school offer?

- What are the most popular majors and is mine on that list?

- Do I want to be involved in a sorority/fraternity?

- Will I have any scholarships or grants that affect where I can go?

- Do I want a philosophical or religious college?

You may not know the answers to all these questions yet. Many of them will only come after you have taken some tours, read your research and talked to your team. Giving them some thought now, however, will give you a head start.

What to Look for in a College

When you start your college search, you have to find a happy balance between being optimistic and realistic. Look at the GPA and ACT/SAT scores that each college lists and analyze those numbers in relationship to yours. If a college's cut-off on the SAT verbal score is 510 and yours is 520, go ahead and apply — it's a "safety" college. What if your score is 480? Give it a try — it's a "fairly good chance" college. How about a score of 410? Not likely — but you could still apply to this college; just don't hold your breath. Be willing to stretch a little and know that those numbers are not carved in stone but are general guidelines.

The colleges profiled in this book do more than just accept B students. They are dedicated to helping them. They may offer a first-year general studies, remedial or transition class to help get you started. Many offer on-campus writing clinics and tutoring services. When you get in touch with the representatives from these colleges, be prepared to ask them what services they might offer. Can you record lectures? Are there faculty advisers for each student? Are classes offered to help with the transition to college? Even if they don't have any plans in place (which is unlikely) your request might be just enough to implement one.

Let's take an up-close look at each of these options for a moment. It's important for you to think about which of these features is important to you and will help you succeed in college. Take notes so that when you contact a college rep or admissions officer, you can ask if these choices exist at the school:

TUTORING: A variety of types of tutoring are available on virtually every campus. The only question is what format you prefer. You can check into peer tutoring from either a classmate or friend; faculty tutoring from a willing professor; in-depth tutoring from a teacher's assistant or at special on-campus centers and clinics. While some tutors may charge a fee, most services tend to be free. When you speak with a college rep, ask what might be available if you should need extra assistance.

COUNSELING: While tutoring is helpful to understanding a certain assignment or class subject, counseling is a wider scope. A counselor will help you make bigger decisions like what major to choose, what classes to take and in what direction you should go to achieve your goal. An academic counselor will not only help you reach academic goals, but he or she also will often help you with emotional and mental stress. To do your best academically, you need to be in good shape mentally. Counselors can recommend resources, give suggestions and tips, connect you with helpful mentors or organizations and much more.

The most important thing any student can do when searching for a college is to keep an open mind. When I make recommendations to students for a college, sometimes they say, "I haven't heard of that one so it must not be any good." They have this concept that only the ones mentioned in the papers are decent. It drives me crazy! You have to take the time to decide what YOU want from a school and then start choosing possibilities. Find a school that fits YOU and not the other way around. Look outside the box.

Also, please take the time to really understand financial aid as part of the college puzzle. The topic is near and dear to me because I grew up with a middle class background and I could not afford the state school. You do not want to graduate with $50,000 in college loans.

— Todd Johnson,
College Admissions Partners

CLASS SIZE AND PROFESSOR/ STUDENT RATIO: One of the biggest advantages of small colleges is their small class size. While many universities, even the really large ones, state that their average class size is between 10 and 30, a number of small colleges have fewer students per class. Instead of 22:1 student to professor ratios, they may have 5:1. This can be good because your professors are much more likely to be aware of you; if you are struggling or having a problem, they will be more apt to recognize it and reach out. Small classes mean you can ask more questions and discuss things on a deeper level. It also frequently means that participation will play a role in your overall grade.

There are many positive things about small classes, but some students might say that small classes have a negative side as well. For example, if you miss class, professors know (in a class of several hundred, it is a lot less noticeable, believe me!). If your homework isn't turned in, it will be observed right away as well. Truthfully, these can be good things. Professors who notice you are getting behind can remind you to catch up before you've dug your hole so deep that it takes a miracle to pass the class.

Overall, small classes can make the transition from high school to college easier. You will not feel so much like a minnow floundering in a huge ocean. You will get to know your fellow classmates much easier and quicker if there are a half dozen in your class rather than hundreds. Smaller classes often create more of a sense of cooperation between students rather than competition. Instead of trying to do better than

A College Whose Door Is Always Open

The core philosophy of the community college in America can be captured in the phrase "access and excellence." Community colleges, like all institutions of higher education, struggle to be excellent. But when it comes to "access," there is no struggle at all; community colleges are the access institutions of the 21st century.

The community college has emerged as the institution of the second chance — even the third and fourth chance. Community colleges take great pride in their "open-door philosophy," which means that any student who has graduated from high school or who has reached a certain age will be admitted. This philosophy and practice is remarkably different from those of most four-year colleges and universities. Historically, most four-year colleges and universities require that students meet certain criteria for admission, eliminating those who are under-prepared or unqualified to compete.

Community colleges are willing to give all applicants an opportunity to succeed regardless of their history. That does not mean that an unprepared student will be admitted into a very challenging program such as nursing or engineering technology. Instead, through assessment and advising, students who are not pre-pared for more challenging work will be guided into developmental education programs where they will receive special tutoring and courses in which they can develop the skills for more advanced work.

The focus of the community college — through its faculty and innovative pro-grams and practices — is to help students succeed, regardless of their level of achievement when they enter.

— Terry O'Banion, former president of the League for Innovation in the Community College

another person, you will only be trying to do better than you have done before — and that is the best kind of competition there is.

It's important to go beyond the statistics when you look at the numbers you find for professor/student ratio. Ask students who attend the school how much they interact with their professors and how much of an effort the professors make to help their students. More important than the ratio of professors to students is how involved the professors will be in your studies.

TEACHING STYLES: Another question to look into when choosing your college is what different teaching styles the school may offer. What emphasis does it have on lab time? Is there a period of internship? How much of class time is comprised of hands-on activities for kinesthetic learners? How much is pre-printed or written in forms that are student-friendly for visual learners? How much can be taped for auditory learners? Are there many field trips? All these options can make learning easier for many students. They are alternatives to the typical lecture/listen teaching format that has dominated your education up until now. Colleges offer new ways to learn and excel.

PASS/FAIL or CREDIT/NO CREDIT CLASSES: Not all colleges offer classes with pass/fail grading systems but a number of them have used it effectively, including the following: Millikin University, University of Iowa, University of Illinois, Ohio State University, Stanford University, Tufts, University of California (Berkeley), Syracuse University, Pennsylvania State University, Pomona College and Grinnell College.

There are certainly a number of perks to this type of grading system. It often encourages students to explore classes that they might otherwise have ignored. For example, if you are an English major, you may not be brave enough to take an advanced math class because you will be surrounded by students who excel in math and competing with them might be overwhelming. However, if you know that you are only going to have to achieve a passing grade, you might be willing to go for it. With pass/fail, there is often less pressure on you; conversely, you may mistakenly think that you don't have to try at all (then you are just wasting everyone's time!).

"Getting the right college is not a game to be won, but a match to be made."

— David Miller, director of college counseling at Stevenson School, Pebble Beach, California

In addition to regular classes, some types of learning fit the pass/fail system better than the traditional A, B, C, D and F. This is especially true for laboratory experiments, hands-on activities, thesis work and research.

Is there a downside to this type of grading system? Naturally. Some of these courses can't be counted toward your major. While taking a class that doesn't count toward your major may seem unwise, it can be a smart move. You might discover a new passion, interest or direction for your education. You might also discover that you are better at a subject than you had imagined. Pass/Fail classes might even lead you to decide on a supplemental course of study, a double major— or you might even consider changing your major. Think of the Pass/Fail credit simply as an invitation to go down another new college pathway.

THE EMPHASIS ON FINAL EXAMS: Another option to explore is how much influence final exams have on your overall grades. If you are the type who suffers from test anxiety (more on that later) or just does not test well, you want to look for colleges that offer options to traditional testing. Maybe oral tests are possible. Maybe you can earn most of your grades through homework, class participation or other activities.

SUPPORT NETWORK AND LEVEL OF COMPETITION: Besides the formal support network provided by the school from tutoring and counseling, some colleges offer an informal support network. You will want to find out more about this. Do students tend to help each other or compete against each other? At some schools, students frequently work together on group projects or have study sessions together. At other schools, students work more independently. This is especially important if you learn better in a group environment.

SPECIAL PROGRAMS: Investigate what kind of special programs the colleges may offer. For example, some colleges offer co-op programs in which students are able to spend a semester gaining hands-on work experience with a company while earning credits. Most schools have study-abroad programs that allow some students to study internationally, but they vary in their size and scope. Special programs like these may appeal to you and may be just what you need to get motivated.

POSSIBLE AND POPULAR MAJORS: As you look through colleges listed in this book, take special note of the majors listed with each one. These are the most popular majors associated with the particular school. Why is it important to choose a college that features your major? It is just like going shopping. If you really want a pair of boot-cut jeans, you aren't going to go to a shoe store. You want to go where the clerks know what you are talking about and can lead you directly to many choices that fit your needs, right? It's the same thing with a college. If you want to be in computer tech, a college that specializes in art may not be the best choice. You want the school that is familiar with your major and can offer a strong faculty and curriculum in your choice.

You also want to check with a college rep for a school that interests you and ask if you can have a double major at that college (and not just CAN YOU, but will you get the support and guidance you need if you choose to) or can you create your own major. The more options you have, the better the chance of having a college education tailored to your unique needs and the stronger the possibility of overall success.

What if you are undecided about your major when you start your college search? Relax — you are far from being the only one. Make a list of the most likely areas you'd like to explore and then look to see which colleges offer them. It is a first step and that's where every journey begins.

Where to Find Out More about Colleges

■ **College fairs.** Dozens or even hundreds of college representatives will come to your town for college fairs. This is your opportunity to ask questions and get a personal perspective from those associated with these colleges without leaving the city limits. Get a list of upcoming college fairs from your counselor or at www.nacac.com/fairs.html.

■ **College representatives at your school.** Be sure to meet representatives from colleges when they come to your school! You may be tempted to spend the time doing something else, but these events are designed to give you an opportunity to learn a lot about various colleges. You may also be meeting people who will eventually review your application, should you decide to submit one to any of the schools involved. If you make a good impression, your chances of admission may improve.

■ **College catalogs/view books.** These may vary from a simple, colorful tri-fold pamphlet to a 40-page catalog, complete with DVD and/or CD, business cards with contact names, testimonials from students and dozens of photo-

My biggest piece of advice is that there IS a school for everyone and you WILL be accepted. Remember, you have power over your own life. Get connected with knowledgeable people, invest in books like this one and in the Fiske's Guide and Princeton Review's 361 Best Colleges. Check out U.S. News and World Report's "A+ Schools for B Students."

In your junior year, start making plans. Use the summer before your senior year the best way you can. Look for opportunities that open doors and windows for you—think big. If you can't find something, start your own. My son and his friends started a driveway sealing business and did great. Paint, mow lawns—show initiative. It will be a great topic for the essay you should be working on before summer ends.

When school starts again, take the most challenging curriculum you are capable of handling. If your school is small and does not offer the more advanced courses, look elsewhere: go online, take distance learning classes or check out the community college.

— Shirley Bloomquist, MA
College and Educational Counselor

graphs. Read them through carefully because they can answer many of your questions.

■ **College websites.** Whether you look online at home, in the library or at school, take the time to look over the websites of some of the colleges you are interested in. They almost always have a FYI/FAQ section that will provide answers to basic questions. You also get a chance to see what the campus looks like, what some students have to say about the place (all glowing, of course!) and much more.

■ **College alumni.** For great suggestions and insight into a college, see if you can get in touch with someone who actually attended it. It might be your cousin, your father's co-worker, someone your guidance counselor suggested or a person the college itself refers to you. Make a list of questions for that person ahead of time so you are sure to cover what you most want to know. If the person graduated more than a few years ago, some information might not be as current as you need, but you can still learn some important facts.

■ **College visits and tours.** While this topic will be discussed in greater depth later in this book, it is important to say at this point that college visits must be given the value that they deserve. Nothing makes a place come alive as much as visiting it. You can read about a university in every possible source, but you can't really know it until you visit it. That's when you can personally taste the cafeteria creations, hear the conversations in the student union and see the layout of the dorms in some of the residence halls. Go on a tour with your class, counselor, friends or family. The information you will gather is immeasurable.

■ **College online virtual tours.** While going to a college in person is the best option, it is not always possible for a variety of reasons. In that case, be sure to at least go to a college's website and check out its virtual tour. You can get a better idea of whether this is the kind of place that calls to you — or not.

■ **Guidance counselors.** These wonderful people can give you a lot of helpful information about individual colleges. They may have printed material, website suggestions, contact names and more. Just ask!

■ **The school or local community library.** While this book is a great source for finding out about schools that welcome B and C students, there are tons more books out there that list college options. Check them out and look up the schools in which you are most interested. You'll find out useful information that can help you in your decision making. Spend some time just browsing through these books. You may encounter some colleges that you have not heard of before but that are intriguing possibilities.

- **Current college students.** Are there any students in your neighborhood or community already going to a college that interests you? Ask if you can meet for a snack and a chat and have all those questions you haven't been able to ask anyone else ready. Currently enrolled students are the real "been-there-done-that" experts. They will tell you the real truth about college life, not just what the writers of the college's marketing materials want you to know. If you can't find a college student in your area, go to the college and dialog with the students there. Can't get to the campus? Give the place a call and ask the admissions officer to connect you with some students.

- **Decoding college lingo 101.** When you are reading college literature (and believe me, you will get a TON of it), look for key words that will tell you more about how they evaluate applications. For example, they may say that they do a "comprehensive" review of a student's application. Typically, this means they will look beyond the numbers to things like background, extracurricular activities, essays, interviews, recommendations and more. Check online to see if the colleges you are interested in list information about their admissions process online; it might give you some great insight into how they make their decisions.

- **Right from admissions itself.** Skip the middle men and the media and go straight to the college's admissions office. Call and ask to speak with an admissions officer. Be honest. Explain your situation and ask what your chances of admission are or what you might be able to do to improve those chances. You might get some fantastic insider information (the legal kind!).

Visit Colleges Sooner Rather than Later

Don't wait a moment longer to go and visit schools. Seeing is believing! Reading about a place in a book or online is fine for background information, but it is a visit that will give you the true feel of the college's atmosphere, attitudes and activities. (To find out what college tours are like, check out the website www.campustours.com).

Patrick O'Brien, former admissions officer and consultant-ambassador for the ACT, says, "The more opportunities to visit college campuses

College Score Sheet

Name of school: _____

Date visited: _____

Who went with me: _____

Contacts I made at the school: _____

_____

FOOD	1	2	3	4	5	6	7	8	9	10
CAMPUS	1	2	3	4	5	6	7	8	9	10
DORMS	1	2	3	4	5	6	7	8	9	10
GREEK	1	2	3	4	5	6	7	8	9	10
COMMUNITY	1	2	3	4	5	6	7	8	9	10
_____	1	2	3	4	5	6	7	8	9	10
_____	1	2	3	4	5	6	7	8	9	10

TOTAL SCORE: _____

Questions:

How does this place make me feel? _____

Best thing about this place: _____

_____

_____

Worst thing about this place: _____

_____

What is the city like? _____

as a junior or in the first part of senior year, the better. And don't just go for the standard college tour of the campus and facilities. Check out the dorms and dorm life," he advises. "Insist on visiting a class in a field of interest—it will show you how the college academic system really works."

Try not to visit colleges during summer, however. As O'Brien says, "Never visit a campus when school is not in session; that's like visiting your high school on a weekend—dullsville." Don't depend on Mom, Dad or your guidance counselor to contact the school for a tour either. Do it yourself; it shows that college that you have initiative.

When you go for a campus tour, take part of your college-finding team with you so that you can get their impressions of each place too. Don't spend your time exploring the things you can get from the school's website. Pretend you are an anthropologist from the future and study the place like we study primitive cultures today. Watch the students interact, check out the food sources, find out how the place accepts those from different ethnic, political or religious backgrounds, gays or married couples. Read the posters in the buildings and the bulletin boards in dorms. What announcements do they have? What are some of the upcoming events and activities? Do they have a choir, band or orchestra? How about a drama group? Hang out in the student union and see what goes on there. Is there a lot of diversity on the campus? Go by the bookstore and see what souvenirs you like. Check out the shopping area around the campus. Pick up a campus newspaper to read later.

Remembering all your impressions of the places you have seen will not be easy. After you have seen a couple of campuses, facts and opinions will begin to mesh and soon you will find yourself asking which college had that great library. Do you remember what campus had those huge trees and large green lawns? To prevent this from happening, make up a form to write down your thoughts as you tour a place. You can create a form that reminds you to give schools a score of 1 (horrible) to 10 (perfection itself), and that offers a spot for general comments, thoughts and questions to follow up on later.

On the opposite page is an example of the kind of form you could use. If you don't like it, my feelings aren't hurt. Create your own! Design it the way that fits best for you.

The Sky's the Limit

Once you start looking for colleges, you'll be overwhelmed at how many great choices there are. In fact, your problem may be that you have too many options!

After you have a list of colleges, the next step is to fill out the applications. This is your opportunity to make your case (why you should be accepted) to each college. While most colleges do look at the numbers from your GPA, SAT and ACT scores, they will also look to your character. They will want to know your aspirations, your passions, your level of responsibility and maturity and how you choose to spend your time. Who inspires you? Who influences you? What do you expect of yourself? College admissions officers see countless numbers of applications, many with high numbers, but it is the student that shows integrity, curiosity, originality and independence that will catch their eyes. Unlike grading those little #2 pencil-filled dots on the standardized tests, this kind of information is much harder to measure. The college application will go a long way to help paint that very unique portrait of you as a person.

But before we hit the application, let's take the next chapter to look at some things you can do now to make sure you maximize your time in high school and set yourself up to create the strongest application possible.

Don't Get Caught Up in the Frenzy

Many students get totally caught up in the college admissions frenzy without actually realizing that there are more than 4,000 colleges in the United States that have to stay open, so they are looking for students. In other words, you have a much better chance of getting in than you think.

Some advice for you:

■ Remember that it is not what college you get into but what you do while you are there that matters the most.

■ Even if you think you cannot get into a college, apply anyway.

■ Make sure to apply to colleges other than just your favorite one. Even if you consider them a back-up plan, take the time to make a list and apply.

■ Be true to yourself about what you want out of a college experience. If you really do not want one that is academically rigorous, that's totally fine. Just be up front about it.

■ If one certain college is your dream but you don't fit the academic requirements, apply anyway. If you stand out in any way at all, you just may make it in after all.

— Laura Jeanne Hammond, Editor in Chief
Next Step Magazine

CHAPTER TWO

• • • • • • • • •

It's Never Too Late:

Take the Necessary Steps to Make a Change for the Better Right Now

Procrastination (pro-kras-ten-a-shun): that annoying habit that tends to follow us throughout our lives, convincing us that we can easily put off until tomorrow what we should be doing today (or yesterday) and not have to pay any consequences. (For an example, see the character of Scarlett O'Hara in the classic *Gone with the Wind*, who coined the phrase, "Fiddle-dee-dee, I'll think about it tomorrow!")

We've all done it. You will start the project/diet/chore/report/whatever tomorrow. Tomorrow, as little red-headed Annie reminded everyone in a relatively annoying song, is always a day away. It's eternally full of promise and potential. Unfortunately, when tomorrow arrives, it's today already, so we just repeat the mantra and everything is bumped one more time.

When it comes to getting ready for college, procrastination can be positively lethal. You already know that multiple forms have to be turned in early, from applications to financial aid requests. It doesn't stop there.

If your grades and test scores are not where you want them to be, there are no overnight miracles, potions or cures you can use. But there are steps you can take to brighten the picture a bit, especially if you are still in your sophomore or junior year.

Here is the list. Read it now (don't wait until tomorrow!) and you will already have a leg up on the competition. Some of these things are fairly simple; others take a lot of self-discipline. Fortunately, that is good practice for your college days ahead.

(1) Improve your grades ASAP.

Don't try to get out of improving your grades just because the school year is already partially over. Unless it's less then two weeks until summer vacation, there is still time to make a difference in that GPA. Here are some great ideas to try—TODAY, not tomorrow or next week. Don't be a Scarlett.

First of all, don't generalize your grades or the challenges of certain subject areas. If you're like most students (or human beings for that matter), you're stronger in some subjects than others. Think about which subjects give you the most trouble. Pinpoint the class or classes. Now narrow it down further. WHAT in that class is tough for you? In English, is it the reading or the writing? Is it the grammar or the composition? If it's science, is the difficulty in the lab or in reading the text? What formula or concept in math is bogging you down? If you can be specific about the problem, it is easier to find steps that will help you change things.

Once you know what issues are giving you the most trouble, do something about it. Here are just a few suggestions:

- ❑ Ask your teacher for help before or after class.
- ❑ Find a student who can help explain certain concepts.
- ❑ Join or create a study group.
- ❑ Get a tutor.
- ❑ Ask your parents for help.

What else can you do? If you are not already doing so, TAKE NOTES. By taking down what the teacher is saying and putting it in your own words, you are focusing and repeating key information. These notes should be as organized and neat as possible and then they should be read over at least once a day to make sure the material is sinking in. Studies have proven that you can learn far more reading short amounts of material each day rather than cramming lots of details in a few hours.

Go over your past tests, quizzes, worksheets and homework assignments. If you did something wrong on them, make sure you understand what it was. If you don't, then ask. There is nothing wrong with making mistakes if you turn around and use the experience for learning and understanding more.

Lastly, check to see if there is a way to earn some extra credit in the class where you are struggling. If there is, do it. It will help your overall grade and make a better impression on your teacher.

(2) Reorganize your priority list.

At the risk of sounding like your parents (and one day, you will realize how intelligent they really are), one of the most important steps you can take in high school is to make your studies a top priority. Does that mean that you will never see your friends and that you must give up any semblance of a social life? No. Instead, it simply means that when you think about your day, school should be high on the list, somewhere below breathing, eating and drinking, but way above watching *The Three Stooges* marathon on television.

Please remember that difficulty of admissions does NOT equal quality of education. Just because a school is really difficult to get accepted into does not guarantee that it is the highest quality or best fit for you. Keep an open mind. If you haven't heard of the college, it doesn't mean that it isn't a wonderful place. I am personally biased towards small colleges—they give you individual attention, professors and other administrators know your name and you have the chance to develop the academic self-confidence you need.

— Judith Mackenzie
Mackenzie College Consulting

If you have homework and your best friend calls and asks you to come over and hang out, give it some thought. Do your best to look beyond the fun of the moment to the potential reward down the road. It's not easy—but it is the mature thing to do (so be sure and let your parents know you made the responsible decision and earn a few brownie points in the process).

By making school a priority, other things will fall into line. Doing homework and studying for tests means better grades, and better grades mean a higher GPA and most likely a better performance on the SAT or ACT. In turn, both of those will strengthen your chances of getting into more colleges. Amanda (Mandy) Warhurst Webster, senior associate director of admissions at Salve Regina University, says, "Students must realize that the senior year is very important. You have to remain focused on academics and come in with a very strong first semester."

(3) Use your summers wisely.

Counting down the days to summer break is an educational tradition. Imagining how you are going to spend those long, hot, lazy summer days can keep you occupied for hours. Chances are that your plans include sleeping in, being with friends, finding a beach, exploring a career as a couch potato and generally doing as little as possible. Without ruling out those possibilities, why not include a few things that could actually raise your chance of college admission? Here are a few possibilities:

■ **Get a job that will teach you important skills.** Colleges value students who work because it demonstrates responsibility and maturity. The skills you gain will also help you move up the ladder so that the next job you have will be better.

- **Read that list of books your English teacher handed out.** Doing this will not only give you a head start on the fall but will also help you prepare for the standardized tests.

- **Volunteer in your community.** Colleges like to see students who are involved and give back to their neighborhood or community. Plus, think of the sense of satisfaction that you'll receive from helping an elementary school child read or by making the life of a senior citizen less lonely.

- **Take a summer school class at your high school or a community college.** You can do this to review material from a class that you didn't do as well in or to get a jump start on your classes for the fall. The biggest question that college admissions officers ask when reviewing your application is this: Will you be able to handle the academic courses at this college? Show that you will by taking a class.

You still have lots of days to be lazy or sleep in, so find a balance.

(4) Start on that college essay NOW.

College essays (as you'll see in Chapter Four) can be extremely helpful in getting admitted to colleges. Don't wait to plan what you will say in an essay until you have to actually write it. Begin to brainstorm ideas and work on the basics you will need to know to write an outstanding essay. Don't put it off! That would be like waiting until the homecoming game to work on your tackling or waiting until the debate tournament to think about what position you are taking on an issue. Start now!

Brush up on basic English skills and start thinking about what ideas you might want to write about. Refer to the sample questions listed in Chapter Four and think about how you would answer each one. Go to the library and check out a book on writing a quality, winning college essay. Read the samples to get a feel for what admissions officers seem to prefer. Think how you would approach the same or similar topic. Line up your reasons, examples and anecdotes now, not later.

(5) Get to know your guidance counselor.

For many students, the guidance counselor is just one of those people in the background of your high school life. You rarely see him or her except on special occasions (or if you are in trouble). You have time to change all that! Schedule a visit with your guidance counselor. Ask for tips on how to improve your chances of getting into college. Ask for help in searching out the best options. A guidance counselor is a person that is there to help you, so make yourself accessible. Ask questions. Follow up on advice.

(6) *Shed the fluff and take advanced placement, honors or college prep courses.*

A number of colleges do some rearranging of your grades that you might not be aware of. They will look at the classes you took in high school, throw out the "fluff" classes and recalculate the "core" classes. Journalism, shop, drama, home economics—all gone. Only science, math and English might remain. For many students, this is an unpleasant surprise because the grades they got in their elective classes were the ones responsible for driving up their overall GPA. Knowing this, you might want to choose different classes for your junior and senior years. Throw out the easy classes and take advanced placement or college prep courses instead. Some suggestions include these classes: algebra, geometry, foreign language, laboratory science and English. The honest fact is that a B in a core class will benefit you more than an A in any fluff class.

Patrick O'Brien adds, "Junior year for many is like boot camp, or to say it another way, it's more like college while the frosh and sophomore years are more like middle school. It is a breakthrough year with greater opportunities but also greater challenges. More self-direction is expected," he adds. "You should expect it of yourself. Keep all things in balance."

Mark Campbell, vice president for enrollment management at McKendree College, advises high school students, "Don't be tempted to take the soft senior year. Continue to develop your writing!"

Here is a helpful chart for converting your grades over to the point system used for computing GPAs.

A	4.0
A-	3.7
B+	3.3
B	3.0
B-	2.7
C+	2.3
C	2.0
C-	1.7
D+	1.3
D	1.0
D-	0.7
F	0.0

(7) Get passionately involved in your community.

Another factor that can help you get accepted into college is a history of being actively involved in your community in some way. Don't wait until the summer of your senior year to do this. Start looking around now for ways to play a part in your community. Make sure that you are sincere; don't become involved just to impress the admissions departments of colleges. Do it to learn and explore, and to discover more about yourself. Find a place of service that is in an area of great interest to you. Then you will find your passion, and it will mean more to you than just wanting to look good on a piece of paper. And there's another plus—you will be able to write or talk about that passion in your essay or interview.

Some possible areas in which to get involved include volunteering at places such as these:

- schools
- crisis intervention centers
- homeless shelters
- park and recreation centers
- community gardens
- nursing homes
- libraries
- hunger relief centers
- humane society
- theatres

(8) Get a coach, tutor, mentor and/or study buddy.

Just like it is better to study several days before a test rather than several hours (or minutes!) before, why wait to find someone who can help you succeed in so many ways? If you are not doing well in a class, do not hesitate to ask for help. Talk to your teachers. Get a tutor. Find a student who will study with you. Hire a study coach. Learn from a mentor. Do what you need to do now to improve those grades, as well as your own enthusiasm, dedication and passion.

If the term "mentor" is new to you, here is some helpful information. A mentor is a guide and counselor, someone that gives advice and helps you think through decisions. The term "mentor" carries with it the connotation that the person brings a certain knowledge that comes from wisdom and experience—in other words, a mentor is someone who "knows the ropes"—a friend, coach, tutor, teacher, counselor or even a relative that has been where you are. Research has shown that mentoring relationships can help students to develop work ethics and a sense of responsibility, as well as help raise self-esteem, strengthen communication skills and improve personal relationships. The skills that mentors can teach you will most likely help in high school and certainly in college.

The Top Five Facts about Learning Disabilities

When someone has a learning disability, what he or she should be able to do is different from what he or she is able to do. Learning disabilities are invisible, life-long conditions. You can't tell by looking at a person that he or she has one, and learning disabilities can't be cured. One in every ten people has a learning disability.

A learning disability may mean you have difficulty with any of the following:

- spoken language
- written language
- coordination
- self-control
- organizational skills
- attention
- memory

FACT 1: People with LD are smart. People with LD have average to above average intelligence. Some people prefer to think of LD as a "different learning style" or a "learning difference." That's because you CAN learn, but the way in which you learn is different. You have a unique learning style.

FACT 2: There are many types of LD.

Dyslexia is usually thought of as a reading disability although it also means having problems using language in many forms.

Dyscalculia causes people to have problems doing arithmetic and understanding math concepts. Many people have issues with math, but a person with dyscalculia has a much more difficult time solving basic math problems.

Dysgraphia is a writing disorder that causes people to have difficulty forming letters or writing within a certain space.

Dyspraxia is a problem with the body's system of motion. Dyspraxia makes it difficult for a person to control and coordinate his or her movements.

Auditory memory and processing disability describes problems people have in understanding or remembering words or sounds because their brains don't understand language the way typical brains do.

FACT 3: LD is hereditary. No one knows the exact cause of LD but it is believed to be a problem with the central nervous system, meaning it is neurological. LD also tends to run in families. You may discover that one of your guardians or grandparents had trouble at school. LD is not caused by too much sugar, guardians who aren't strict enough or allergies.

FACT 4: LD must be assessed by a psychologist. Diagnosing LD involves a number of things. You and your guardians will be interviewed to find out what kind of problems you have had, how long you have had them and how seriously they have affected you. Your teachers should be interviewed as well.

You will be given several tests. These aren't the same kind of tests you take in school. Instead, the person testing you will ask you questions and get you to complete certain tasks. Once the tests are finished, the examiner looks at how you are doing at school and compares that with how you should be doing given how smart you are (your intelligence). If there is a difference between these that can't be explained by other reasons, then a diagnosis of LD is often made.

FACT 5: There is no cure for LD but lots can be done to help. One of the most important things you can do to help yourself is to understand what your particular LD is. It is also important for you to recognize and work on your strengths. Your guardians and teachers will help you learn about how to cope with your learning problems better by teaching strategies that can minimize their effect.

Source: Reprinted with permission from the Learning Disabilities Association of BC

(9) Make sure you aren't working "around" an undiagnosed learning disability.

If you have been continually struggling in school and it has been showing up in your grades and test scores, make sure that you have been tested for learning disabilities. It is possible that you have an undiagnosed issue that has caused you to develop a different learning style. Talk to your guidance counselor or family physician. Many of the colleges today welcome students with various learning disabilities and they have special programs geared especially for them.

Not sure what qualifies as a learning disability? It's a blanket term that covers everything from not being able to sit still in class to not being able to read very well. There are many people who dislike the phrase "learning disability." They believe that instead of calling areas of challenge "disabilities," people should realize that some students simply have found other approaches to gaining knowledge that are perhaps different from most people's ways of learning.

Review the information about learning disabilities from an organization called the Learning Disabilities Association of BC. Know the facts about learning disabilities.

Worried that learning disabilities will interfere with your education? There are many successful people who have made the "LD" list, such as Whoopi Goldberg, Magic Johnson, Nelson Rockefeller, Jay Leno and Charles Schwab. Not too shabby, eh? You wouldn't mind being in such good company, would you?

(10) Take classes at your local junior college.

Start your college career while you are still in high school by taking classes at your local junior or community college. Many of these institutions are open to the idea. Terry O'Banion, former president of the League for Innovation in the Community College, explains the possibilities. "In the last decade or so, many high schools and community colleges have created articulated programs to allow students enrolled in high school to take courses for community college credit," she says. "Called 'dual or concurrent enrollment,' the practice is very widespread and is likely to expand in the next few years.

"The practice emerged because able high school students often exhaust the supply of solid courses by their senior year; there is no reason to wait until they graduate from high school to begin taking college-level courses," adds O'Banion. "Additionally, community colleges and high schools in the same region share common purposes of preparing students for the workforce or for further education, and they can enhance that purpose by creating opportunities for high school students to take courses at the local community college to round out their schedules," she concludes.

Tonia Johnson, associate director of admission at Guilford College, also discourages students from leaving school early in their senior year. Just because you have all the credits you need doesn't mean you need to cut your day short. A better plan is to use this time to do something that will impress admissions officers. "Take courses somewhere, get involved in an internship, but use the time wisely," she says.

Regardless of the stage at which you need to make changes, don't look back at your mistakes: look forward to your possibilities. Making that difference can be enough to get your admissions application placed in the "accepted" pile instead of that other stack. Write out a list of the top ten things you want to change, pin it up and give it the attention it needs. You might be surprised at the results!

GETTING IN

Beyond the Basic Application Form:

Explaining Weaknesses and Building on Strengths

CHAPTER THREE
• • • • • • • • • •

GPAs, SATs and ACTs, Oh My!

Let's face it. If you're reading this book, it means those wonderful acronyms in the title of this chapter are not among your strong points. For one reason or another, your overall GPA or your test scores are just not that remarkable.

What can you do about that? One possibility is to check out the colleges that do not require standardized test scores as part of their admissions process. "What?" you ask in amazement. There are colleges that don't want those all important numbers? That's right. In fact, there are more than 700 of them and they can all be found at www.fairtest.org.

Why would some colleges choose not to rely on ACT and SAT scores? Here is how Fair Test explains it:

> *"Test scores are biased and unreliable.* Standardized college admissions tests are biased, imprecise and unreliable, and therefore should not be required for any college admissions process or scholarship award. If test scores are optional, students who feel that their strengths are reflected by their SAT or ACT scores can submit them, while those whose abilities are better demonstrated by grades, recommendations, a portfolio or a special project are assured that these will be taken into full account. Sometimes admissions officers use low test scores to automatically reject qualified candidates without even considering their schoolwork. That's simply not fair.

> *"Test scores are nearly useless in college admission.* Research shows that the SAT and ACT do not help colleges and universities make significantly better admissions decisions. The University of Chicago Press book, *The Case Against the SAT* found that the SAT is 'statistically irrelevant' in college admission. It also proves that the SAT undermines the goal of diversity by reducing the number of qualified minority and lower-income students who are admitted."

Some Thoughts from College and University Officials on the SAT and ACT

"Schools that use the SAT are throwing away a third of their talent."
—William Hiss, Dean of Enrollment at Bates College

"While this test has some ability to predict student performance in the first year of college, it falls far short of predicting overall academic or career success and a host of other aptitudes that educators and society value, such as intellectual curiosity, motivation, persistence, leadership, creativity, civic engagement and social conscience."
—Joanne Creighton, President of Mount Holyoke College

"The negative impact of the SATs falls disproportionately on African Americans and Latinos. If you are about things like diversity in your student body, the SAT can be an impediment."
—Christopher Hooker-Haring, Dean of Admission at Muhlenberg College

Reprinted with permission of FairTest (www.fairtest.org)

If you are applying to a school that requires SAT or ACT scores, Fair Test encourages you to ask some important questions including these:

- How does your school use the SAT and/or ACT?

- Are cut-off scores used? If so, do they apply to general admissions or to particular programs?

- Does your school use any statistical formula which includes SAT/ACT scores to judge applicants' academic records?

- Do you take possible coaching into account when considering ACT or SAT scores?

- How does your college report SAT and ACT scores in handbooks and brochures?

- Does this college report simple averages or a range of scores? Does this include all entering students' scores in these figures, in compliance with the Good Practice Principles of the National Association for College Admission Counseling?

So, if all of this is true, why do most colleges rely so heavily on the results from standardized tests? It's a matter of "measurement." If you think about it, an A at a high school in Chicago may be different than an A at a high school in Los Angeles. In fact, an A at two high schools in the same school district or even with two different physics teachers at the same high school may be different. Because schools have varying ways of awarding grades and varying levels of difficulty, colleges need a uniform way to measure students. The SAT and ACT have become those measures. A great deal of importance is given to the scores achieved on them.

In fact, a good performance on college-entrance tests has become the focus of many a student's "free" time past the hours when the high school doors are closed for the day. In recent years, "test prep" has become more than just an option. It's a booming business! During the last few years, it has grown from $100 million to more than triple that. More and more students are putting out big bucks to prepare themselves to take the SAT.

So while standardized tests may be unreliable and not every college requires them, it doesn't look like they are going away anytime soon. If you are applying to a college that requires test scores, then you have little choice but to "bite the bullet" and take the test.

Meet the New Tests

As you probably know, the SAT and ACT tests have recently been changed. Let's take a look at these "new" exams:

SAT Reasoning Test (www.collegeboard.com)

- The exam has three sections—Critical Reading, Math and Writing—each scored between 200 and 800 points for a total possible score of 2400.

- The Critical Reading section is 70 minutes long with two 25-minute sections and one 20-minute section. It contains reading comprehension, sentence completion and paragraph-length critical reading sections. This section replaces the old verbal section.

- The Math section is 70 minutes long with two 25-minute sections and one 20-minute section. It contains multiple-choice questions and student-produced responses on numbers and operations, algebra, geometry and statistics, probability and data analysis.

- The Writing section contains a 25-minute essay that is first and a 35-minute multiple choice section that has questions on identifying sentence errors, improving sentences and improving paragraphs.

ACT (www.actstudent.org)

■ This exam has four multiple-choice tests and an optional Writing test. There is a score for each of the four tests (English, Math, Reading and Science) from 1 (low) to 36 (high), and the composite score is the average of the four test scores between 1 and 36.

■ The English section has 75 questions in 45 minutes that test standard written English (punctuation, grammar and usage, sentence structure) and rhetorical skills (strategy, organization, style).

■ The Mathematics section has 60 questions in 60 minutes that test pre-algebra (23 percent), elementary algebra (17 percent), intermediate algebra (15 percent), coordinate geometry (15 percent), plane geometry (23 percent) and trigonometry (7 percent).

■ The Reading section has 40 questions in 35 minutes that test reading comprehension.

■ The Science section has 40 questions in 35 minutes that test the "interpretation, analysis, evaluation, reasoning and problem-solving skills" of natural sciences.

■ The optional Writing section has one essay prompt in 30 minutes that tests writing skills.

Tips for Getting a Higher Score

It goes without saying that doing well on the standardized college entrance exams (ACT/SAT) helps you get in the front door of most colleges. There are dozens of books to tell you how to do well on these standardized tests, so I will not attempt to do it here. Instead, here's a quick list of the most basic things you can do to assure that you do the best you can:

In my opinion, the way our culture is shaped today means that college is still a learning time for students. We should not expect to drop them off, drive away and Boom! they are adults. Colleges understand that your performance in high school is not who you are. They want to help you in the process of becoming an adult.

In your junior year, if not before, step back and take a careful look at your study skills. Are you really doing the best that you can? Is there some area that you can improve on? Be sure to use any outside help you can. High school teachers are usually very willing to help you reach your potential, so just ask. You can meet after school or use your school's free tutoring services. Take advantage of those opportunities to improve your grades.

— Sarah Wilburn
Campus Bound

- Make a decision that the test is important to you and that you will give it time and effort.

- Get familiar with the test format so that this is not a surprise to you. Know what each test will cover. You can get free sample exams from the creators of the exams by going to www.collegeboard.com for the SAT and www.act.org for the ACT.

- Consider hiring a coach or tutor to help you prepare for the tests. There are intensive test preparation courses available from companies like Princeton Review (www.review.com) and Kaplan (www.kaplan.com), but there are also lower-cost options from community colleges and maybe even your high school.

- Go to the library or bookstore and start looking at all the test prep books. They come in several different formats. A recent trend is exciting novels of all kinds that entertain you while they introduce you to all of the vocabulary words you need to know for the test. Check the stories out at www.amazon.com or use a search engine to find "vocabulary SAT novels." The stories are so captivating that you completely forget that you are learning at the same time. SAT and ACT prep books are easy to find and will de-mystify the process for you.

- Check out websites on the Internet for test help. Just put "SAT test preparation" in the search box. Here are just a few of the many out there:

  www.review.com
  www.kaplan.com
  www.testprepreview.com
  www.number2.com
  www.act-sat-prep.com
  www.4tests.com
  www.petersons.com/testprepchannel

A last bit of advice before you take one of these standardized tests: Do not attempt to cram for them; it will never work. This is not that type of test. Instead go into the test well rested, following a good breakfast. Take the entire three hours and 35 minutes to complete it. Don't rush. If you get done early, just take the time to go back over it. Don't panic when you see other students turning in their tests when you are far from done. Everyone has a different test pace and getting done faster is not an indication of how anyone did on the test. Know that you did the best you could and despite the scores, forge ahead. Colleges are waiting for you!

Taking the Credit; Taking the Blame

There will come a time within the application, essay or interview where you will be expected to either explain or discuss your SAT/ACT score and GPA. It's better to offer an explanation than to ignore your scores or GPA and hope that the admissions officers don't notice them. In fact, they will notice them, and without an explanation, they will have no reason to give you the benefit of the doubt.

Remember that admissions officers are human beings. They have made mistakes or struggled in some way in their lives. They will understand and listen, so take the time to explain honestly why you believe your numbers are not as high as you had hoped they would be.

Here is a list of the general do's and don'ts that you need to remember when discussing your less-than-stellar numbers. The key is to be honest at all times.

DO: Explain any circumstances that may have affected your numbers such as these:	**DON'T:**
frequent moves	whine
test anxiety or health issues	complain
learning disabilities	place blame on others (parents, teachers, etc.)
part-time jobs	adopt a "poor me" attitude
extenuating personal or family issues	be emotional

As you can see, it's important to take responsibility for your performance. Instead of making excuses or blaming others, state the facts and own up to how you did. There are legitimate and understandable reasons for not doing as well as you are capable of doing. Some of these reasons were listed above. But make sure that you do not confuse explanations with excuses. Not having a date to the spring formal is not a good reason.

Also have a balance between providing enough information to make your case but not so much information that your explanation is overwhelming. For example, you might write that having a severely ill parent affected your ability to concentrate on your studies for a semester, but you don't need to also provide the detail of every medical procedure your parent has had.

If your grades are low in a specific subject, explain this. You can describe how you have sought extra help in the subject or how you took a summer school class to make sure you really understood the material, but it's still a weak area. You can also explain that you plan to major in another subject area in which you are stronger when you reach college.

It's important as well to note any progress that you've made. If you have since improved your grades in a subject area or overall, indicate this and explain that you have a renewed commitment to your studies.

Once you have discussed this topic, you can move on to focus on your strengths instead. Without dwelling on the negative, you have the opportunity to highlight how much you have to offer the college.

Include a Resume to Highlight What You _Have_ Accomplished

Many colleges will let you submit a resume. You may already have one on hand thanks to summer job searches. This can provide a beginning. The resume you used for looking for a summer part-time job might give

---

How Will My SAT Essay Be Graded?

Each essay will be scored independently by two high school and college teachers. Neither scorer will know what points the other one gave. Each reader will assign the essay a score ranging from 1 to 6. Essays with a 6 are outstanding, with few to no errors at all. These essays are built on a main point that is supported by stories, examples and reasons. Essays with scores of 6 are organized, focused, coherent, smooth and are indicative of a wide vocabulary. But not every essay is a 6. Let's look at what other scores can mean:

- A score of 5 indicates that the essay is effective, without being stellar. It is effective with only a few grammar/usage/mechanics errors.

- Essays that are scored with a 4 are considered competent, but with some gaps in quality.

- An essay with a score of 3 is adequate but has a number of errors, including grammar/usage/mechanics, vocabulary, focus or development.

- A score of 2 means that the essay is seriously limited with a number of weaknesses.

- An essay that is scored with a 1 is severely flawed.

For more detailed information on how the scoring is done, check out the College Board website at www.collegeboard.com.

A Word About Test Anxiety

Feeling worried or pressured about taking a test is normal. Indeed, a slight edginess can often enhance your performance. However, if the worry turns into panic and/or fear and makes it almost impossible to study or take the test, you probably are suffering from test anxiety.

Test anxiety can strike before and/or during a test. It can make you feel physically sick, from a headache or nausea to faintness and hyperventilating. You might have a dry mouth, pounding heart or sweaty hands or be unusually emotional. It is often very difficult to concentrate at all.

How can you combat it? Here are some tips:

1. **Be prepared as much as possible for the test.** The SAT and ACT are cumulative exams that assess years of study in high school. They are not tests for which you can "cram." Get a good study guide and become familiar with what the SAT and ACT test. Try a few of the practice tests. Then relax and just do your best.

2. **Take good care of yourself.** Get enough sleep, eat healthy and get some regular exercise. Don't have any coffee before the test because caffeine increases your level of anxiety.

3. **Learn how to relax.** Sounds simple, but it can be challenging when your body and mind are trying to do just the opposite. Like with other things, practice is the key. Spend time learning how to think about each muscle group in your body. Start with your feet. Tighten them and then let them go. Work your way all the way up to your head. Breathe slowly and deeply.

4. **Replace negative thoughts with positive ones.** Instead of telling yourself, "I am just going to blow this entire test," say, "This may be a difficult test but I will do the best I can on it." Visualize yourself doing well on the test.

5. **When you are taking the test, remember those deep, slow breaths.** Be sure to read the test directions carefully. If you don't know a question, skip it and go back later.

6. **If you find yourself tensing up during the test, put down your pencil, take a few deep breaths, relax your neck and shoulders and then go back to it.** Go to another question or problem and come back to the one that made you anxious. Sometimes answering a few problems that you *do know* will help you remember the answer to the one that threw you a curve.

7. **When you are done, do something fun.** See a movie, go out to eat, meet with a friend or just take a well-deserved nap.

you some quality information to use, but it probably will need changes before you share it with a college. Why? Two reasons: one, time has most likely passed since you wrote it and there may be new things to add, and two, your intention is different. You aren't trying to impress a potential employer so that he or she will give you a weekly paycheck. This time, the goal is to impress a college admissions officer and get you through the front door of the school.

Resumes are like the *Cliffs Notes* of your academic/educational and community life. They are the condensed version of the great stuff you have accomplished thus far. Resumes can be very effective. Here are some tips:

- Have high-quality paper.

- Choose a font size and style that is easy to read (at least 12 and below 18 and Arial, Times New Roman, Garamond or Franklin Gothic Book).

- Do not handwrite this resume. Even if you have to use the school or library computer, make sure this is neat and looks professional.

- Many word processing programs include a built-in resume wizard, so check and see if you can find one. This template walks you right through where to put what and then puts it in a format that looks great.

Here is what you need to include on your resume:

- full name
- current address
- telephone number (home and cell)
- email address
- all awards or honors you have earned
- all forms of community service
- all part-/full-time jobs
- references
- sports and extracurricular involvement—remember that these can be in school or outside of school!

One of the most important aspects of the resume is to include the pertinent details that truly explain what you have accomplished. For

123 4th St.
Anytown, USA 10000

Phone 555-555-5555
Fax 555-555-5556
E-mail anystudent@aol.com

Chris Smith

Community Involvement

Volunteered for six months (2007) at The Boys and Girls Club: helped organize and guide 30 children between the ages of 8 and 13 in multiple after-school activities. Learned skills of organization, teamwork, cooperation and discipline.

Intern at Wheels Unlimited, my grandfather's bicycle repair shop, after school for two years (2005-2007). Learned how to serve customers, run a register and basic mechanics/engineering skills.

Extracurricular Activities

Participated in the Chess Club (2005) and the Debate Club (2006-2007). Director of the Drama Club (2006) and President of the Ski Club (2007).

Employment

June-August 2006 20 hours a week at Marin County Public Library

June-August 2007 18 hours a week at the Community Theatre

Education

2004-2007 East County High School

Summer 2006 Theatre Workshop

Summer 2006 Sign Language 101 at St. Martin's Community College

References

Mr. Bob Smith, Youth Coordinator at the Boys and Girls Club, 555-222-1111

Mrs. Jean Youngblood, English/Language Arts Teacher, East County High School, 555-982-1120

Mr. Rod Cooper, High School Debate Coach, 555-888-1210

Miss Lindsay Francis, Professor of Sign Language, St. Martin's Community College, 555-333-0101

Awards received

Debate Team Regional First Prize, 2006

First Place, State Library Essay Contest, 2006

Heart of Gold, Volunteer Ribbon, 2007

example, if you worked as a volunteer at a local children's day care center, include how many children you worked with and what responsibilities you held. This is the place where you can really shine in ways that your numbers do not reflect.

On the previous page is an example of a typical type of resume you might want to include in your application. Look it over to see how you can adapt it to your needs.

After you have done all this hard work, don't blow it by not checking your spelling and grammar. The greatest resume will make a rotten impression if it has errors. Have someone else read over it before you finalize it. They may catch a mistake you missed—or remember something wonderful that you forgot to include.

A resume gives the opportunity to share with the college more than your grades and test scores. It gives them a snapshot of your achievements that will really help them understand what you have to offer.

CHAPTER FOUR

. . . .

Winning in Writing:

The All-Important College Essay

Not every college requires an essay, but most of them want to see one. If you are applying at one of the colleges that do not require ACT or SAT scores, for example, the college essay is extremely important. Bottom line: The chances are pretty good you will have to write an essay. And, putting aside your fears for a moment, you will come to realize that this is a good thing.

For many admissions officers, your essay is the first chance they get to see the real you. They already know your grades, test scores and what classes you have taken for the last four years, but they don't know YOU. Sure, they are looking at how well you remember those grammar and punctuation rules, as well as what kind of vocabulary you use, but they also want a glimpse of your personality, ambitions, talents, goals and dreams.

College essays have become such an important part of the admissions process that there are many books dedicated to showing you how to write them. Many also give sample essays to read from students who were accepted by colleges. One excellent book is *Accepted! 50 Successful College Admission Essays* by Gen Tanabe and Kelly Tanabe. Check out the many websites on the Net dedicated to the topic.

Be aware there are unscrupulous companies and people willing (for a price) to take the headache out of your hands and write the essay for you. Yes, you can buy your college essay. Is this ethical? What do you think? Not only is this wrong but it won't help you get into college. Purchased essays are never able to convey the real you to a college. Don't ask a friend or relative to write it for you either. The admissions officers are good at spotting styles that don't fit with students. Also consider that if you turn in a perfect paper, but your GPA in English class has always been a B or less, a red flag will pop up immediately.

TYPICAL ESSAY QUESTIONS

- Describe your most significant personal experience. How has it influenced you?

- Identify and discuss a problem facing your generation.

- What have you read that has had a special significance to you? Explain why.

- Describe a person or experience of particular importance to you.

- Describe the reasons that influenced you in selecting your intended major field of study.

- If you could travel through time and interview a prominent figure in the arts, politics, religion or science, whom would you choose and why?

- Describe your experience in living in a racially, culturally or ethnically diverse environment; what do you expect to need to know to live successfully in the multi-cultural society of the future?

- Make up a question, state it clearly and answer it. Feel free to use your imagination, recognizing that those who read it will not mind being entertained.

- Indicate what you consider your best qualities to be and describe how your college education will be of assistance to you in sharing these qualities and your accomplishments with others.

- Evaluate a significant experience, achievement or risk that you have taken and its impact on you.

- Indicate a person, character in fiction, a historical figure or a creative work (as in art, music, etc.) that has had a significant influence on you and describe that influence.

- Why do you want to spend two to six years of your life at a particular college, graduate school or professional school? How is the degree necessary to the fulfillment of your goals?

- Use this space to let us know something about you that we might not learn from the rest of your application.

- How have you grown and developed over the four years of your high school career?

- What is the biggest risk you have ever taken? Explain why you took it and what you learned afterward.

- Discuss some issue of personal, local or national concern and why it is important to you.

- Write about your favorite book or film and tell why it has influenced you.

- Relate the most humorous experience in your life.

- You have just finished writing your 300-page autobiography. Please submit page 217.

But the best reason for writing your own essay is that regardless of your skill, you can write a successful essay that will reflect your personality and your passion for life. It's not as hard as you might imagine! Read on to learn how.

The questions and/or topics you might be given to write about in college essays vary a great deal in subject area. Regardless of the question, the point is to say who you are. You will show that in how you respond, what anecdotes you use, what examples you include and so on.

Essay Mistakes to Avoid from the Get Go

Remember that you want your essay to stand out from the others in the pile on that admission officer's desk. You want to make a favorable and memorable impression and you want the reader of the essay to feel as if he or she is getting to know you. To make sure that your essay sounds unique and individual, take care to avoid certain pitfalls; for example, don't respond with the answers that everyone else does. If you are asked to write about a book you have read, don't pick the one that all high school students were required to read. Pick something unusual or different, a book that tells the admissions personnel something about you for choosing it. It does not matter if the admissions officer has ever heard of it. What matters is how you explain why it was an important book to you.

If you are asked to write about an event in your life, go beyond just describing it. Show how it affected your life and how you are different because of it. The trick here is not writing what everyone else does. Along with Dr. Seuss essays, admissions officers weary of reading essays that focus on the "I've seen the light" philosophy. You lost the game, but achieved a goal. Your parents got divorced/took drugs and it taught you a lesson. You had this favorite teacher or coach. It's one thing to write about something that you learned from the experience, but it's over the top to write that you've found the purpose of life through these experiences. It's easy to think that you have to be profound and philosophical when you write this essay, but the truth is that admissions officers see more than enough of this approach.

Other things to avoid:

Don't try to be cute by adding poetry or illustrations unless they directly relate to your topic or your specific talent, don't use unusually fancy paper and never handwrite the essay. While it is okay to be emotional, do not whine, complain or be sarcastic. Avoid using current films, actors or television shows for your examples, and don't try to sell yourself. Represent the special person you are, but don't sound like an overzealous salesman working on commission. Don't use anyone else's idea even if it is interesting. It won't sound like you and your support will sound hollow.

Be funny, be enthusiastic, be reflective—but make sure it is not something that you and 4,000 other students wrote about. Go beyond the expected and you will get noticed. The college essay is often the deciding factor in whether you are accepted or rejected. You want your words to push you over the top.

Putting Words on Paper

College essays are typically 250 to 500 words. That is about one to two pages of typing, double spaced. According to the Common Application (www.commonapp.org), that limit is a guideline because colleges do not actually count the words. They won't mind if it is a little shorter or longer because quality is far more important than quantity. "College admissions officers are far more concerned that the essay is well written, proofread (not just spell-checked), well thought out, etc. Do not get caught up in the 'micro' (words, spacing, font size, color of ink)," states the website. "They are looking for the 'macro': does the student write well and what can they learn about this person from his/her essay?" Their website has more helpful information on what you will find on many college application forms.

Once you know the question, sit down and brainstorm possible answers. Just let your mind wander around the topic and write it all down with-

---

This is Your Chance!

Quite often, the college application essay is the perfect opportunity to tackle the subject of your less-than-stellar quality test scores or GPA. Many times you can tie the question you are asked to write about to the subject of your strengths and weaknesses. If you can directly address the issue in your essay, do so. Look back over the list of the most commonly asked questions. Can you see how you could relate your strengths to the topic? For example, "Use this space to let us know something about you that we might not learn from the rest of your application." You could explain how you have been persistent, dedicated, strong, determined, creative or any other admirable trait through examples. You can show the admissions officers that while your numbers may not be the strongest they have seen, you are a bright, skilled and wonderful student that would be an excellent addition to any college. Think of the essay as your time to shine!

out judgment or self-censorship. When you have run out of ideas, start going through what you have. What looks best? Throw out the things you could only write a paragraph about and keep the ideas that you can build into several pages of examples and facts that support a topic sentence. Look for the ones that make you feel emotional; that probably means they impacted your life in some way. Then choose one.

Now, write out an outline, just like you have done for other papers and reports you've done in school. What are the main points you want to cover? What details go under each point? For example, imagine that you have been asked to write about something you have read that was significant to you. Some points you might want to cover include these: Why you chose to read the book, how you felt while reading it, what new perspectives or points of view the author taught you, what questions the material raised in your mind, what you learned from the experience.

Once your outline is done, it is time to write your first draft (and yes, that means there will be second, third and more drafts before you're done). Do not start your essay with any of the following opening sentences:

- My name is Kevin Jones and I …

- I was born in Los Angeles, California, and …

- My college admissions essay is going to be about …

- I am writing this because I really want to go to your college...

- This is the story of my life so far …

- I am such a great person that you will want to read my story …

- My parents, Jean and Jasper Carpenter, first moved …

These are boring lead-ins and you will most likely have lost the reader's attention in the very first paragraph. Start with something interesting, eye-catching and unique. Grab the admissions officer's attention by writing something that will make him or her put down that cup of coffee, sit up straight in the chair and want to read what comes next.

Your first draft should be written without worrying about grammar, spelling or punctuation. You want to get your best thoughts down first, without being slowed down by rules. In case you don't remember the basic structure from endless English classes, you need the minimum of a five-paragraph essay. It should look pretty much like this:

INTRODUCTION thesis statement
BODY: Paragraph 2 support for thesis statement
BODY: Paragraph 3 support for thesis statement
BODY: Paragraph 4 support for thesis statement
CONCLUSION summary of main points

When you are done, show the first draft to your friends and family. Ask their opinions. Should you give more detail? Was everything clear? Did it represent your personality? Is this how they would have imagined you answering the question? Listen carefully to their feedback so you can use it in your revisions.

Now write a second draft, pulling in any extra details you remembered and keeping others' comments in mind. This time, fix any spelling, grammar or punctuation errors. Share it with a favorite teacher or your guidance counselor. Get their comments. Go back to the desk. Go through it again, keeping the new feedback in mind. Run spell check (but do not depend on it) and print. You're ready.

What If I'm Not a Writer?

It is entirely possible that you are a whiz at math or a mad scientist, and writing just isn't your forte. If this is true, the college essay may be all that much more intimidating. So let's give your essay some thought before you begin to put words on paper.

Here are some ways to take your brilliant ideas and eventually come up with an essay. Which one sounds best to you?

- Get a tape recorder and tell what you would like to have in your essay. Consider this your first draft. Listen to it and refine it and when it centers on what you want to say,

Let Me Explain . . .

Remember in Chapter 3 how I talked about "taking the credit; taking the blame"? Let's return to this theme for a moment. An essay is one of your best opportunities to explain your grades. If you can do this clearly and honestly without resorting to whining and complaining, then you are doing yourself a huge favor.

Let's take a look at three partial sample essays that explain, in three very different ways, why these students' grades are less than stellar. Can you relate to what they say? How could you write your essay?

Example 1

Reaching and then maintaining high grades has always been a struggle for me. It wasn't that I didn't care about school, because I did. Basically, there were so many issues going on inside my house that I rarely had a moment to give to homework or studying. I have a younger brother named Kevin and he has cerebral palsy. He has to spend most of his time in a wheelchair and since both of my parents work, it is my job to take care of him as soon as I get home from school each afternoon. I don't mind doing it, but it really makes it hard for me to sit down and study for more than a few minutes at a time. Sometimes it also meant that I was up later than I should have been and then I was tired for class the next day.

Has your family experienced something that has made it harder for you to study and maintain good grades? It might be an illness or sickness, moving, divorce, a parent in the military, etc. Think about it for awhile. Maybe to help your family you have had to work two jobs. Perhaps you have had to help out in the family business. What are some reasons that you simply could not study or do as well in school as you had hoped?

Example 2

The only person that I can blame my poor grades on is me. For the first two years of high school, I just did not put the effort and time into my classes that they deserved. I spent most of my time playing sports and spending time with my friends. In my junior year, however, that all changed. One of my best friends died in an automobile accident. It came as quite a shock to me. I guess, like a lot of other teenagers, I thought I was immortal and this accident proved me wrong. Moreover, it made me realize that time really is limited and if I wanted to go to college and pursue music, I had to start taking school a lot more seriously. Since that time, I have been working to make high school my first priority. It has not been easy and I am still struggling in a couple of my classes, but my GPA has steadily gone up.

Does this story sound familiar? Did something happen to you during your high school years that changed your perspective on things? Did you blow off school for a while and then something got your attention focused in a different direction? If you admit that once you didn't do so great but you're better now and why, it can be quite persuasive.

Example 3

My GPA is low for one reason and that is math. My teacher was very supportive and spent a great deal of extra time tutoring me but it never seemed to work. For whatever reason, math just continues to be incredibly difficult for me. As abysmal as I am at numbers, however, I excel with words. I love to read the writings of other authors as well as pen my own. I have kept journals since I was six years old and have written more than 100 short stories. I've won a number of local and regional contests and truly believe that my future will center on the publishing world. In the meantime, however, my math grades will keep pulling down my GPA and I will keep muddling my way through numbers while I am covering my notebooks with words.

Is there an area in which you stand out from the pack and another that is a constant struggle? Talk about it. Explain this challenge and what you have done to address it and even compensate for it. It is okay to honestly state that you are not as strong in one subject as you are in another. Show how you use that experience to fuel your productivity in areas where you do excel.

either type it as you listen or ask someone else to transcribe it for you.

- Sit down and talk to your parents or a special friend about your response to the essay question or topic. As you speak, have that person make a list or an outline of what points you mention. Once you have a basic roadmap, it can be easier to start writing the essay.

- Find some friends who are writers and ask for their tips, ideas and suggestions. Have one of them tutor you through the process as you write the essay.

- Get some books from the library that have sample essays and see if you can use them as inspiration.

- Ask your English teacher for some guidance in putting your ideas on paper.

- Check to see if the college you are applying to allows for some flexibility in the format of your essay. If so, you might be able to write it as a lab report or some other format that feels more comfortable to you. You might also see if a college will accept a verbal essay rather than a written one.

- Write the essay as best you can and then let someone who writes very well go over it for suggestions, corrections and revisions.

Out of Your Hands

It is done, gone and out of your hands. What happens to your essay now? That depends on the college. At least one person will read your essay. At smaller, more intimate colleges, it will probably be read by more than one person. Quite often the first person to see it is an admissions officer, commonly an alumnus of the college or someone with a strong background in education. If there are multiple readings, your essay passes next to another admissions officer or perhaps a director. At some colleges, it will even be presented to an entire admissions committee.

The college essay is important, so give it the time, attention and effort it deserves. In turn, the colleges will give your essay the time, attention and effort it deserves.

Winning in Admission—With Someone Else's Words

There is another important element of the admissions process that we don't want to overlook—personal reference letters. This time you don't have to sell yourself with your words; other people will do the job for you.

Whom should you ask to write a letter of reference? Common sense says to make it someone who likes you, right? Just don't make it your grandmother, best friend or boyfriend. Sure, they like you—even love you—but you need a letter that will show how a person has evaluated you as a potential student, not something about how you are the best granddaughter, friend or girlfriend in the world. Here are some potential people to ask:

- co-workers, employers or supervisors

- teachers

- coaches

- other school faculty

- your pastor

- karate instructor or sponsor of other activities outside of school

- if you have done volunteer work, ask the organization's leader

It may be tricky to ask someone at school for a letter of recommendation if you haven't done well in his/her class but don't rule it out. Explain to your teacher or counselor what you are trying to accomplish and you may find you have more of an ally than you had originally thought. If you have a reason for not performing to your full potential, let your teacher know. Explaining your circumstances can help your teacher write a more supportive letter that gives a fuller picture of who you are.

How do you go about asking for a letter of reference? Ask in person rather than by email or telephone. This way you can show how much it would mean to you to have this individual's personal recommendation.

Be sure to give the person plenty of time to write a quality letter. Don't walk up to your boss at the end of the shift and say, "Before I go home tonight, could you write a reference letter for me?" Ask weeks ahead if possible. If there are word limits or other restrictions on the letter's format, be sure to tell the person before he or she begins writing.

Some people may not know how to write a personal reference letter, so be ready to tell them what it should include. Provide a resume or summary of some of your achievements to help the different individuals that you ask to write letters, and include a stamped, addressed envelope to the school. The typical letter should be about one to two pages in length and should include these elements:

- The identity of the writer

- The writer's relationship to you (teacher/student; employer/ employee, etc.)

- Why the writer has chosen to recommend you as a potential candidate for college

- Examples and illustrations of the strong points that he or she has observed in you

- An overall evaluation of you as a student, community volunteer, all-around person

- A conclusion

Afterwards, always, always, always show your appreciation and gratitude for each person's help. A thank you note is really good manners, but a direct and sincere thank you face to face is great too.

CHAPTER FIVE

• • • • • • • • •

Winning in Words:

The Also-Important College Interview

You may or may not have won over those admissions officers or committee members with your written words, so now it's time to dazzle them with your verbal wit. The college interview is important as it is another chance to show a school just who you are, why you want to attend their college and why they should count themselves lucky to get you (in a humble fashion, of course). It is also another chance to explain why your numbers are not as high as they could be.

While not all colleges require an interview, if you are given the opportunity, take it. Interviews may be held at the college with an admissions officer, which requires a trip to the school. But sometimes interviews are conducted in your community by local alumni. You should look forward to the opportunity of an interview. In fact, you might find it easier to discuss issues face to face rather than on paper.

Of course, unlike the essay, an interview doesn't afford you the chance to brainstorm, outline, think about, mull over, ponder and weigh the questions. Your responses are going to be on the spot, so preparation is the key to not looking like a befuddled idiot desperately searching for the right answers.

What kinds of questions will you be asked during the interview? They are similar to the kinds of questions that are used as essay topics. But the essay has just one question to answer or one topic to explore. In the interview, however, you typically answer a number of questions and converse with an interviewer or panel for 15 minutes to an hour. Topics to be discussed are often divided into categories like school/classes, teachers, extracurricular activities, community, college and the world in general. Here are some typical examples. As you read these questions, think about how you would answer each one.

- How would you describe your high school?

- How do you fit into your school?

- If you could change one thing about your school, what would it be? Why?

- What has been your favorite/least favorite class in school?

- Who was your favorite/least favorite teacher in school? Why?

- How do you spend your free time and/or summers?

- Do you have a hobby of some kind? Tell me about it.

- Why are you interested in coming to this college?

- Where do you see yourself four years from now?

- What would you like to change about yourself?

- What are the three words that best describe you?

- What accomplishment are you most proud of?

Don't Just Talk About You

Since the interviewers are real people, they value real conversations. Which would you prefer: listening to a one-hour soliloquy with Socratic references on the merits of academia as perceived through the eyes of an 18-year-old, or participating in an intriguing conversation about current events, life experiences and personal opinions? Needless to say, interviewers prefer the latter as well.

Throughout your interviews, remind yourself that your goal is to achieve two-way conversation. Be careful of any interview where the subject is you and you dominate the interview talking about your accomplishments. Don't worry about trying to mention all your achievements—your interviewer will ask about them. At the same time, however, this is not the only thing the interview is about.

Common sense tells us that most people enjoy talking about themselves, and interviewers are no different. Your interviewers volunteered for this job because they enjoyed their college experience and they like talking to potential students. Interviewers are usually the kind of people who love to give advice to young prospects. Think of this as a time not only for your interviewers to learn about you but also for you to find out as much as you can about them and their experiences.

Reprinted with permission from *Get into Any College* by Gen and Kelly Tanabe

■ Why do you think you are a good match for this college?

■ What do you think about _____ (current event, literature, art, music or other contemporary subject)?

How do I respond to questions like "Tell me about your greatest failure" or "What is your biggest weakness?"

Contrary to what it may seem, these are not trick questions. They ask you to examine yourself closely and to be honest. Admissions officers often ask questions like these to draw out meaningful experiences in your life that show you have coped with a variety of challenges. To prepare for a question like this, just think a moment about what kind of difficult moments you have had to deal with in your life. Did your parents get divorced? Did you lose a friend? Think about what you have had to struggle with. Did you have trouble with a certain subject? How did you overcome your difficulty? What personality trait gives you the most trouble? What do you do about it? When you answer a question like this, you may just find out some amazing things about yourself that you had not realized yet!

Who will ask you these questions? It depends on the college. It may be an admissions officer, another student, faculty member, alumnus or panel of interviewers.

Keep in mind that a college interview is usually more like a casual chat over coffee, not a white-light-in-your-face interrogation. If you have a good sense of humor, the interview is the time to show it. If you have a talent, skill or ability that just did not fit on the application form or in your essay, speak now or forever hold your peace. If you can, find out if the interview is considered to be informational (just getting some facts about you and a time for questions and answers) or evaluative (part of the admissions criteria).

Feeling nervous as you go into the interview is understandable. In a way, it is a good thing because it will give you that extra boost of adrenaline you need to keep on your toes and pay attention. A person who isn't at least a little bit nervous may not do as well as one who is!

To make this less of a stressful event, practice what you are going to say ahead of time. Entertain your friends and family with it. Speak in front of the mirror or to an understanding guidance counselor. Prepare an

Your Interview Homework

Remember those college brochures filled with pictures, statistics and text cultivating dust balls under your bed? Dig them out before your interview and do something really radical—read them! It is not necessary to read them cover to cover, but knowing such basic facts as where the school is located, what kind of environment it has, some of the courses it offers and some of the activities you may choose to participate in is a good idea. It does not impress interviewers to discover that students who are applying to their beloved alma mater do not even know what state it is located in or that the college is single sex. (There was an applicant who actually made it to the interview before he learned that the college he was applying to was an all-women school!)

Try to talk to relatives or friends who attend or have attended the college. They can give you insights into the college that are not found in the glossy brochures. The more you know the better.

Doing your homework will allow you to be able to ask intelligent questions. You are making the most important decision of your life so far. It makes sense that you would have a question or two about it. Having prepared questions not only helps create the two-way conversation dynamic, but it also demonstrates that you are serious about attending the college.

Not all questions are good questions, and in particular, avoid asking those obvious ones where the answers are on the first page of the college's brochure. Instead, the best questions to ask your interviewers are those that make them reflect on their own experiences, require them to do a little thinking and elicit an opinion. Making your interviewers think or express their opinions makes the interviews more interesting for them and makes your question seem insightful and probing. Some examples:

- What do you think about the X department?
- How did the small/large class size affect your education?
- How did X college prepare you for your career?
- What was the best opportunity you felt X university provided you?
- What is the best/worst aspect of X university or X city?
- If you had to do it again, what would you do differently?

Think of some more questions like these and write them on a list with the most interesting ones at the top. Take this list into the interviews and refer to them when the conversation begins to stall and when your interviewers ask you if you have any questions.

Reprinted with permission from *Get into Any College* by Gen and Kelly Tanabe

The Moment of Truth

What happens when the admissions officer asks you, "How do you explain the fact that your SAT score or GPA is a little less than wonderful?" First, expect it. That way you can prepare for it. If it doesn't happen, then whew! you are off the hook. If it does, you're ready. Second, be honest. Don't say there was a computer error or you really did better than that. Third, don't place blame. Don't try and put those numbers off on rotten teachers, stupid tests or unfair grading. On the other hand, you can explain with a truthful assessment of factors that have affected your life. Was there a crisis during that time? Did you have to work extra hours that cut into study time? Were you heavily involved with sports or other extracurricular activities? Did you find high school boring or stifling? Without accusing others, tell the interviewer why you believe those numbers do not represent your real potential.

What should you do if the admissions officer does not ask about your numbers? That's a judgment call, and the answer rests with your gut instinct. If the interview has gone really well and you feel like you have established a good rapport with the officer, explaining those numbers without being asked can be seen as admirable. If you have not clicked with the officer, however, and the interview has had some awkward pauses, you might want to just skip this so things don't go downhill.

answer for all the possible questions so you are ready, no matter which one the officer may ask.

The bottom line of the interview is simple—it is not the end all, be all of the admissions process. It will not usually make or break your acceptance. The person talking to you is a human being and may well have gone through the exact same thing you are going through right now. This means you will glimpse some compassion, empathy and even a smile during the interview. Relax, take a few deep breaths and let the special person that you are shine out!

According to the people at www.collegeboard.com, there are 13 things to avoid in a college interview. Are you paying attention? Here they are!

Don't:

■ Be late

■ Memorize speeches—instead sound natural and conversational

- Ask questions covered by the college catalog

- Chew gum

- Wear lots of cologne or perfume

- Swear or use too much slang

- Be arrogant—there's a fine line between being confident and boasting

- Lie—it will come back to haunt you

- Respond with only "yes" or "no" answers

- Tell the school it's your safety or last choice

- Be rude to the receptionist or any other staff you meet

- Bring a parent into the interview

- Refuse an interview

During the interview, more than your words count. While you don't have to come to the interview in a suit and tie or wear a dress, you shouldn't show up in shorts and tank top either. Be professional in your appearance. As you talk to the interviewer, sit up straight and don't fidget. Be sure to make eye contact. Never interrupt, and shake hands at the beginning and the end.

Your college interview is also a chance for you to ask questions. By doing so, you often show initiative and curiosity—two traits most colleges are looking for in their students. Ask if the officer has any advice for you, ask a question about your potential major or ask about dorm activities and college lifestyle. Find out if there will be a new student orientation program, what activities are available for freshmen, what part-time job opportunities there are in the area or end with a zinger like, "Is there anything you would like to know about me in order to help you make a fair and final decision about my application?"

The interview is a unique opportunity to establish rapport with a person who previously only knew you as numbers and words on paper. Use it wisely and show the interviewer(s) what a fantastic person you really are!

PAYING

B Students Can
Win Scholarships Too

CHAPTER SIX
• • • • • • • • •

B Students Can Win Scholarships Too

"My GPA is not that hot…and my SAT scores were lousy because I had a temperature/didn't get enough sleep/forgot to prepare/had an argument with my boyfriend, so I wonder if I can even get into college. But heck, college costs thousands and thousands of dollars and my family cannot afford that. Why even apply? My parents don't have the money and scholarships only go to the straight A students anyway…"

Have you had that conversation with yourself? If so, you aren't the first and certainly won't be the last to do so. But be advised: Such thinking is a big mistake.

Without question, college costs a lot, and most families struggle to find enough money to pay for it. But those scholarships you keep hearing about are not just for the eggheads or overachievers who excelled in everything from U.S. history to trigonometry.

So who exactly gets scholarships besides those with high numbers? Let's take a look.

Students who show genuine financial need

And you thought growing up without a Porsche in the driveway was a bad thing? Scholarships were originally set up for these very students. They were put into place to support students' families financially so that college could be possible for many more than just those who can afford it. If your family has a genuine need to help you attend college, many scholarships may be available for you. The key to snatching one of them is simple: be honest about ALL your numbers, including finances; don't try to fudge those income levels. That isn't honest, and you will get caught. Also be prepared to show any extenuating circumstances behind those numbers. Was your mother laid off? Was there a medical emergency? Does your family have three kids in college already? These are important factors to include.

Myth:
You need straight A's to win money for college

The Truth: While straight A's certainly don't hurt your chances of winning [scholarships and awards for college], you may be tempted to place too much importance on your grades. Many scholarships are based on criteria other than grades and are awarded for specific skills or talents such as linguistic, athletic or artistic ability. Even for scholarships in which grades are considered, GPA is often not the most important factor. What's more important is that you best match the qualities the scholarship committee seeks. Most students who win scholarships do not have the highest GPA. Don't let the lack of a perfect transcript prevent you from applying for scholarships.

— Gen and Kelly Tanabe, *Get Free Cash for College*

Students with a disability or illness

Not that you would wish for one, but if you happen to have a documented disability or illness, there is assistance for you because of it. A number of organizations support students with some kind of physical challenge. Scholarships are available from such sources as the Alexander Graham Bell Association, American Foundation for the Blind, Hemophilia Resources of America and the National Center for Learning Disabilities.

Students with specific majors

Already know what you want to do with the rest of your life? Countless organizations support young people who are pursuing certain careers. You must show that you are genuinely passionate about whatever field it might be, from digital photography to interior design. You will need to let the scholarship people know how you found out about the field, who mentored or inspired you, how your dedication grew and what skills you learned or developed. Have truthful, profound stories ready to share. Have you started your own business in this career already? Have you supported your fascination through volunteer work? Do you have recommendations from people in a related field? These are the factors that will help a committee select you above all others for that cash. Consider these examples: The American Nursery and Landscape Association has money for those who love flowers, trees and the outdoors. The Arabian Horse Foundation helps those who adore horses. Other organizations have money for those whose focus is cooking, construction, forestry, hospitality, the performing arts and more.

Students who show leadership

Are you known for taking charge and putting things together? Do you already have a few groupies that really like you? Scholarship committees are impressed with young people who have shown some form of leadership. If you have helped others by using your abilities in organization and guidance, or if you have inspired others, then this is the place to let it be known.

What have you done? Show it, don't just tell it. Give concrete examples such as letters of recommendation, photographs and projects. Point out the responsibilities you have taken on and what they have taught you. Places like the Financial Service Centers of America, the Coca-Cola Scholars Foundation and Discover Card promote their own businesses by sharing their profits with students like you.

Students with particular religious backgrounds

If you have been wondering if God has been listening to those prayers, this might be your answer. To promote the growth and development of their religion or denomination, many church organizations offer students college scholarships. Okay, time for real honesty here. Do not try to get one of these scholarships or awards if the only times you go to church are to attend weddings, funerals and pray right before a major test. You have to be a true believer and show it through your active involvement with the church. Perhaps you lead a youth group, work in the church nursery, take classes from the pastor or participate in other areas of ministry. It is common to see scholarships from the Methodist, Catholic, Baptist and Presbyterian churches.

Students with superior athletic ability

Love to chase some kind of ball around? If you are the star football, basketball, baseball, tennis, golf or track star, chances are there is a college or organization that wants to give you the money to go to college. As Gen and Kelly Tanabe say in their book on scholarships, "Athletic scholarships are the Holy Grail. At their best, they can cover tuition and fees, room and board and books. That's not bad for doing something that you enjoy." Not sure if your sport is covered? Even the Ice Skating Institute of American Education Foundation and the National Archery Association have money to share. Check it out!

Students with a specific ethnic background

Time to look through your family tree. To celebrate their history and culture, some ethnic organizations are willing to give you money for school. This helps increase the number of minorities on campuses and also encourages students to go into professions they might have ignored or otherwise overlooked. Many groups are represented, including such organizations as the Sons of Norway and the National Italian American Foundation. Look for information regarding your heritage.

Students with hobbies

And your friends tried to say you were wasting your time! Not so. Scholarships are out there for young people who have serious hobbies. Of course, you have to show that you don't just pursue this hobby on rainy weekend afternoons, but that you are involved on a regular basis. You also want to prove dedication to this hobby by showing a consistent effort to improve the skills it takes to be good at what you do. Perhaps your hobby has even led you to awards and honors or even to the creation of your own business.

Discuss how this hobby has affected your life and what skills it has taught you. Be sure to include letters of recommendation from people who have seen what you are capable of. Do you spend hours doing graphic design on your computer? Have you sold some of your original logos to local companies? The Rhythm and Hues Studios might have money for you. Is photography all you can think about? Have you had your own displays at local stores? Do people call you to take pictures at their weddings or parties? Have your shots already popped up in the community newspaper? Talk to the National Press Photographers Foundation. Whatever your hobby, it's worth doing a little research to see if there are organizations with scholarships and awards for students just like you!

Students with parents who have generous employers

Check out your mom and/or dad's places of employment. It is not uncommon for businesses and corporations to include in their employee package some scholarship money for workers' children. Ask your parents to read through their employee handbooks again or just ask some questions. Who knows what hidden benefits your parent will find?

I hope you're convinced by now that just as colleges will happily take students with less-than-stellar grades and test scores, so will they just as happily take students who do not come from the wealthiest families. Financial aid is a huge part of college admissions and one that often means you can get that education you once told yourself was way out of reach. It's time to start an all-new conversation with yourself. Try something along these lines: "Hey, colleges really DO like me, and my family really CAN afford it now. So, what am I waiting for?" There you go.

Where to Find Scholarships

For most students, the hunt for scholarships is a short one. Many start with a scholarship book or head to the Internet. Unfortunately, most students end their search after exhausting these two sources.

Big mistake!

Books and the Internet are only the tip of the iceberg, and neither comes close to listing all the available scholarships. If you do your own detective work and canvass the community, you will uncover additional awards. Keep in mind that local scholarships may have smaller overall awards, but the chances of your winning them are much higher. Here's where to begin:

High school. The first stop in your scholarship hunt should be the high school counseling office. When an organization establishes a new scholarship (awards are created every year), high schools are the first places to get a notice. Over the years, most counseling offices have assembled a long list of scholarships. Don't reinvent the wheel if the counselor has already collected the information. Also remember that some high schools give out a set number of scholarships to their students each year and often less than that apply. In other words, all you would have to do to get the scholarship is fill out the papers!

Prospective colleges. Contact the financial aid office at every school you are interested in attending. Not only do the colleges themselves offer scholarships, but their financial aid offices also maintain lists of outside opportunities.

Civic and community organizations. Every community is home to dozens of civic organizations, such as the Rotary Club, Lions Club, Knights of Columbus, American Legion, Elks Club and VFW. Part of their mission is to support the community by awarding scholarships.

Businesses big and small. Many businesses such as newspapers, shopping malls, supermarkets and retailers offer scholarships to local students. For example, every Wal-Mart and Target store awards scholarships to students in the community. To find these opportunities, contact the manager at these businesses. You can get a list of businesses from the chamber of commerce or in the reference section of the public library.

Parent's employers/union. If your parents work for a large company, have them ask the human resources department about scholarships. If they are limited to the children of employees, there may be little competition for these awards. Also, if your parents are a member of a union, have them ask the union representative about scholarships.

Professional or trade associations. From accounting to zoology, every profession has its own associations, and many of these professional associations use scholarships to encourage students to enter the field. Start by looking at groups related to your future career.

Religious organizations. Your church or temple may offer scholarships to support members. If your local church does not have a scholarship program, check with the national headquarters.

Ethnic and cultural organizations. To promote a certain culture, develop leaders or encourage members to pursue higher education, many ethnic organizations sponsor scholarships.

State and local governments. Make those tax dollars work for you by taking advantage of financial aid from state and local governments. Each state has a higher education agency that provides information on financial aid, and many administer state-based grant and loan programs. Closer to home, your county or city government may have awards for students in the community.

Private foundations and charities. As part of their mission to help the community, private foundations and charities often offer scholarships. To find these scholarships, visit your library and ask the reference librarian for a directory of local charities and foundations.

Friends and family. The more people who know you are looking for scholarships, the better. Friends and family members can be invaluable scholarship scouts as they go about their daily business. Scholarship opportunities have been uncovered on supermarket bulletin boards, standing in line at a bank, even on a bottle of aspirin. You never know where a scholarship will be publicized and who can help you to find it.

The Internet. Thousands of scholarships are just a click away. Websites such as College Answer (www.collegeanswer.com) make it easy to find scholarships free-of-charge. Although the Internet is a valuable resource, it is not a magic solution. Remember to use all the resources available to you.

Reprinted with permission from *Sallie Mae How to Pay for College* by Gen and Kelly Tanabe.

Where Not to Find Scholarships

Watch out for scams. You already know this but it bears repeating: if it sounds too good to be true, it most likely is. Avoid any scholarship that asks you for payment, promises scholarships that NO ONE else has access to or asks for too much personal information like your social security number or bank account information.

Setting Your Priorities

Once you start searching for possible scholarships, you may easily find that there are so many that you are somewhat overwhelmed. Too many scholarships, too little time! It will help if you take time to prioritize them, i.e. decide which ones are the best fit for you. Ask yourself the following questions to help narrow down the list:

- How do you fit the mission or point of the award? Does it sound just like you or do you only match about 3 out of the 10 criteria?

- How much do academics count in each of the scholarships? Most organizations provide this information. If the only mention is a minimum GPA and yours is above that, you are set.

- How many awards are being given out? What are your overall chances of getting one?

- What is the scope of the competition? You will have a better chance of winning a scholarship that is only open to students in your county than one that is nationwide.

- How much is the award? Is it enough to make a difference? Consider the amount given, but don't just apply to the scholarships with the largest prizes because those often have the most competition.

Scholarship Essays

Scholarship essays and college admissions essays are not the same thing. When you are scheduling time to write your scholarship and college admissions essays, remember that the two are very different. While an admissions essay is geared to providing college admissions officers with an overall picture of who you are, the scholarship essay is targeted to the purpose of the scholarship itself. The people reading this are looking for something specific about you. For example, if you are applying for a sports scholarship, include information on the reason you play, what you have learned and how you have improved. If the scholarship is for future teachers, write about your experience with children and teaching or tutoring. Don't just list these things either in some kind of bulleted format. Instead, talk about the why, how or what behind it all. How did you get involved? What new perspectives have you learned? Why do you want to pursue this further?

Time to recycle. You have been throwing your soda cans and water bottles in recycling containers for years now, so keep up the spirit and see if you can recycle any of your essays. The good news is that, naturally, this saves you time and effort. The bad news is that it isn't quite that simple. Before you decide to use Essay B for scholarship XYZ, make sure it actually fits. Read the question carefully and make sure you are addressing it specifically. You may be able to tweak certain parts of an essay and adapt something written for one college or scholarship to meet the criteria of others.

I hope you've seen from this chapter that scholarships are a possibility for any student, regardless of college-entrance exam scores or GPA. There are awards given for every background, talent or achievement. Many scholarship or award committees don't count grades or test scores as the most important factor. It is well worth taking some time to prioritize the scholarships you apply for. Then write the best application and essay that you can. With that combination, you have a good chance of winning funds for college.

SECTION | **4**

COPING

Tips for Thriving

CHAPTER **SEVEN**

• • • • • • • • • •

What Is Due When:

The Top Ten of Time Management

No matter how you feel about cloning now, by the time you have been in college for a few months you will be a staunch fan of the concept. The possibility of being in two places at one time will sound like the perfect solution, if only it were possible.

For many of us, college is the very first time that we find ourselves with so much to do and so little time to do it. Suddenly, 24 hours is simply not enough. You have classes, friends, homework, a hobby or two, perhaps sports practice or a part-time job. Oh yes, and time for sleeping, eating and basic hygiene. Squeezing all that into one day is not just difficult, it can border on impossible. Help is on the way. Turn this list into your daily mantra.

What you need to realize about college life (and you will hear this over and over, so be prepared) is that all of a sudden responsibility is on you and you alone. Did you just grin…or gulp? Just imagine you are Spiderman and that you whisper, "With great power comes great responsibility." There are no parents to look over your shoulder and remind/nag you to get things done. Your professors may be too busy to notice what you are and are not doing. There is no one to report to, and no one is keeping track of your activities. If a project gets done, it's because you did it. If it doesn't, well, you know where the blame lies, right? It takes a combination of practice, dedication, organization and most of all self-discipline to make sure you cover everything. This is where you get to prove how grown up and mature you truly are. Are you ready? Here are some tips.

(1) So much work, so little time

Even if you are an English major and you only know enough basic math to balance your checkbook each month, take a minute and fiddle around with these numbers. Start with the standard 24 hours in each day. That's all you get, no matter who you know or what you do.

Write the numbers 1 to 24 on a piece of paper. Label 1 through 8 SLEEP. Certainly there will be times where your shuteye will be more or less than eight hours, but use this as an average for now. Next look at your class schedule and figure out how many hours a day you are actually sitting in the classroom or lab. While that can change, let's say four hours a day for now. So you can label hours 9, 10, 11 and 12 SCHOOL. Mark hours 13, 14 and 15 for EATING. If you have a four-hour part-time job, you'll need to mark hours 16, 17, 18 and 19 WORK. You now have a mere five hours left for everything from sports practice, exercise and studying to hanging out with friends and those tedious duties like showering, brushing your teeth, changing clothes and doing laundry.

You Don't Gotta Get A's But You Do Gotta Give 100 Percent

When I applied to college, I did not get into my top choice. It wasn't until I had finished going to UCLA and then business school that I realized it was my essays and not my grades that caused that to happen. I worked for six or seven years in the business field but finally returned to college admissions because I felt drawn there. Five years ago, I launched my own business, Headed for College. I want to help kids find a great match and believe that the lower the GPA, the more value I can bring to the situation.

As I tell my clients and my own kids, you will never hear me say, "You gotta get A's." All I ask is that you give 100 percent and from there, we can build a lot of choices. If you are only giving 80 percent, you are wasting many opportunities.

I spend 20 to 25 hours working with a student, but that is after I have put 15 to 30 hours into putting together a great list of possible schools for each one. I ask them, "When you go to college, what will you do differently than you did in high school? What services will you take advantage of to help improve things?"

Remember that it is never too late to make some changes. Any upward trend in grades is seen very positively by colleges and can be included in your application form and/or essays. A number of colleges will see this and take time to look at the trend and give you the benefit of the doubt.

I also encourage students to go on virtual or actual tours of colleges. What may sound less than intriguing on paper may look much more interesting when you can see the campus, the dorms, surrounding area and so on. It may be just what you need to reconsider colleges you had previously overlooked.

— Jennifer Tabbush MBA, CEP Headed for College

Can you see the problem? Too easily, we begin to rely on weekends to catch up what we missed during the week. Unfortunately, those days are usually busier than weekdays. If your time is not carefully scheduled, something will get left out and it might be the important things like homework and classes.

When it comes to scheduling things, remember Murphy's Law of Time: Time goes faster than you expect and everything takes longer than you think.

(2) Falling in love with the syllabus

When you go to class and the professor hands out the syllabus, take a moment to focus your full attention on it. Appreciate it. Respect it. It is one of the most important things you will ever be given while you are in college. In virtually every syllabus, there is a list of what you will be expected to do for each week of class. It will list homework assignments, quizzes (except those dreaded pop quizzes), reports and papers. Just think of it as a roadmap to consult repeatedly as you take off on a long journey. The syllabus will keep you from getting lost.

Most syllabi contain other vital information as well, including sections on these things:

- where class is held

- how to contact the professor

- grading plan, i.e. how much of your grade depends on test scores, papers, projects, etc.

- course description

- course objectives

- course topics

- required texts and supplies

- attendance requirements

- classroom rules of conduct

- class schedule of tests, quizzes, papers, projects and homework assignments and when they are due

At first, you may say, "Heck, I don't need this silly old syllabus because the professor will remind us all when a test or paper is due, right?"

Not quite. That may have been the case in high school, but no longer. Classes are bigger, professors are busier. Many of them expect you to be responsible enough (there is that word again) to monitor what is due when. And let's face it, it is no fun to walk into class and find out there is a test you didn't study for.

When you get back to your room after that first class, take out the syllabus and grab a highlighter or two. Go through each line and highlight those important due dates. Remember that if you have a test, you need to plan time to study. If you have a paper, you must schedule time for researching at the library or on the Internet, as well as hours for outlining and writing.

How will you keep up with it all? Once you have worked your way through the syllabus for each class, you will take the information—those assignment, project and test due dates—and put it into…into what?… your day planner…tip three. (Great segue, don't you think?)

(3) Sticking to the plan

Even though you may have laughed at or even made fun of those people who always walked around with those nerdy day planners in their arms, you are about to join their ranks. A day planner is your key to managing time, so let's take a look at what it can do for you.

The first step to creating a good day planner is to pick one you like. Head out to the office supply store or college bookstore and browse the day planner section of the store. Does one appeal to you more than another? Does the shape and size feel right? Do you like plain or fancy? Lines or no lines? Whatever you like is fine, as long as it has a monthly or weekly calendar and pages for you to write out what you are going to do each day. Make your selection and purchase the one that fits you. Then make that day planner your own; add stickers, photos, drawings, whatever you need to personalize it. If you want to take the high-tech route, an electronic planner works too.

Open up the day planner to the current month and write down all time commitments you have. Write them in pencil, however, so you can change things if necessary without making a scratched up mess. Be sure to include class time, work, any kind of practice, meetings with friends, study groups or other regular activities. Now add the due dates for your quizzes, tests, papers and projects. Do this for as many months as you have data for. (It gives you an excuse to count how many days until spring break.)

Writing it all down is a wonderful thing to do, but it is meaningless if you do not open up and LOOK at the day planner on a regular basis.

Consult it multiple times a day to make sure that you are keeping up with everything. If a friend asks you to the movies, check the book. If you want to join a group that has regular meetings, look at the book. Carry the day planner with you wherever you go. Jam it into your backpack. Stick it in a pocket. Shove it in a purse. Got the point? Use it. Look at it. Live by it.

(4) Making a list; checking it twice...or more

Do you remember all those lists your parents seemed to have around the house? Your mom may have made grocery lists or bills-to-be-paid lists. Your dad might have made lists of what he needed to get from Home Depot. Maybe you have even kept lists of your favorite books or bands, your top ten movies or the foods you liked best in your sack lunches.

College is the perfect place to either start the list habit or simply continue it. Make a list of what you have to do for each project or paper. For example, if you have to write a research paper, chunk it down into steps like choosing a topic, writing an outline, researching the Net, going to the library, writing the first draft and so on. Once you know all the steps, you can put them where they belong on the list. Do this for each class and anything else that might require daily attention.

Here are two sample days from a student's list:

MONDAY

Get books on Plato from the library

Run one mile for track and time it

Study for tomorrow's literature quiz

Biology lab

Science class from 10-12

TUESDAY

English class from 2-4

Work from 6-8

Write English outline on Plato

Meet with Dan and Kevin at 9

Call Mom and ask for more money

A list like this will help ensure that you don't waste time. You won't spend time wondering what you are supposed to do next or have to stop and look it up again. These lists will also work wonderfully with your day planner. While it has overall due dates, your list will have things broken down into steps. Can you guess the most important part about a list? Put it where you can see it, whether pinned to your bulletin board or inserted in your day planner. Just choose a place that you will see daily, which brings us to another point: Update the list daily. If the professor changes the date the project is due, indicate this in your day planner and on your list. When you have accomplished something, check it off your list. Watch for the thrill as you achieve the items on your list. You will also know if you have missed something, you should add it to the next day's list.

What You Eat Counts

"If a freshman puts on 15 extra pounds from drinking beer alone, then that is a problem. But even if the extra weight comes from a mixture of beer and junk food, or junk food alone, I would urge you to do your best not to fall victim to this rite of passage. In the first place, it shows a lack of maturity—that without Mom constantly looking over your shoulder, you can't keep yourself from gorging on pizza and chips. It also means that you're probably not eating right, as I doubt that you're piling on the broccoli and carrots too. (It's not uncommon for college students to get diseases that come from not eating a proper diet and that are usually found only among the very poor who can't afford to eat the right foods.) Such extra weight may also indicate that you're not getting enough exercise. And, finally, it might start you on a lifetime of food problems, and that's definitely not one of the lessons you want to include in your college education."

— Dr. Ruth Westheimer, *Dr. Ruth's Guide to College Life*

---

(5) Basic elements of life

Whether you are rushing to complete an assignment, trying to make it to work on time or squeezing in an unexpected track practice, it's easy to overlook two simple things: sleeping and eating. You cut out a little sleep here, skip a meal or two there. It isn't much—but it builds up.

The student who doesn't get enough sleep and food may accomplish more, but in the end, it will all fall apart. Students who allow themselves to become depleted will lose more time than they gain. (Advice on the inevitable but occasional all-nighter can be found in Chapter Eight.) They will be tired, cranky and more susceptible to getting sick.

You must take time to eat well and sleep at least seven hours a night or everything you gained by skipping both will be lost when you are exhausted or ill. Here are two examples of what can happen when you neglect basic needs like sleeping and eating. They may seem to be on opposite ends of the spectrum, but they really are quite similar because they both deal with control.

The first problem is one that faces a growing number of young people today: undereating, including anorexia and bulimia. These eating disorders happen when the number of calories plummets due to limited or restricted eating, while physical activity increases. It may start out as just skipping a few meals to spend that time doing something else, but it can turn into a potentially fatal condition. If you find yourself missing meals on purpose and your weight dropping significantly, especially if this is accompanied by signs of depression or anxiety, it's time to talk to someone. Get to the health center, talk to a friend or call home.

On the other hand, you might experience what is sometimes called "The Freshman 15." According to Roberta Anding, a spokesperson of the American Dietetic Association, about 60 percent of college students gain five to 25 pounds during their first year of school. It goes back to that "my parents aren't looking" philosophy. You can order pizza every night and don't have to get any fruits or vegetables as you go through the cafeteria line. You get to make the decision about what you are—and are not—going to eat. Ah! The power! Ah, the scales!

To avoid either of these two extremes, try these simple steps:

- Keep healthy snacks in your dorm room

- Eat your heaviest meals in the first part of the day, not the last

- Carry healthy snacks in your purse or backpack

- Avoid sugary, carb-laden foods when you finally do eat

- Do not skip meals; at least have some fruit, a granola bar or some sort of healthy snack

For more suggestions, check out the Healing Well website at http://healingwell.healthology.com.

(6) The best time...

You have been trying to convince your parents for years that you study best late at night, right? You've launched multiple campaigns to get them to let you stay up really late, and finally you have the chance to do it all the time. You are in a place and situation where you can find out if your late-night study preference is a good idea—or not.

But don't just assume that you are right. Experiment a little. Study at night, in the morning and in the middle of the afternoon. Which seems to be the most effective? When are you most alert and receptive to information? You need to find what works best for you. (And if it turns out to be early morning like your parents told you, we promise not to tell.)

(7) ...and place

While you were trying to convince your parents that you study best after midnight, you might have also been telling them that you did it best in your room with loud music playing, or even with a few friends around. Once again, it's time to put that theory to the test.

Conduct a few experiments. Study in your room, at the library, in the lounge, at a friend's house or in the fraternity or sorority house. Study in silence or surrounded by music, people or television. Study on the bed, in a soft chair or a hard chair. Sit at a desk or lie on your bed. Try bright lights and dim lights. Even the type of music you listen to can have an influence on how successful study time is. Try classical, country, gospel, opera, rock, blues, jazz, oldies or Broadway soundtracks. What seems to work best for you? How does the material soak in the best? What is distracting and what is not? For some students, trying to read material and understand it in complete silence is a treat; for others, it is torture. Simple sounds like water dripping, clocks ticking or phones ringing can drive some people crazy, and others will not even notice them. Once you have found what works for you, stick with it.

Be sure to avoid internal distractions as well. Your ability to study can be compromised by simple things like being hungry, tired or sick. Extreme worry, boredom or even a drive for perfectionism can interfere with being able to concentrate. If you become aware of any of these factors, they need to be addressed, just as much as time and location do.

(8) And in your spare time...

Not that you have much of it, mind you...but what spare time you do have should be used wisely. There are so many options to choose from and as you have found out already, there are only a few hours to give. Here is just a short list:

- sports
- clubs and organizations
- study groups

- part-time jobs
- meet with friends
- party
- volunteer work

When thinking about what to do in your spare time, consider what activities might bring you the most fulfillment. It's vital that you balance the fun with the work (see Chapter Eight). Too much of one or the other makes you a cranky student. Too much fun means that you're falling down in the academic department, while not enough fun means you will end up stressed and burned out.

(9) Fitting in a job

Should you work while you are in college? For many students, not working isn't an option. They must work to make ends meet for books, supplies and other costs not covered by scholarships, grants and parents. If working is an option, however, give it some serious thought. As you saw earlier in the chapter, time is precious in college, and work will definitely take up a lot of your time and energy.

In 2002, a report entitled *At What Cost?* was issued by the Public Interest Research Group Higher Education Project (www.pirg.org). It looked at how employment affected college students. Here is what the report found:

- 74 percent of full-time students work while attending school

- Of those, 84 percent identify themselves as primarily working to meet college expenses

- 46 percent of full-time working students work 25 or more hours a week

- 42 percent of these students reported that working hurt their grades

- 53 percent of full-time working students who work 25 or more hours a week reported that employment limited their class schedule and 38 percent said that work limited their class choice

- 63 percent of full-time working students who work 25 or more hours a week reported that they would not be able to afford college if they did not work

■ One in five full-time working students works 35 or more hours a week

As you can see, working may be essential to college survival, but it comes at a high price. Before you just accept the fact that you will have to work in college, do your scholarship/loan/grant homework. Start with Gen and Kelly Tanabe's book *Sallie Mae How to Pay for College*. It can give you a lot of information on finding ways to pay for college other than working every spare moment.

If you do have to get a job, see if you can find something that will give you added experience in your field of study. If you're studying animal medicine, work at a veterinarian's office, for example. Another option is work-study, which you may be offered as part of your financial aid package. The benefits of work-study are that your job will most likely be conveniently located on campus and your employer will be flexible to arranging your work schedule around your classes. Also, be sure to put your schedule into your day planner and on your daily list. You will have to pay extra attention to sleeping enough and eating well because you will need all the energy you can muster to keep up with the demands of college life.

(10) The most effective piece of equipment you will ever purchase

Any guesses? Is it the perfect day planner? The toughest backpack? Maybe even the most high-tech computer? Good guesses, but the actual answer is (drum roll, please) a quality alarm clock. Being up on time is essential to getting to class and getting each day started the right way, so get a good one. Make sure the alarm rings loudly and that you place the clock far enough away from your bed that you have to get up to turn it off. Never hit the snooze button. It's dangerous and addictive.

Remember that while time management may sound like a pain, you will get used to it. After you do, the results will be less stress and more efficiency, which in turn will provide you with time to learn and play.

CHAPTER **EIGHT**

• • • • • • • • • • •

Am I Having Fun Yet? The Top Ten of Balancing Social Life and Studies

A philosopher once said (ok, this is a bit paraphrased), "Virtue comes from following a course of action somewhere between the extreme of too much and that of too little." Another way to put it is "all things in moderation." Or simply, balance.

How can you balance all that you will be asked to juggle in college? Here are some helpful hints:

(1) The scoop on groups

By putting together a study group, you can blend two things at once: seeing your friends and getting your studying done. It is often easier to understand information when you are with others who are learning the same thing. You can bounce questions off one another and gain different perspectives on the material, and if one of you grasps a certain concept first, he/she can explain it to the others in the group in a way that might make more sense to them.

If you decide to organize a study group, keep a few things in mind:

- Always select people who have the same goal as you—and that doesn't mean how much pizza you can eat while cramming for a math test. You want to choose people who want to learn this information for the purpose of performing well in class.

- Look around your class and see which students seem to really be paying attention, taking notes, asking questions and responding to the professor. They are the ones you want to ask to be part of your study group.

- Most groups work best if there are more than three and less than seven. Too many of you and it turns from studying to partying.

College Students and Stress

Dr. Gregory Hall, Bentley College

Mind and body are integrated as can be seen with the issue of stress. It is no secret that psychological stress and physical illness are related. Stress triggers physiological and chemical (hormones) changes in the body. Physical illness is commonly accompanied with increased stress. Thus, as we learn to manage stress we must address physical as well as psychological factors. As you consider the following tips, keep in mind that maintaining balance between your intellectual, social and personal development is the key to a well-adjusted college experience.

- ■ Add a physical workout to your schedule at least every other day. One does not need to be gifted athletically to accomplish this. You can jog, power walk, use stepper, rowing or biking machines, swim or any other form of exercise. Do not see this as "recreational time" that can be blown off. Physical activity is a great way to insure that life's minor stresses do not build.

- ■ Set both long-term (this semester or this year) and short-term (this day or this week) goals. Write them down. Make them part of your time-management schedule.

- ■ Manage your time. Develop a schedule that provides for academic, social and physical time. Follow the schedule! Seek the help of an adviser in developing better time-management skills.

- ■ Each day find 20 minutes of "alone time" to relax. Take a walk, write in a journal or meditate.

- ■ Don't sweat the small stuff...always ask yourself if the issue at hand is worth getting upset about. If it isn't affecting your goal achievement, it may not be worth fretting over.

- ■ Humor and positive thinking are important tools in stress management.

- ■ Most importantly, communicate! Talking to persons whom you trust, be they a friend, roommate, family member, professor, significant other or co-worker, about issues of concern is helpful. We all need someone to listen.

Reprinted with permission of *CampusBlues.com*.

When you are in your groups, use your time efficiently. Quiz one another over the material you've been working on. Ask questions if you don't understand something. Often the best teacher is another student.

(2) Choose wisely, young student

You may well be overwhelmed with social opportunities at school. There are meetings for everyone that span a gamut of interests and hobbies. There are often hundreds of classmates to meet and spend time with. There are sports programs and sororities/fraternities to join. Your biggest complication will be making sure you do all these extracurricular activities in moderation. Before you commit to anything, get that day planner back out and make sure you really have time for it. Social life in college is very important, but it is not the primary reason you are there.

(3) Dating—not high school anymore

If you think about the social aspects of college, dating is certainly one of the first subjects to come up. Most likely, you will be dating during your college years. In fact, many students meet their future spouses during college. Advice about dating and sexuality is not within the scope of this book, except to say that both of them take time and you will have to balance that with your studies as well.

For some great advice on sexuality and the college student, check out the websites www.smartersex.org and teensexuality.studentcenter.org.

(4) Ignoring temptation; do more than say "no"

Along with the many new educational and social opportunities that can come your way with college, there are also temptations. Certainly drugs is one of these. You may be sick of hearing "Just say no," so instead just say you've got too many other things to do with your time (and money!) than spend them on drugs. They are expensive, dangerous and carry the potential to destroy everything you have been working so hard for all these years. Common physical changes from drug use include lack of physical coordination (forget sports), puffy face, running nose, hacking cough and excessive sweating (forget dating), hyperactivity and tremors (forget sitting in class). Behavioral changes are often worse, including moodiness, nervousness, lack of concentration and depression. Doesn't sound like much fun—why risk it?

You can find some terrific info on the Net about the nasty effects of drug use. The National Mental Health Association's web site has some good data at www.nimh.nih.gov/publicat/students.cfm. So does a user-friendly site called Facts on Tap (www.factsontap.org). Check 'em out.

(5) Just a few drinks...

Alcohol carries just as many dangers as drugs—perhaps even more since it is often easier and cheaper to get. Any "decent" party on campus features non-stop beer, right? Well, before you start thinking about all those great partying weekends ahead of you, keep in mind that according to a Harvard study, 31 percent of college students "meet the clinical criteria for alcohol abuse" (Harvard School of Public Health College Alcohol Study (CAS) www.hsph.harvard.edu/cas). According to the *Alcohol Policies Report* from the Center for Science in the Public Interest, college presidents believe that binge drinking is the most serious problem on campus (Source: www.cspinet.org/booze/collfact1.htm). They also stated that frequent binge drinkers are 21 times more likely to miss class, fall behind in school work, get hurt and get in trouble with campus police.

In *A Call to Action: Changing the Culture of Drinking at U.S. Colleges* (written by the College Task Force of the National Advisory Council of Alcohol Abuse and Alcoholism), statistics include these:

- 1,400 college students die each year from alcohol-related injuries

- 500,000 college students were injured under the influence of alcohol

- 600,000 college students are assaulted by students who have been drinking

- 70,000 college students are victims of alcohol-related sexual assault

- 150,000 college students develop an alcohol-related health problem

Are beer and hard liquor really worth all this? If you are convinced that drinking really is a part of college life, at least use some common sense and be...here's that word again...*responsible.*

(6) All Greek to you—or not

A great many colleges offer the chance to join on-campus sororities and fraternities. Whether or not you choose to join one is completely up to you and your personality. Just be aware that if you do, membership will require time. Get out that day planner!

From the outside looking in, the Greek life may look perfect. While many people cherish the time they once spent in a fraternity or sorority, there are aspects you should be aware of before you make your final decision.

First, there is the time involved. You are making a commitment to participate in activities including rush, community service and social events.

Second, there is a monetary commitment. If you are on a tight budget, you should know that membership can range from $100 to $900 per semester.

Don't get me wrong. Becoming part of a campus's Greek life can be delightful. If you want to meet more people and have some great friends, this is one good way to do it, and membership in a sorority or fraternity can teach you some terrific lessons regarding leadership, socializing and teamwork.

(7) Dorm life...hmmm...fun!

Years from now, when you look back at your college experience, you will most likely sigh wistfully, remembering wonderful times you had in your dorm room. While some students may live in off-campus housing, the majority will be in a dorm on campus. Some colleges require that you live in a dorm for at least the first year. You will make some great friends, learn how to live with and get along with others and hopefully like your roommate.

Dorms often sponsor activities, from television marathons to singing contests to slumber parties. If you take the time to join in now and then, you will find that you suddenly not only know a lot more people on campus, but they are also living so close to you that getting together is nooooooo problem. As the people at www.collegeboard.com say, "The dorms can help jump start your social life, ease the transition to life on your own and introduce you to a diverse group of people. Sure, living in a dorm can have its drawbacks—no privacy, crowded bathrooms, weird roommates. But most people find that the rewards outweigh the frustrations."

(8) Feeling low

College is exciting, fun, demanding—and stressful. It's easy to feel overwhelmed by everything! There are increased academic demands, the changes of a new environment, financial responsibilities, a shift in social life and exposure to new people and possibilities. Stress can turn into depression almost before you realize it. You should be aware that depression manifests itself differently in each person. Some are always irritated. Others cry, and still others never say a word.

According to the National Institute for Mental Health, there are major symptoms of depression that you can learn to watch for:

- Sadness, anxiety or "empty" feelings

- Decreased energy, fatigue, feeling "slowed down"

- Loss of interest or pleasure in usual activities

- Sleep disturbances (insomnia, oversleeping or waking much earlier than usual)

- Appetite and weight changes (either loss or gain)

- Feelings of hopelessness, guilt and worthlessness

- Thoughts of death or suicide, or suicide attempts

- Difficulty concentrating, making decisions or remembering things

- Irritability or excessive crying

- Chronic aches and pains not explained by another physical condition

A less intense type of depression, dysthymia, involves long-term, chronic symptoms that are less severe but keep a person from functioning at his or her full ability and from feeling well.

In bipolar illness (also known as manic-depressive illness), cycles of depression alternate with cycles of elation and increased activity known as mania.

What can be done if you find you are suffering from some or all of these symptoms? Just recognizing them is a good first step. Next, find someone to talk to about what you are experiencing. Don't ignore it. Speak with your residential assistant or in more serious cases seek professional help.

(9) Same day, different people

One of the biggest perks of college life is an introduction to the wide world of diversity. If you grew up in a small town, this will be especially evident. You will most likely be surrounded by students from all ethnic groups, from whites and African-Americans to Hispanic to Asian and Native American. There will be international students from countries around the world. You will meet gays, lesbians and bisexuals. With every class, there comes the opportunity for a diversity of students—tall, short;

blonde, brunette; single and married. Some students will have come from poor backgrounds, others from wealthy families. The small-town students will sit right next to the students from New York City or Chicago. This is a wonderful opportunity for you to learn about other people and find out how different—and how alike—they all are. Don't waste it.

(10) Pulling the inevitable all-nighter

Chances are you will pull a number of all-nighters—sessions where you forfeit sleep to study or finish a paper or project. Maybe you fell behind, maybe you need more time to understand a concept or 12, maybe you just found out about tomorrow's test, maybe it's mid-terms or finals week or maybe you just want to study more than you usually do. Whatever the reason, if you are going to do it, do it right.

First of all, have food and drink nearby. You will need it to keep up your strength and provide some necessary energy. Have something in your room and take regular breaks to snack. As much as you would like to stock up on lattes and M and M's, you will be better off with some fruit

Advice on Sleep

If you're planning your class schedule before you actually arrive at college, be sure to leave some mornings free so that you can sleep late. You can only go so many days in a row on four or five hours' rest.

Pack some earplugs. There will be nights when you're utterly exhausted and will need to conk out before dawn. Remember, sleep deprivation has been used as a form of torture, so don't suffer needlessly.

Cat naps can be quite refreshing. Even 15 minutes' worth of sleep in between classes can keep you going.

Don't abuse caffeine, in whatever form. You need to sleep to absorb what you are studying, so staying up all night before an exam will only have a negative impact.

If you really are having problems staying awake in class, go to see your RA. This is one roommate problem where there is the potential for help. If others in your dorm report having the same problem, then you can switch roommates so that you share quarters with someone who also likes to get to sleep at a reasonable hour.

— Dr. Ruth Westheimer, *Dr. Ruth's Guide to College Life*

and juice or water. Too much caffeine and/or sugar will just make you jittery instead of energetic.

Choose a place to study that is not terribly comfortable. Make the chair harder than you prefer, keep it cool in the room and don't grab any pillows or blankets. Keep far, far away from soft chairs, couches or beds. You may think you're just pausing for a rest but the next thing you know, it can be 9 a.m. and you didn't get near the studying done that you needed.

Give yourself incentives. When you finish a chapter, you will have a snack, call a friend, take a quick shower or whatever would be rewarding for you.

As odd as it sounds, try to have fun with an all-nighter. When you were in high school, the idea of staying up all night like this would have been exciting. Enjoy it. Listen to your favorite music and just relish the moment. You might not have this chance again for years.

If you can arrange it, pull your all-nighter with a friend...or six. If you are all studying for the same test, you can quiz each other. Just having other friends with you will automatically make it more fun and help keep you awake.

Keep in mind that all-nighters are occasional events. They should never be depended on for keeping up with your classes. They are a measure of last resort because too many of them will turn you into an exhausted student, not a successful one.

One of my goals is to reverse the frenzy of students thinking they cannot get into quality colleges if they do not make straight A's. I also want to help students to take a breath, settle in and think about college beyond the admissions period. They have to take the time to think about what it is they want and what they are interested in. Students tend to have tunnel vision, so focused on getting IN, that they don't look beyond it. They often want some kind of magic formula. "How many clubs do I have to join each year to get into XXX college?" Instead, please focus on who you are and what your passions are. College is all about expanding and experiencing and being there because you want to be.

— Laurie Nimmo
Career Center and College Admissions Coordinator/Independent College Advising

CHAPTER **NINE**

. . . .

Where's Mom When I Need Her?

The Top Ten of Living on Your Own

Living on your own is wonderful, exhilarating, empowering and... often a lot more work than you had ever anticipated. You will most likely be utterly amazed at how much your mom, dad or other guardian did on a daily basis for you that you never really noticed. It will become quite evident when those services suddenly disappear and you have to give thought to bizarre things like buying the toothpaste you like most or fixing buttons that fell off your shirt.

If you live in the dorm, some of life's basics are taken care of. You don't have to worry about paying the electricity, heat or water bills like you might if you lived off campus (unless you're renting and then that is often the landlord's headache, not yours). No matter where you live, however, you may be easily overwhelmed at what you have to take care of beyond just going to class and keeping up with your studies.

The best piece of advice when it comes to living on your own is to start practicing while you are still at home and can falter with fewer consequences. Ask someone to show you how to properly do laundry. Learn to cook some simple meals. Talk to a parent about how to budget money. Find out where you can find that special flavor of toothpaste or your favorite shampoo. (Perhaps you already know all this! In that case, congratulations. When you get to college, you might be able to teach your dorm mates a thing or two.)

In case you don't know already or aren't planning to learn before you get to college, here is a list of some basics you will need to make this powerful position of living alone a little easier.

(1) Smart laundry

Laundry will be one of the most important life skills you need. If you are going to community college (and living at home) or if you head to your parents' house every weekend, you might be able to avoid this chore for a while. But face it, one day you really will have to do this without help, so why not start now when your learning curve is at its peak?

Hopefully you have spent your life not dividing things into black and white (including everything from people to what to report on your tax returns). However, this is one time where you can throw out that rule. Divide your clothes into dark and light before washing them. (At what point you decide something is officially "dirty" is up to you. Chances are, it will be much later than what your mother would have liked and just before it can stand up on its own in your closet.)

Most clothes are easy to separate, but what about that black and white shirt or the red and pink skirt? Go with darks and hope for the best.

Before laundering anything, check the label in the clothes. You might have something that requires special handling, like that delicate sweater with the beading on it. You might also have clothing that is dry cleaning only. These will take extra effort, either to put together enough for a delicate load in the washer or a trip to the closest dry cleaner.

Once it is time to hit the dorm's laundry room or the college's laundromat, keep the following rules in mind:

- Have lots and lots of quarters on hand.

- Check the pockets of everything you wash to make sure they don't contain money, tickets, tissues or anything else that could be damaged.

- Don't overload the washer or the dryer.

- Fold the clothes when they come out of the dryer and you won't have to iron them as much (if at all) later. If you're asking, "What's an iron?", then just don't worry about it. You're used to wrinkles by now.

If you think that doing laundry is so awful that it belongs on one level of Dante's version of hell,

Laundry is sorted into two piles. Dirty and Offensive. Dirty may be worn again. Offensive must be washed. Learn the compost method of cleaning in which the heat and weight from the top of the pile cleans the clothes on the bottom of the pile.

—Youth minister Steve Case at Windermere Union United Church of Christ, excerpt from www.youthspecialities.com

consider asking someone else to do it for you. You could barter—you could help them with math class for an hour for each load done, or you could just pay them.

(2) Beating the health inspector

If health inspectors came to dorm rooms, colleges and universities across the country would be shut down for multiple violations. Keeping a dorm room clean seems simple. After all, it's not very big and there are only one or two of you in there most of the time. So how does it manage to look like a hurricane went through anyway? Just consider it a talent.

Keeping your dorm room clean doesn't mean it has to look like your house back home did. You probably don't have the time, energy or interest in keeping it that clean. Some simple tricks can help though. Try these:

- Put up a bulletin board to hold all your important papers so they aren't all over the place.

- Make your bed every morning before you do anything else. It sounds like a drag, but you will be surprised at what a difference it makes. In such a small room, your bed often serves as the place to sleep, eat, rest, study, talk and relax. If it's all rumpled up, you will be less likely to use it. To simplify making it, have a large comforter instead of a bedspread so that you can just take hold of everything and yank, smooth and you're finished. While keeping tons of things on your bed may seem like a good idea at first, you may find yourself whittling it down as days go by if you have to move it every night and replace it all every morning.

- Dust around things once a month, unless company is coming. If it's your parents, pick everything up and dust carefully. Wait for them to mutter to each other about how much you have matured since you left for college.

- Set up a special place to keep your backpack and/or purse or wallet. Always put it there and it won't get lost in the daily shuffle.

- If you have a sink in your room, clean it at least once a week. There are disinfecting wipes that just require a quick wipe-down. If not, be prepared for rainbow-colored growths, something that is not only unsightly but also can make you sick.

(3) Ya gotta eat!

Perhaps one of the biggest complaints about adjusting to college life is the food. Most students eat in the cafeteria, and while some are pretty darn good, others aren't. Here are a few suggestions for dealing with not getting your favorite meals anymore.

- Keep some food in your dorm room. A small fridge is a great thing to ask for when your grandparents want to get you something for your room.

- Be open minded to new foods. Don't turn your nose up and act "picky" (That's what little kids do, not big, tough college students).

- Eat out now and again, as long as you keep within your budget and don't overdo it.

- Order pizza occasionally, but watch out for those Freshman 15.

- Go grocery shopping and keep actual food for a basic meal in your room rather than just snacks.

- Learn some basic cooking skills. Many dorms have small kitchens where you can prepare your own meals. How tough is a microwavable pot pie anyway?

(4) What's a budget again?

Whether you are paying for college with your parent's money, a scholarship, working or a combination of all three, you will need to learn how to budget. This will come in mighty handy when you are living on your own after school too.

A budget should be firm but not inflexible. Life always presents a few surprises along the way that will require you to adjust where your money is going, but you still should have a standard plan to follow.

Budgeting is not that complicated a process. It is a matter of making a list of your expenses and income and finding a balance between the two.

When you look at your expenses, figure how much you will need for these things:

- tuition

- rent/room and board

There are No Perfect Students

Don't be caught unaware when it comes time to apply to colleges. As early as you can (sophomore year is great, junior is okay and senior is almost too late), be familiar with your overall academic standing. What is your GPA? How do your test scores look? Don't just look at your report card and then put it away. Be cognizant of your position.

Also take time to learn what different colleges require. To do this, you will have to do your homework. Learn the lingo and the terms they use. Then apply it to what you know about your grades and your goals. Remember that there is no perfect student. We all have weaknesses, so figure yours out so that you can start working on them.

Although taking a challenging AP core of classes looks good, it doesn't if you are in over your head and struggling. If you can't handle these classes, be honest and say so and do as well as possible in regular classes instead. Focus on colleges that look beyond GPAs and test scores and are more liberal and open to B students.

— Marjorie Ann Goode
   Educational Consultant/School Counselor

- car payments
- car insurance
- parking fees
- utilities
- entertainment
- gasoline
- food
- hygiene stuff
- clothing
- car repair
- books
- phone bills
- dating

The first five are usually preset amounts and are absolutely due on time. They are considered "fixed" costs. The others are "variable," meaning the lifestyle choices you make can affect the amounts. If you cut back on eating out, going to movies and other entertainment, that expense is quickly reduced. You can do a lot to affect those numbers just by making decisions to do so. It takes discipline, but it is possible. After all, your parents have been doing it for years!

The next thing you do is look at what money you have coming in. This can come from sources such as these:

- parents

- grants

- scholarships

- loans

- jobs

Those were the easy steps. Now for the more difficult part: comparing the two lists. Add up the numbers on both lists. It doesn't take a math major to figure out that if your monthly expenses are running more than your income, something has to change. This is where you go back to your list of variable expenses and start paring them down as much as possible to get those two sums a lot closer. If you get stuck, give your parents a call. No, not to get more money but to ask for budgeting advice.

(5) I'm out of everything. Where do I get dental floss?

Before you leave home, make a list of the hygiene supplies you like the best. Take the list and do one of two things: Give it to your parents and

Beware of Credit Cards

Special warning: Despite the incredibly cutesy commercials credit card companies keep putting on the television and in magazines and the offers of free T-shirts on campus, credit cards are not the solution to running low on money. Credit cards (which deservedly should be referred to as debt cards since that's what happens to a lot of people when they rely on those handy pieces of plastic) are risky for most people. For young adults newly on their own, credit cards can be poison. With interest rates that are often double and triple regular rates and stiff penalties for spending over the limit or for late payments, your small purchases can turn into giant problems. Credit cards should be used for unexpected emergencies and primarily with parental permission. You have years ahead of you to struggle with dealing with the chronic seduction of credit cards; don't start now.

have them buy a dozen of each so you don't have to face running out for a long time, or find out where each product can be purchased and keep the list in your dorm's desk drawer for quick and easy referencing. Things you might want to include are items such as these: soap, perfume/cologne, deodorant, toothpaste, dental floss, makeup, lotions, shaving cream and razors. Of course, a third option is to send the list to your grandparents or favorite aunt or uncle and hope that they take pity and send you "Keeping Clean" care packages.

(6) Learning to do without

While you may have used two cars and a U-Haul to move all your stuff to college, most students don't. They pack what they can fit into one car and settle for that. The luxuries you had at home are just not going to be available at college. For instance, while many students bring their own computers with them, some are not able to do this. In that case, check how to get access to one. It can be your roommate's (with permission, of course!), a college computer, one at the library, whatever you can find.

I believe that a typical high school curriculum just does not work for everybody. For some kids, it is just not a good fit, and sometimes it is just something that you have to get through to get to the next step. College is such a wonderful experience that it is more than worth what you might have to trudge through to get to it. College offers classes to turn you on, to feed your passion. In the meantime, take extra-curricular activities if you can and remember, school changes and it does get better.

— Maureen McQuaid
College Focus LLC

Other luxuries that you once took for granted while living at home but now may miss desperately, are a stereo, refrigerator and television. There are several solutions to this. Hope your roommate has one and is generous, try to pick one up at a local thrift store, start making your Christmas lists now and put aside money any chance you get until you can afford one. There is one more option—get used to not having them. Just think how much you will appreciate them again once you get back home for holidays or weekends.

(7) Dad, where do I put the oil?

If you are going to have a car at college, learn some simple repairs. Start with the very basics like changing a flat tire, changing the oil and checking the battery. These are easy tasks to do and can be unbelievably convenient in important moments. Learning to do simple maintenance on your own car can save you money; first, because you won't have to pay someone else to change the oil, for example, and second, because routine maintenance can prevent future repairs that become necessary when simple problems that were neglected turn into major break-downs.

You can get information for car maintenance and simple repairs from several sources. There are tons of books on car care, from simple to advanced mechanics. You can also try asking someone in your family to show you or you could take a shop class in high school that will teach what you need to know.

(8) I feel crummy

The first time you feel sick at college can feel mighty lonely. Maybe you miss the chicken soup your older sister made for you or the way your mom felt your forehead to monitor your temperature. Just remember that most every college has its own infirmary or health center, so find out where it is located and use it. They are there to give you confidential and competent help. Friends can help you keep up on what you are missing in class and they might even run to the store to get you another bottle of your favorite soda and some crackers. If worse comes to worst, call home and get unconditional sympathy.

(9) Late night stroll…or not

Everyone has watched a scary movie where the plucky heroine takes off into the dark, dank, dreary basement of a house, armed with nothing other than a wavering candle, right? You shout at the television screen, "You idiot! At least take a flashlight so you can hit someone over the

Know Yourself

It is essential that you KNOW YOURSELF. Do not be driven by what you THINK should happen but by your own preferences, personality, skills, traits and abilities. Put a rubber band around all of that and your test scores and GPA before approaching colleges. All of my clients take the Myers-Briggs test before we start working together. It helps them pinpoint these elements and then we can choose colleges that allow them to grow, thrive and become stronger, better individuals.

I ask each one of my students, on a scale from 1 to 10, how much effort they put into their high school courses. One means they were able to turn oxygen into carbon dioxide. Ten means they did everything they were supposed to do and much more. Even the highest ranking students tend to say 7 or 8, leaving room for improvement. It was okay to be at that level then—but it is not okay to stay there. It isn't about where you have been but where you are going and what you need to do to get there. Kids with 3.1 or so GPAs are solid kids—and they can be superstars!

— Todd Fothergill
   President of Strategies for College

head with it. What are you thinking going there all alone? You know better!" You can be sure that if you head out across campus alone at night, someone will be shouting the same thing at you. College life is wonderful, but it has its problems, and crime on campus is one of them. Don't complicate your life by putting yourself at risk unnecessarily. Finals are stressful enough; you don't need to add staying safe to your list of things to worry about.

Here are some important rules to keep in mind about campus safety. Heed them well. Hint: This is a good one to make a copy of and pin up on your wall or bulletin board.

DORM SAFETY

- Don't let anyone into the dorm that you don't personally know. (This goes for pizza deliverymen too!)

- Keep your dorm room door locked all through the night and whenever you are gone. If you leave to go to the laundry room, bathroom or another friend's dorm room, lock your door behind you.

- Never, ever lend your dorm room key to anyone.

PARKING LOT SAFETY

- Keep your car locked at all times.

- Don't keep your valuables out where someone can see them. Put them in your trunk, under the seats or bring them into your room with you.

- Never walk out to your car alone at night. Have someone go with you, even if it is your campus' escort service or a security guard.

- Have your keys ready in your hand as you approach the car.

- Check the back seat before getting into the car.

PERSONAL SAFETY

- Never walk alone—especially at night. Remember the girl in the horror movie? You're smarter than that!

- Walk only in well-lit areas, not dark alleys or shortcuts.

- Trust your instincts. If you feel a place or situation is dangerous, you just may be right. Play it safe and go to a populated area or call campus security on your cell phone.

- Find out where all campus emergency phones are located.

PARTY SAFETY

- Don't go to a party alone.

- Drink responsibly.

- Always tell your friends where you are going.

- Take a cell phone with you.

- Have the number of a local taxi service and/or the campus bus service on your person at all times.

DATING SAFETY

- Find out who your date is before you go out.

- Know his/her first and last name and address. Where does he/she go to school? Where does he/she work?

- Tell your friends exactly who you are going with and where you are going.

- Set up a time to check in and if you don't, your friends should call for help.

- Carry a cell phone at all times.

- Stay in public places on your date.

- Have a way to get home should the date not go quite as well as you hoped.

Keep in mind that while these precautions may seem a little paranoid, they are important. In 1986, a freshman named Jeanne Clery was sleeping in her dorm room at Lehigh University. She was murdered there and her parents discovered that the campus had not told anyone about the 38 violent crimes that had already occurred on the campus. They helped pass the Jeanne Clery Disclosure of Campus Security Policy and Campus Crime Statistics Act. It is a federal law that requires colleges and universities across the country to disclose information about crimes on and around their campuses. This law is enforced by the U.S. Department of Education. It requires the following:

- Schools must publish an annual report disclosing campus security policies and three years' worth of selected crime statistics.

- Schools must make timely warnings to the campus community about crimes that pose an ongoing threat to students and employees.

- Each institution with a police or security department must have a public crime log.

- The U.S. Department of Education centrally collects and disseminates the crime statistics.

- Campus sexual assault victims are assured of certain basic rights.

- Schools that fail to comply can be fined by the DOE.

Source: www.securityoncampus.org

(10) How am I supposed to get there?

One of the biggest things students tend to miss when they get to college is transportation. Mom and Dad (and their respective cars) are no longer available. Some colleges will not allow first-year students to have their own cars on campus. So how do you get from one place to another? Well, the first obvious choice for campus travel is your feet. You will probably never do as much walking in your life as you do that first year of college. (That's good though. It will help work off those extra pounds from all the pizza!) Spend some big bucks on comfy walking shoes. They will become your new best friends.

A bicycle is a great way to get places faster and get exercise to boot. Invest in a good bike lock to keep it safe and sound. Never park your bike and leave it unlocked.

If you want to go off campus, check into local buses. They often run near the campus to help students get where they need to go. You might also talk to other students with cars to see about carpooling into the city.

Being on your own is wonderful. You will be amazed at how fast your life changes and how you learn to accept responsibilities that you had never thought about before. The key is being prepared so that you don't have to recover from shock before you can start learning. Don't wait. Get as many skills under your belt as you can now and you will be relieved later.

You are Not Defined by Your Grades

Always remember that you are NOT defined by your grades. When you begin to think about possible colleges, take the time to think, imagine and dream. What do you want to do? What are your talents? What path do you want to follow?

There are so many elements to think about when selecting a college. If at all possible, take the time to visit the campus when students are there. Look around and see if you feel comfortable. Talk to as many students and faculty as you can. Look at the programs offered. Here are some additional questions you should be thinking about when looking at colleges:

■ Location: do you want to be in a large city, the beautiful outdoors or something in between?

■ Size: do you want a large campus or a small one? Do you want large or small classes?

■ Religion: is the presence or lack of religion a factor?

■ Climate: what kind of weather do you prefer?

■ Curriculum: what programs are you most interested in taking?

■ Atmosphere: Intellectual? Social? A blend?

■ Cost: is this a factor? Is financial aid possible?

■ Dorms: do you want to live on campus or off? Alone or with someone?

■ Sports: do you want to play any special one? Watch any? What type and level?

■ Organizations and clubs: What type do you want to be a part of? Do you want to be in a fraternity/sorority?

■ Culture: are theatre, art and music opportunities a high priority?

■ Diversity: do you want to be surrounded by a lot of people like yourself or people who are distinctly different in a myriad of ways?

Although it is unlikely that you will find one perfect college that fits each and every one of your preferences, you can find those that meet most, and the rest you can compromise on.

Always remember that every single person has the ability to be successful—and that includes you.

— Marilyn Emerson
   Independent Educational Consultant

THE COLLEGES

A Guide to the Colleges that Welcome B Students

COLLEGE DIRECTORY
• • • • • • • • • • • • •

A Guide to the Colleges that Welcome B Students

As a B or C student, you have many options when it comes to finding a college that is right for you. In fact, there are far more colleges that want you than you could ever apply to in a single year. Your challenge will not be finding the right college but narrowing down your list of possibilities.

As you will see, not all colleges require certain GPAs or test scores to make it past the velvet rope. Now it's time to meet some of the schools that not only accept B and C students but that also embrace them. These colleges are competitive and offer the highest quality educations, but they also recognize that students like you have much to offer and are committed to ensuring your success.

How These Colleges Were Chosen

All the colleges and universities listed in this directory were chosen for several reasons.

- ■ **They each offer very high quality educations.** Just because the colleges listed here accept students with less-than-perfect scores doesn't mean that they sacrifice quality. These schools are committed to preparing you for your future.

- ■ **B and C students are welcome.** These colleges have test scores and GPA averages that fit well with the typical B student's range. In addition, the schools offer programs such as tutoring or mentoring that will help students succeed once they are in college.

- ■ **They are competitive.** While not as selective as many of the colleges at the top of news magazines' lists, the schools listed here do have standards for admission. Because they generally draw from a smaller geographic area, community colleges are not included.

- ■ **They offer diversity.** These schools represent all parts of the country and all sizes, from small to large.

The Profiles

The college profiles have the essential information you need to determine if the school is a good fit for you academically, financially and career-wise. Here are some important definitions to help you make the most of the profiles:

Percentage of applicants admitted: This statistic gives a general sense of the level of competitiveness of the college and represents the undergraduate admission rate.

Average GPA range: This is the average high school GPA of admitted undergraduates.

SAT/ACT range: These numbers represent the range between the 25th and 75th percentile of scores of accepted undergraduate students, or the middle 50 percent. In other words, for a range of 500 to 600 on the math SAT exam, 25 percent of accepted students scored below 500, 25 percent scored above 600 and 50 percent scored between 500 and 600.

Number of undergraduates: Knowing this number gives you an indication of what the campus life will be like, as well as the size and scope of the school.

Costs: While it's useful to know the costs of tuition, fees, books and supplies and room and board, keep in mind that most students do not pay the full sticker price of a college. Financial aid and scholarships can bring the costs of college down.

Favorite majors: This list represents the largest programs offered at the college.

The B features: These are the features offered by the colleges that can be especially helpful for B students. Included are tutoring programs, the faculty-student ratio and programs to ease the transition from high school to college. You'll see the active role each college is taking in helping their students succeed.

Featured profiles: Certain profiles are much longer than others. This is because at these schools, the admissions department took time to speak at length about their welcoming policies for B students.

Special Request: If you get in touch with any of the places here, be sure to tell them that you found them here!

Adelphi University

Garden City, NY

Address: One South Ave., P.O. Box 701, Garden City,
NY 11530-0701
Phone: 1-800-ADELPHI or 516-877-3050
Admissions email: admissions@adelphi.edu
Admissions contact: Christine Murphy, director of admissions
Website: www.adelphi.edu

Admissions Stats

Percentage of applicants admitted: 69.6% of freshman
applicants
Average GPA range: 3.3-3.4
SAT range: 480-580 critical reading, 490-590 math
ACT range: 22-25 composite, 22-26 English, 20-26 math

Size

Number of undergraduates: 4,161

Cost

Tuition and fees: $20,900
Books and supplies: $1,000
On campus room and board and other expenses: $11,800
Off campus room and board and other expenses: $10,000

Academics

Favorite majors: education, business, social sciences, health
professions and related clinical arts, visual and performing arts,
psychology

Student Life

The campus: Chartered in 1896, Adelphi was the first institution of
higher education for the liberal arts and sciences on Long Island. Its
main campus is in Garden City, New York, and it also has centers in
Manhattan, Hauppauge and Poughkeepsie, New York. The campus
covers 75 lush acres and has six residence halls. It is 45 minutes
away from New York City.

The students: Undergraduate students come from 38 states and
45 foreign countries.

The B Features

This school has offered a General Studies program since 1985. According to the university, it is designed for "motivated high school seniors who demonstrate the potential for academic success, but who have not met the traditional academic admission requirements. Counselors, faculty members and administrators identify potentially successful candidates on the basis of their applications and letters of recommendation, as well as through personal interviews." The program offers small classes and personal advisement for each student. At the end of the year, students who have met all of the requirements continue as sophomores in the school's other undergraduate programs.

Insight

"Our admissions process is holistic," says Esther Goodcuff, associate vice president for enrollment management and student affairs. "We carefully read every single piece of documentation in each application. Our General Studies program is not a remedial program but one that challenges students, while at the same time supports them. Our faculty does individual tutoring outside of class, and students are given an academic counselor to help with college transition issues." Goodcuff says that Adelphi's admissions department looks at trends in how students have been performing in high school, watching for an upward movement. "Letters of recommendation and the essay also give us a sense of just who you are," she adds. "We look for students who are highly motivated and truly want to do well."

Student Perspective

Crispin Booker from Brooklyn, New York is majoring in computer management and information systems. A graduate of Lafayette High School, he was a member of the varsity basketball team during his junior and senior year. He managed to maintain a 3.0 average during his senior year when he was the captain of the team and participated in community service projects with the Key Club.

"My expectations were to attend a prestigious university, which would provide me with the tools and opportunities to compete in a tough job market and to make a difference in my life and others," he says. "Plus, I wanted to learn in a diverse academic environment that would allow me to share my experiences with those from other ethnic backgrounds. Adelphi University has met my expectations, giving me a sense of direction in my life. The rigorous course work from the General Studies program and the diversity among the professors and students has helped me to focus and excel. In addition, I believe the program has prepared me for a demanding job market.

I was able to take several challenging courses such as math, psychology, history, philosophy and English.

"I ultimately chose Adelphi because of its proximity to home and the prestigious General Studies program," he explains. "I also enjoyed the fact that it's close to New York City and I would have more job opportunities coming out of a well-known university like Adelphi. My short-term goals are to complete my bachelor's in computer management and information systems or history. My career goals are to complete law school and become a corporate lawyer.

"The experiences with my classmates are ones to remember," he adds. "I've met all types of people during the program and made many friends due to the various group assignments. In addition to the assignments, we got a chance to network and bond since a majority of us have to complete the same work and we can help each other. My experiences with my professors will result in lasting friendships because we spend so much time together during tutoring and counseling sessions," he continues. "They have helped me start my college career in a positive way, especially by reviewing my papers. Plus, I've really connected with my professors because of the individual attention they provide.

"I have found that the most challenging part about college is time management because there are so many things to do on campus, and so many people to meet. I learned that it is beneficial to set aside study time so I won't fall behind in the General Studies program," says Booker. "I like campus life because there are so many activities to participate in. I'm the vice president of the Adelphi chapter of NAACP and also participate in other minority-based organizations. In addition," he concludes, "I work two on-campus jobs, one in operations and the other security."

The New York Times describes Adelphi as "thriving" and Jay Matthews of *The Washington Post* says Adelphi is "one of 100 hidden higher education jewels."

Agnes Scott College *

Decatur, GA

Address: 141 E. College Way, Decatur, GA 30030-3797
Phone: 404-471-6285
Admissions email: admissions@agnesscott.edu
Website: www.agnesscott.edu

Admissions Stats

Percentage of applicants admitted: 53%
SAT range: 565-680 critical reading, 520-630 math, 540-660 writing
ACT range: 24-29 composite

Size

Number of undergraduates: 848

Cost

Tuition and fees: $25,685
Books and supplies: $700
On campus room and board and other expenses: $9,890
Off campus room and board and other expenses: $3,400

Academics

Favorite majors: social sciences, astrophysics, biological and biomedical sciences, psychology, English language and literature/letters, German, math, economics

---

The B Features

Besides being the setting for the horror flick Scream 2, Agnes Scott offers smaller classes, often with less than a half dozen students. The school offers "talking study halls," centers with tables and comfy chairs where students can gather to discuss homework assignments as a group. Every student is given an admission counselor who works with the student from beginning to end on the application process.

* All women college

Albertson College of Idaho

Caldwell, ID

Address: 2112 Cleveland Boulevard, Caldwell, ID 83605-4432
Phone: 208-459-5306
Admissions email: admissions@albertson.edu
Website: www.albertson.edu

Admissions Stats

Percentage of applicants admitted: 74.2%
SAT range: 490-640 critical reading, 490-630 math, 478-620 writing
ACT range: 22-28 composite, 21-29 English, 21-27 math

Size

Number of undergraduates: 818

Cost

Tuition and fees: $16,670
Books and supplies: $800
On campus room and board and other expenses: $7,491
Off campus room and board and other expenses: $5,750

Academics

Favorite majors: biological and biomedical sciences, psychology, history, visual and performing arts, social sciences, business, management, marketing and related support services

The B Features

All freshmen at this college must go through the First Year Experience, which consists of three parts and is geared to help each student connect "personally, academically and socially with their peers and with the College."

Part one of the Experience is called the First Year Book and consists of assigning a specific book to be read and then campus events such as speakers, contests, movies and discussions are centered around it. This helps students have a common point to begin talking and making friends.

The second part is Student Mentor, which links first-year students with junior or senior student mentors. The mentor's role is to help each new student get involved in campus activities and to guide them to helpful resources.

The third part is First Year Advising in which several advisors are dedicated to helping first-year students transition from high school to college life.

Albion College

Albion, MI

Address: 611 E. Porter St., Albion, MI 49224
Phone: 517-629-0321
Admissions email: admissions@albion.edu
Website: www.albion.edu

Admissions Stats

Percentage of applicants admitted: 87%
SAT range: 510-640 critical reading, 520-630 math
ACT range: 22-27 composite, 21-28 English, 21-27 math

Size

Number of undergraduates: 1548

Cost

Tuition and fees: $26,112
Books and supplies: $700
On campus room and board and other expenses: $8,196
Off campus room and board and other expenses: $7,236

Academics

Favorite majors: social sciences, psychology, biological and bio-medical sciences, English language and literature/letters, business, management, marketing and related support services, economics, premed/prelaw

The B Features

Albion wants its new students to transition well into college life and provides a First Year Experience, as others do. It offers Common Reading, followed up by presentations by the author, as well as a program called Student Orientation, Advising and Registration (SOAR). This takes place in May before the freshman year begins and is two days of touring the campus, meeting people, eating in the dining hall, speaking to faculty, planning student schedules and even registering for fall classes. The first three days of the first year center around fun get-acquainted activities such as skits, singing, lectures, ice cream breaks and even comedians.

Albion offers classes smaller than 20 students, and many undergrads speak highly of the casual and friendly attitudes of the entire faculty.

Albright College

Reading, PA

Address: 1621 N. 13th St., Reading, PA 19612-5234
Phone: 610-921-7512
Admissions email: Send email through the college's website
Website: www.albright.edu

Admissions Stats

Percentage of applicants admitted: 54.5%
SAT range: 460-550 critical reading, 460-560 math
ACT range: NA

Size

Number of undergraduates: 2,112

Costs

Tuition and fees: $26,620
Books and supplies: $800
On campus room and board and other expenses: $9,358
Off campus room and board and other expenses: NA

Academics

Favorite majors: business, management, marketing and related support services, psychology, social sciences, computer and information sciences and support services, history and visual and performing arts

The B Features

At Albright, students have the ability to focus on a single field of study, or combine several to create an individualized major. The college offers a Learning Resource Center that is open daily for free individual tutoring or group sessions. There is a Writing Center that gives students the chance to have their papers proofread and edited before they are turned in. The Center offers workshops on time management, test taking tips, study skills and success strategies. Students with learning disabilities can contact the vice president of student services for individual arrangements. Class sizes average 15 to 20 people with general classes slightly larger and advanced classes sometimes having less than 10 students.

Alcorn State University

Alcorn State, MS

Address: 1000 ASU Dr., Alcorn State, MS 39096
Phone: 601-877-6147
Admissions email: admissions@lorman.alcorn.edu
Website: www.alcorn.edu

Admissions Stats

Percentage of applicants admitted: 34.7%
SAT range: A minimum score of 790 is required.
ACT range: 16-20 composite, 16-21 English, 15-18 math

Size

Number of undergraduates: 3,554

Costs

Tuition and fees: $4,156 in state; $9,332 out of state
Books and supplies: $1,345
On campus room and board and other expenses: $9,098
Off campus room and board and other expenses: $10,077

Academics

Favorite majors: liberal arts and sciences, general studies and humanities, business, management, marketing and related support services, health professions and related clinical services, education, biological and biomedical services

---

The B Features

This is primarily an African American college, although about 8 percent of the students are Caucasian or of other ethnic backgrounds. Classes are small, and College for Excellence is offered for all freshmen, returning and transfer students. This program plans, supervises and coordinates all academic experiences of these students. It has an advising and tutoring staff and state of the art computer labs. Professional advisors support students by helping them adjust to college life, teaching them about Alcorn and its policies, exploring career options and solving any problems that come along. Additionally, staff is available to teach good test-taking, studying and time management skills and to monitor progress. Students who need additional help in reading, writing or thinking skills are assisted so that they can quickly reach college-level proficiency.

Alfred University

Alfred, NY

Address: One Saxon Dr., Alfred, NY 14802-1205
Phone: 607-871-2115
Admissions email: admwww@alfred.edu
Website: www.alfred.edu

Admissions Stats

Percentage of applicants admitted: 77%
SAT range: 500-620 critical reading, 520-610 math
ACT range: 22-27 composite, 20-26 English, 20-26 math

Size

Number of undergraduates: 1,961

Costs

Tuition and fees: $22,100
Books and supplies: $850
On campus room and board and other expenses: $11,000
Off campus room and board and other expenses: $11,000

Academics

Favorite majors: visual and performing arts, engineering, business, management, marketing and related support services, psychology, communication, journalism and related programs

---

The B Features

Rumored to have been the inspiration for the 1980s sit-com *Northern Exposure*, this college is quiet and small but active. The school is especially known for its School of Engineering's glass and ceramic programs and is one of the few schools that offer a degree in Ceramic Engineering. Classes are typically less than 10 students at Alfred. The general atmosphere appeals to the back-to-nature student who likes cold and snowy winters. Each applicant is considered individually and with true, personal attention.

Anna Maria College

Paxton, MA

Address: 50 Sunset Lane, Paxton, MA 01612
Phone: 508-849-3360
Admissions email: admissions@annamaria.edu
Website: www.annamaria.edu

Admissions Stats

Percentage of applicants admitted: 80%
SAT range: 946 average composite
ACT range: 17-18 average composite

Size

Number of undergraduates: less than 1000

Costs

Tuition and fees: $31,000
Books and supplies: NA
On campus room and board and other expenses: $8,000
Off campus room and board and other expenses: NA

Academics

Favorite majors: criminal justice, nursing, business, music and art therapy and fire science

---

The B Features

This Roman Catholic college was founded by the Sisters of St. Anne. An interview with admissions stated that Anna Maria is a "best kept secret." They offer an $8,000 scholarship based upon involvement in the high school community and the community at large. The best advice for students who do not have straight A's is to APPLY! Anna Maria is among the many non-Ivy league colleges that will educate and prepare you for graduate school or a career, and B students are qualified to apply. Anna Maria does not require minimum scores on the SAT. In addition, the admissions department states that there are many B and C students who are highly involved in their high school and are welcomed at Anna Maria!

Arizona State University

Tempe, AZ

Address: P.O. Box 870112, Tempe, AZ 85287-0112
Phone: 480-965-7788
Admissions email: askasu@asu.edu
Website: www.asu.edu

Admissions Stats

Percentage of applicants admitted: 80%
SAT range: 490-600 critical reading, 500-620 math
ACT range: 20-26 composite, 19-26 English, 20-27 math

Size

Number of undergraduates: 39,690

Costs

Tuition and fees: $ 15,847 out of state, $4,688 in state
Books and supplies: $950
On campus room and board and other expenses: $10,722
Off campus room and board and other expenses: $10,722

Academics

Favorite majors: history, business, psychology, geology, anthropology, music, landscape architecture, accountancy

---

The B Features

Like other colleges, ASU offers First Year Experience for freshmen. According to the college, this program is designed to "provide a strong foundation for all first-year students and students in transition that will foster their academic and personal success. We will achieve this mission by providing academic support services, opportunities for the exchange of ideas, workshops, generating and supporting research and scholarship, hosting visiting scholars and practitioners, faculty interaction within living and learning communities, administering a website and student involvement opportunities with the university community."

The Learning Resource Center offers tutoring to help students develop study skills and strategies. This nationally certified program offers tutoring in more than 100 courses, either in a group or individual settings. Peer coaching teaches time management, study habits and test-taking skills. The program also includes software training and Academic Skills Workshops.

Assumption College

. . . .

Worcester, MA

Address: 500 Salisbury St., Worchester MA 01609-1296
Phone: 888-882-7786
Admissions email: asmiss@assumption.edu
Website: www.assumption.edu

Admissions Stats

Percentage of applicants admitted: 74.4%
SAT range: 480-580 critical reading, 485-590 math
ACT range: 20-24 composite, 19-24 English, 18-25 math

Size

Number of undergraduates: 2,443

Costs

Tuition and fees: $26,060
Books and supplies: $850
On campus room and board and other expenses: $10,700
Off campus room and board and other expenses: $10,700

Academics

Favorite majors: business management, marketing and related support services, communication, journalism and related programs, English language and literature/letters, psychology, health professions and related clinical sciences, social sciences and history

---

The B Features

At the end of June, a comprehensive two-day orientation program is given to help new students and their parents become familiar with all aspects of college life. The Academic Support Center, located in the library, is open to all students and staffed by trained peer tutors in many areas including writing, math, foreign languages, economics, finance, accounting, physics, chemistry, philosophy and more. Course-specific group tutorials are conducted each semester and one-on-one tutorials can be easily arranged. Study skills workshops are offered to all students and those with learning needs or ESL can meet with the director for additional assistance.

Auburn University

· ·

Auburn, AL

Address: 202 Mary Martin Hall, Auburn, AL 36849-5111
Phone: 334-844-4080
Admissions email: admissions@auburn.edu
Website: www.auburn.edu

Admissions Stats

Percentage of applicants admitted: 82%
SAT range: 500-600 critical reading, 520-620 math
ACT range: 21-27 composite, 21-28 English, 20-26 math

Size

Number of undergraduates: 19,254

Costs

Tuition and fees: $5,496 in state; $15,496 out of state
Books and supplies: $1,100
On campus room and board and other expenses: $9,868
Off campus room and board and other expenses: $10,048

Academics

Favorite majors: information technology, biological sciences, software engineering, computer science and agriculture

---

The B Features

Auburn's network of academic advisors is by department or major. Advisors assist students with selecting classes and career planning, and they also give general advice. Some department heads provide information about their departments to prospective applicants as well.

Learning Communities bring together first-year students in the same major to take certain required classes as a group. This enables students to easily form study groups and to navigate classes cooperatively.

Departments also offer help that is basic to a student's field of study. For example, the Auburn Office of Engineering Student Services provides tutoring for freshmen and transfer engineering students who need assistance in entry-level math, chemistry and physics classes. The tutoring is done by volunteer upperclassmen in group or one-on-one sessions.

Augsburg College

Minneapolis, MN

Address: 2211 Riverside Ave., Minneapolis, MN 55454
Phone: 612-330-1001 or 800-788-5678
Admissions email: admissions@augsburg.edu
Admissions contact: Bethany Bierman, assistant director of the Office of Undergraduate Admissions
Website: www.augsburg.edu

Admissions Stats

Percentage of applicants admitted: 77%
Average GPA range: 3.26 (29% have 3.0 or below)
SAT range: 290-610 reading, 485-605 math
ACT range: 20-25 composite, 19-25 English, 18-25 math

Size

Number of undergraduates: 2,916

Costs

Tuition and fees: $24,559
Books and supplies: $125 per class
On campus room and board and other expenses: $6,902
Off campus room and board and other expenses: Varies
Majors offered: More than 50 majors and six graduate programs

Academics

Favorite majors: business, education, psychology, communication, biology and unusual majors that include film, medieval studies, music business, music therapy, and youth and family ministry

Student Life

Augsburg's campus contains all of the amenities you might expect from a small, residential liberal arts college, including a student center, library and fitness center. It also has two large skating arenas for hockey and figure skating, a turf athletic field that is covered by an air-supported dome during the winter months, and a chapel that serves as a sanctuary for daily chapel services as well as for a local congregation's Sunday morning worship service.

Augsburg's campus is set in the heart of the Twin Cities of Minneapolis-St. Paul, with easy access to a multitude of off-campus activities. The campus is just blocks from downtown Minneapolis and the Mississippi River, and it is only a short walk to two light rail stations, with trains that stop at the Mall of America and the international airport. Auggies enjoy theatre, live music, shopping, sports and outdoor recreation and many other activities.

The B Features

Support for academic success is provided through tutoring, academic skills coaching, supplemental instruction and the math, public speaking and writing labs. Augsburg's TRiO/Student Support Services program helps students who are 1) low-income, 2) first-generation enrollees, or 3) disabled (learning or physical) to achieve their bachelor's degrees.

StepUp provides ongoing support to students in chemical recovery who are willing and able to progress toward an academic degree while remaining clean and sober. Students live together in separate, chemical-free housing.

The Center for Learning and Adaptive Student Services (CLASS) assists academically qualified students with learning, attention, psychiatric or other cognitive disabilities reach their individual potential through services and accommodations, while the Access Center supports students with documented physical disabilities.

Insight

"At Augsburg, we realize that grades are only one measure of success," says Bethany Bierman, assistant director of the Office of Undergraduate Admissions. "One of our graduates received a D in high school chemistry and went on to receive a Nobel Prize in chemistry! We are an intentionally diverse community, and with that comes students from a range of academic backgrounds. Yes, we will do a thorough review of an application, but grades are not the only basis on which we accept students. Applicants can demonstrate that they are qualified for Augsburg by the extracurricular activities in which they are involved, including work positions or volunteer work. The difficulty of courses a student has selected in high school is also considered," she adds. "Additionally, letters of recommendation that focus on the character of the student tell us a great deal. Ultimately, Augsburg seeks to accept students who want to use their gifts to make a difference in the world." Bierman states that the school's overall philosophy is that it is "more concerned with the quality and character of the alumni we produce than the incoming GPA of our students. As long as we know that students are working to their full potential, taking their academic work seriously and are seeking to make a difference in their community, we are proud of them, regardless of grades that are B's or C's."

Augusta State University

Augusta, GA

Address: 2500 Walton Way, Augusta, GA 30904-2200
Phone: 706-737-1632
Admissions email: admissions@aug.edu
Website: www.aug.edu

Admissions Stats

Percentage of applicants admitted: 62%
SAT range: 430-540 critical reading, 430-540 math
ACT range: 16-21 composite, 15-20 English, 16-21 math

Size

Number of undergraduates: 5,461

Costs

Tuition and fees: $3,066 in state; $10,748 out of state
Books and supplies: $952
On campus room and board and other expenses: $6,490
Off campus room and board and other expenses: $10,446

Academics

Favorite majors: business, management, marketing and related support services, education, social sciences, psychology and communication, journalism and related programs

The B Features

Struggling students are encouraged to contact the instructor or department head for names of tutors. Some of the departments offer Help Labs. The Department of Learning Support helps students learn to write, do math, read critically, study effectively (i.e. the fundamentals of English, mathematics, reading and study skills) and to make the best possible use of all campus resources available that will help them improve and cope with college-level course work.

Bellarmine University

Louisville, KY

Address: 2001 Newburg Rd., Louisville, KY 40205-0671
Phone: 502-452-8131
Admissions email: admissions@bellarmine.edu
Website: www.bellarmine.edu

Admissions Stats

Percentage of applicants admitted: 61.6%
SAT range: 500-610 critical reading, 520-628 math
ACT range: 22-27 composite, 21-27 English, 20-26 math

Size

Number of undergraduates: 2,287

Costs

Tuition and fees: $24,150
Books and supplies: $644
On campus room and board and other expenses: $11,520
Off campus room and board and other expenses: $12,298

Academics

Favorite majors: psychology, business, management, marketing and related support services, biological and biomedical sciences, health professions and related clinical services, liberal arts and sciences, general studies and humanities

---
The B Features

This college's Academic Resource Center is the place for help with your classes and college career. There are tutors available for the 100- and 200-level classes, both in individual and group study sessions. The staff at ARC will help analyze your essays to improve grammar, style and formatting.

Bellarmine also offers a one-hour credit course called Freshman Focus. It helps freshmen make the transition to college. This program includes reading, writing, discussion and out-of-class activities. The focus of the course is increasing a student's self-awareness and sense of purpose when it comes to his/her education and making important decisions about academic and social lives. Students are graded (A to F) in this class.

Bowie State University

Bowie, MD

Address: 14000 Jericho Park Rd., Bowie, MD 20715-9465
Phone: 301-860-3415
Website: www.bowiestate.edu

Admissions Stats

Percentage of applicants admitted: 74.7%
SAT range: 400-490 critical reading, 495-599 math
ACT range: 16-19 composite

Size

Number of undergraduates: 4,020

Costs

Tuition and fees: $5,730 in state; $15,382 out of state
Books and supplies: $2,678
On campus room and board and other expenses: $8,379
Off campus room and board and other expenses: $10,796

Academics

Favorite majors: business, management, marketing and related support services, social sciences, psychology, computer and information sciences and support services and communications technologies/technicians and support services

---

The B Features

Bowie's Writing Center helps students with English class assignments. The school also has a Student Success and Retention Center, whose motto is "Where Your Successful Tomorrow Begins Today." The center assists students through programs and activities that "foster student academic, social and personal development." It is focused on helping freshmen transition into college life with the aid of placement testing, mentoring and tutorial services.

In addition to these services, Bowie State sponsors the Freshman Seminar course. It is designed to help each student pursue academic excellence and includes lessons about the college's history and its contribution to Maryland. Students learn to critically analyze specific readings that introduce them to concepts in liberal arts and to broaden their understanding of global awareness, critical thinking and oral and written communication skills. According to the college,

"The goal is for students to become academically, personally and socially successful within and beyond the intellectual community."

Mentoring is popular at Bowie State. Mentors are matched with students to help foster a strong relationship that "promotes academic success, retention and the successful graduation of students." Peer mentors are paired with six freshmen based on academic majors.

KEAP, or Knowledge Enriched through Academic Performance, helps students with issues like poor grades and poor attendance. Students with a GPA of 2.0 or lower are required to take part in KEAP.

Bowling Green State University

Bowling Green, OH

Address: 220 McFall Center, Bowling Green, OH 43403
Phone: 419-372-2086
Admissions email: choosebgsu@bgsu.edu
Website: www.bgsu.edu

Admissions Stats

Percentage of applicants admitted: 90.1%
SAT range: 450-560 reading, 450-570 math
ACT range: 19-24 composite, 18-24 English, 18-24 math

Size

Number of undergraduates: 16,079

Costs

Tuition and fees: $9,060 in state; $16,368 out of state
Books and supplies: $1,140
On campus room and board and other expenses: $10,928
Off campus room and board and other expenses: NA

Academics

Favorite majors: education, business, management, marketing and related support services, health professions and related clinical sciences, social sciences, visual and performing arts

---

The B Features

Bowling Green offers the Office of Academic Enhancement (ACEN), which is dedicated to providing advice and academic support to new students so that they can make a smooth transition from high school to college. Students can find tutoring, mentoring, and individualized academic assistance through ACEN, so that they can achieve academic success.

In addition to this, Bowling Green has a Study Skills Center that features computer software, course content video cassettes, a "How to Succeed in..." series of manuals, study tips brochures and charts and tests from various classes. Mentor groups are available for students who are struggling in their coursework. These groups meet once a week for 50-minute sessions. The mentors are students who have earned an A in the course he/she is helping with. Students who are enrolled in a Math or Statistics course are also encouraged to utilize the Math and Stats Tutoring Center. Students can get help on any course writing needed through the Writing Center.

The school offers a class called ACEN 100 which is a College Reading/Learning Skills course. It is designed to improve the basic reading and learning habits of students in topics like vocabulary, note taking, comprehension, time management, test taking and critical thinking.

Bradley University

Peoria, IL

Address: 1501 W. Bradley Ave., Peoria, IL 61625-0001
Phone: 309-677-1000
Admissions email: admissions@bradley.edu
Website: www.bradley.edu

Admissions Stats

Percentage of applicants admitted: 68.7%
SAT range: 540-650 reading, 510-610 math
ACT range: 23-28 composite, 23-29 English, 22-28 math

Size

Number of undergraduates: 5,369

Costs

Tuition and fees: $20,078
Books and supplies: $1,000
On campus room and board and other expenses: $8,860
Off campus room and board and other expenses: NA

Academics

Favorite majors: business, management, marketing and related support services, communication, journalism and related programs, education, engineering, health professions and related clinical sciences, psychology, visual and performing arts

The B Features

Bradley's website states, "We encourage students to apply who feel that they can demonstrate both the academic ability to succeed and the potential to contribute to the total educational experience at Bradley. While our students perform above national averages in strong college preparation curriculums, we do not have a stated minimum rank, grade point average (GPA), or ACT or SAT score. We also recognize that rank and GPA can only be considered meaningful in the context of the quality of the high school attended and the classes that a student takes. It is also very important to our admissions review committee that our students balance academic ability with the other qualities that lead to success at Bradley. Social skills, communications skills, leadership, community service, and unique experiences are important qualities in our admission and scholarship review. Finally, different academic areas have different admission requirements."

Bridgewater State College

Bridgewater, MA

Address: Bridgewater, MA 02325
Phone: 508-531-1237
Admissions email: admission@bridgew.edu
Website: www.bridgew.edu

Admissions Stats

Percentage of applicants admitted: 71%
SAT range: 460-550 reading, 460-560 math
ACT range: 19-24 composite

Size

Number of undergraduates: 7,851

Costs

Tuition and fees: $5,788 in state; $11,928 out of state
Books and supplies: $900
On campus room and board and other expenses: $9,662
Off campus room and board and other expenses: $10,314

Academics

Favorite majors: business, management, marketing and related support services, education, communication, journalism and related programs, psychology, security and protective services, social sciences, visual and performing arts history

The B Features

Bridgewater offers the Academic Achievement Center (AAC) which features learning assistance programs and is home to Second Language Services, the Office of Disability Resources, Tutoring Services, the Writing Studio, Mathematics Services, Study and Research Services and the Communication Laboratory. The college also provides a Core Curriculum that is a skill centered, outcomes-based general education course, designed to help all students prepare for learning in their chosen fields. It is made up of four areas: *skills requirements* (writing, logical reasoning, mathematical reasoning and spoken communication); *core distribution requirements* (arts, humanities, natural and social and behavioral sciences, global culture, multiculturalism, quantitative reasoning and the U.S. Constitution); *seminars* (writing/speaking intensive courses) and *requirements in the major* (connecting the core curriculum to each major).

Bryant University

· ·

Smithfield, RI

Address: 1150 Douglas Pike, Smithfield, RI 02917-1284
Phone: 401-232-6100
Admissions email: admission@bryant.edu
Website: www.bryant.edu

Admissions Stats

Percentage of applicants admitted: 43.8%
SAT range: 490-570 critical reading, 540-620 math
ACT range: 21-25 composite

Size

Number of undergraduates: 3,203

Costs

Tuition and fees: $26,099
Books and supplies: $1,200
On campus room and board and other expenses: $11,693
Off campus room and board and other expenses: $9,900

Academics

Favorite majors: business, management, marketing and related support services, social sciences, computer and information sciences and support services, communication, journalism and related programs, and English language and literature/letters

---

The B Features

Bryant College provides extra help to students through the Academic Center for Excellence (ACE). Each year, more than 1,600 students use its services to help with class performance. ACE's philosophy is that college students are not born with good study skills and habits, and like anything else in life, they require practice on a regular basis. Even students who have great study skills in high school may find that they need extra help in college because it requires different kinds of skills. According to the college, ACE's primary goal is to "help students become self-reliant, independent, confident learners so that they may successfully meet the demands of their chosen academic curricula." They do this through both a tutoring program and study skills instruction in group sessions provided by a combination of staff, peer tutors and faculty.

Along with ACE, Bryant offers a Writing Center. Here you can learn and polish the skills of written communication through one-on-one consultations with staff and tutors. Access is provided through ACE to workshops and printed materials that are helpful tools in honing writing skills.

Caldwell College

· ·

Caldwell, NJ

Address: 9 Ryerson Ave., Caldwell, NJ 07006-6195
Phone: 973-618-3500
Admissions email: admissions@caldwell.edu
Website: www.caldwell.edu

Admissions Stats

Percentage of applicants admitted: 66.5%
SAT range: 440-520 critical reading, 430-530 math
ACT range: NA

Size

Number of undergraduates: 1,685

Costs

Tuition and fees: $20,400
Books and supplies: $950
On campus room and board and other expenses: $9,595
Off campus room and board and other expenses: $5,600

Academics

Favorite majors: business, management, marketing and related support services, psychology, social sciences, security and protective services, education, communication, journalism and related programs

---

The B Features

A variety of support services are available through Caldwell's Academic Support Center. Individual and group tutoring is offered on both a scheduled and drop-in basis. The Writing Center has regular hours also and focuses on helping students become independent critical thinkers and writers. In addition, an online writing lab is another option students may access. Students work with peer or professional tutors and there is no charge for these sessions. A supplemental instruction program is offered during the year in courses that serve large numbers of freshman or sophomores. This course focuses on skills needed to better understand lectures, develop study strategies and prepare for exams. Workshops on note taking, textbook reading, time management and test taking strategies are offered throughout the year.

University of California-Riverside

Riverside, CA

Address: 900 University Ave., Riverside, CA 92521
Phone: 951-827-3411
Admissions email: discover@ucr.edu
Website: www.ucr.edu

Admissions Stats

SAT range: 460-570 critical reading, 490-630 math
ACT range: 18-23 composite, 17-23 English, 18-25 math

Size

Number of undergraduates: 14,555

Costs

Tuition and fees: $6,590 in state; $25,274 out of state
Books and supplies: $1,700
On campus room and board and other expenses: $13,200
Off campus room and board and other expenses: $12,000

Academics

Favorite majors: business, management, marketing and related support services, social sciences, biomedical sciences, plant sciences and entomology, engineering, natural sciences, humanities and arts, education

---

The B Features

Educators, counselors and advanced students help with academic performance through services at the school's Learning Center. Any student who is not satisfied with the grade he/she is getting in a class is welcome, including freshmen and students on academic probation. Virtually all services are free.

The Center's ACE (Assistance Counseling Encouragement) Program is designed specifically for students who have been placed on academic probation. Students enter into an official agreement with a counselor and are expected to commit to the program. Activities include study groups, study skills sessions and tutoring. There is an emphasis on goal-setting and motivation as well.

The Learning Center also offers a program known as ASAP, an acronym that stands for Assisting Students Academically and Personally. This is a peer counseling program that helps first-year students with academic, educational, personal and social needs. Other assistance programs include a basic skills unit, computer lab, study group program and tutorial assistance and support staff.

Campbell University Inc.

Buies Creek, NC

Address: P.O. Box 97, Buies Creek, NC 27506
Phone: 910-893-1200
Admissions email: Contact the university online
Website: www.campbell.edu

Admissions Stats

Percentage of applicants admitted: open admission policy
SAT range: NA
ACT range: NA

Size

Number of undergraduates: 5,014

Costs

Tuition and fees: $16,800
Books and supplies: $1,000
On campus room and board and other expenses: $9,824
Off campus room and board and other expenses: $14,650

Academics

Favorite majors: business, management, marketing and related support services, psychology, social sciences, education, health professions and related clinical services

---

The B Features

Both group and peer tutoring are available at Campbell University, and the school also has a Writing Center. Student support services include workshops on study skills, test taking skills, time management and test anxiety. The school has a program known as the Early Alert System, which puts students in contact with the appropriate campus resources in order to help them to meet their educational goals. Faculty and staff members refer students who are struggling in their academic work, as well as those who are missing class often or who are having trouble adjusting to campus life. The Early Alert System helps to make sure that every student is able to take full advantage of the educational opportunities available at Campbell.

Carroll College

Waukesha, WI

Address: 100 N. East Ave., Waukesha, WI 53186
Phone: 262-524-7220
Admissions email: Contact the college through its website
Website: www.cc.edu

Admissions Stats

Percentage of applicants admitted: 73.7%
SAT range: NA
ACT range: 20-25 composite, 19-25 English, 19-25 math

Size

Number of undergraduates: 2,882

Costs

Tuition and fees: $19,910
Books and supplies: $872
On campus room and board and other expenses: $8,595
Off campus room and board and other expenses: $8,331

Academics

Favorite majors: business, management, marketing and related support services, education, health professions and related clinical services, psychology, biological and biomedical sciences

The B Features

The college's Walter Young Center is open to students who are experiencing academic difficulties as well as emotional ones. Whether it is help for a class or how to get over being homesick, this center is ready to help. Anyone needing assistance in a class can be matched with an academic coach for additional help and resources.

Champlain College

. . . .

Burlington, VT

Address: 163 S. Willard, St., Burlington, VT 05401
Phone: 802-869-2727
Admissions email: admission@champlain.edu
Website: www.champlain.edu

Admissions Stats

Percentage of applicants admitted: 58%
SAT range: 500-610 reading, 500-590 math
ACT range: 20-25 composite, 19-25 English, 19-24 math

Size

Number of undergraduates: 2,470

Costs

Tuition and fees: $16,250
Books and supplies: $500
On campus room and board and other expenses: $10,725
Off campus room and board and other expenses: $5,150

Academics

Favorite majors: business, management, marketing and related support services, liberal arts and sciences, general studies and humanities, computer and information sciences and support services, visual and performing arts

---

The B Features

Champlain offers a number of different centers to help students become and stay academically strong. At the Advising and Registration Center, or ARC, academic advisors provide one-on-one help to students who are choosing courses and planning their majors. At the Student Life Office, various academic support labs in accounting/math, writing and computers are offered as well as peer tutoring and counseling. The school also has Career Services and Health Services departments to help with planning and to give support.

Chowan College

Murfreesboro, NC

Address: One University Place, Murfreesboro, NC 27855
Phone: 252-398-1236
Admissions email: enroll@chowan.edu
Website: www.chowan.edu

Admissions Stats

Percentage of applicants admitted: 51.2%
SAT range: 390-470 critical reading, 380-490 math
ACT range: 14-19 composite

Size

Number of undergraduates: 796

Costs

Tuition and fees: 15,950
Books and supplies: $825
On campus room and board and other expenses: $7,040
Off campus room and board and other expenses: $6,310

Academics

Favorite majors: parks, recreation and leisure and fitness studies, business, management, marketing and related support services, security and protective services, education and communications technologies/technicians and support services

The B Features

Chowan offers its entire student body a tutoring program located in the campus library. Students just request a tutor in any area of study by filling out an online tutor request form. Student tutors work one on one with students to provide this service four nights a week at no cost. Chowan also has Camp 121, a tutoring center that gives students a quiet space for individual studying between the hours of 9 and 5. Individual and group study sessions are frequently held at Camp 121 as well.

Christopher Newport College

Newport News, VA

Address: 1 University Place, Newport News, VA 23606
Phone: 757-594-7015
Admissions email: Contact the college through its website
Website: www.cnu.edu

Admissions Stats

Percentage of applicants admitted: 51.9%
SAT range: 530-620 reading, 530-620 math
ACT range: 22-25 composite, 21-26 English, 20-25 math

Size

Number of undergraduates: 4,536

Costs

Tuition and fees: $6,460 in state; $13,532 out of state
Books and supplies: $850
On campus room and board and other expenses: $10,926
Off campus room and board and other expenses: NA

Academics

Favorite majors: business, management, marketing and related support services, social sciences, communication, journalism and related programs, English language and literature/letters, history, psychology and biological and biomedical services

The B Features

Christopher Newport College provides academic advising and counseling/career services to their students. Their Writing Center offers help to students who are writing papers or projects.

In addition, the school has a Learning Communities program for first-year students. This program involves 18 to 24 students who live together, take two classes together and build strong relationships with the community. This arrangement provides support for the transition from home to college, while also giving each participant a peer mentor to learn from as well as help with setting up study groups, test review sessions, informal group tutoring and more.

University of Cincinnati

Cincinnati, OH

Address: 2624 Clifton Ave., P.O. Box 210091,Cincinnati, OH 45221-0091
Phone: 513-556-1100
Admissions email: admissions@uc.edu
Website: www.uc.edu

Admissions Stats

Percentage of applicants admitted: 51.2%
SAT range: 500-620 critical reading, 500-640 math
ACT range: 21-27 composite, 17-25 English, 17-26 math

Size

Number of undergraduates: 15,960

Costs

Tuition and fees: $9,399 in state; $23,922 out of state
Books and supplies: $830
On campus room and board and other expenses: $13,956
Off campus room and board and other expenses: $13,956

Academics

Favorite majors: business, management, marketing and related support services, engineering, visual and performing arts, English language and literature/letters and health professions and related clinical services

---

The B Features

At the University of Cincinnati, helping new students with lower GPAs get up to speed is usually achieved through the Center for Access and Transition. CAT is geared to help students have the knowledge, skills and resources to earn their degree. This is accomplished through one-on-one advising and individually tailored academic plans. (For an example of this kind of plan, go to the website.) Services include free tutoring and academic skill-enhancing workshops designed to increase GPAs, to improve study skills and time management strategies and to increase classroom attendance.

Each student who is assisted by CAT has an advisor to create the personalized learning agreement. This will show the student how to meet each requirement for his/her major and may include required homework, workshop attendance or use of various campus resources. The plan clearly outlines the student's responsibilities, which commonly include meeting with his/her academic advisor and regular progress reports from instructors.

Tutoring at no charge is available to all UC students and the campus has a Writing Lab and a Math Resource Center for students as well.

Coastal Carolina University

Conway, SC

Address: 755 Highway 544, Conway, SC 29526
Phone: 843-349-2026
Admissions email: admissions@coastal.edu
Website: www.coastal.edu

Admissions Stats

Percentage of applicants admitted: 74%
SAT range: 470-550 reading, 480-570 math
ACT range: 20-23 composite

Size

Number of undergraduates: 6,397

Costs

Tuition and fees: $7,500 instate; $16,190 out of state
Books and supplies: $984
On campus room and board and other expenses: $10,786
Off campus room and board and other expenses: $11,338

Academics

Favorite majors: business, management, marketing and related support services, biological and biomedical sciences, education, social services and psychology

The B Features

At Coastal Carolina, professional academic advising and peer mentoring are available. The school also has a course called UNIV 110, which is designed to develop critical thinking and research skills, to provide community support during the first semester of enrollment, and to acquaint students with the school's resources. Tutoring sessions are offered and there is even a Grammar Hotline to call.

The UNIV 110 course, also know as a "First Year Experience," involves peers, faculty and staff and other members within the community. Students play an active part in forums, workshops, discussions, readings, case studies and community service projects. This includes assignments that might come in various forms, ranging from quizzes, tests and journals to presentations, portfolios and writing projects. In the end, UNIV 110 helps students to develop a clearer and more comprehensive academic and career development plan for the future.

Coe College

Cedar Rapids, IA

Address: 1220 First Ave. NE, Cedar Rapids, IA 52402-5092
Phone: 319-399-8500
Admissions email: admission@coe.edu
Website: www.coe.edu

Admissions Stats

Percentage of applicants admitted: 67.7%
SAT range: 580-688 reading, 600-678 math
ACT range: 22-28 composite

Size

Number of undergraduates: 1,331

Costs

Tuition and fees: $25,120
Books and supplies: $700
On campus room and board and other expenses: $8,750
Off campus room and board and other expenses: NA

Academics

Favorite majors: business, management, marketing and related support services, psychology, social sciences, visual and performing arts, health professions and related clinical services

The B Features

Like a growing number of colleges today, Coe offers a First Year Seminar to help students transition from high school to college. This program emphasizes learning basic writing skills and offers a number of different classes to take to get these skills. To support this, the college has a Writing Center plus a Speaking Center for stronger oral presentations.

College of the Atlantic

Bar Harbor, ME

Address: 105 Eden St., Bar Harbor, ME 04609
Phone: 207-288-5015
Admissions email: inquiry@coa.edu
Website: www.coa.edu/html/admissions.htm

Admissions Stats

Percentage of applicants admitted 66%
SAT range: 540-680
ACT range: 24-30 composite

Size

Number of undergraduates: 290

Costs

Tuition and fees: $29,520
Books and supplies: $600
On campus room and board and other expenses: $8,190
Off campus room and board and other expenses: $3,090

Academics

Favorite majors: human ecology only. According to the school, "COA offers one degree in Human Ecology. Within that degree, we have resource areas in arts and design, human studies and environmental sciences. Our students focus in subjects similar to those offered by other liberal arts schools, including: adolescent psychology, animal behavior, animation, anthropology, agriculture, architecture, art, art history, biology, botany, ceramics, creative writing, conservation biology, design, ecological policy and planning economics, education, farm management, field ecology, filmmaking, green business, history, international policy, law, literature, marine studies, museum studies, music, philosophy, photography, psychology, public policy, women's studies and zoology." The school also states, "We do not have majors but in recent years, many students have tended to focus in international policy, ecological policy, literature/writing, art and design, field ecology, education, green business, philosophy and ethnography."

The B Features

College of the Atlantic makes a statement that has punch to it: "At COA, we focus on a student's creativity, desire to do something, as well as their innate interest in learning." From there, they have a lot of advice on how to become a part of this college.

"COA recognizes that a student's academic passions and desire to make a difference in the world don't always translate into a report card with straight A's. We are looking for students whose passion for learning is driven by the desire to use their learning to do something good in the world, not just to get good grades. We don't require standardized tests in the admission process and once our students enroll, they receive narrative evaluations from their professors at the end of every term. It is up to each student to determine if he/she wants a letter grade in addition to the evaluation.

"Our program emphasizes strong connections between faculty and students, individualized curriculum and hands-on learning. In other words, you direct your education. Our students are encouraged to find their passion and go for it. When they do, learning thrives.

"The nature of our education, with close student-faculty interaction, helps out students to know what they need to do to succeed within a class. We also offer a writing center, staffed by faculty and students, for those who could use extra help in writing. Additional assistance is given to others with special needs.

When asked how students with B averages should apply to COA, the answer was candid and helpful: "Hopefully there is something that you, the student, are passionate about, even if it doesn't seem academic in nature. Emphasize that passion and make a case for the ways in which this interest can translate into work that helps other. Let's say your love is running. Talk about why you love running and what you've learned from it/what skills you've developed because of your love for it. Then present an idea you have for translating this love of running into a future career that has meaning to you and to the good of others. Maybe you want to start a running program for middle school students who haven't been successful academically because you understand that running teaches focus and perseverance—skills needed to be academically successful. Or maybe you want to work in the field of land conservation because you want to maintain wilderness areas that provide the public (including runners) access to nature. Make a clear case for how your goals and interests fit with the academic offerings of the school."

Other advice from COA staff includes the following thoughts: "Choose your recommenders wisely. Don't just go for the teachers who gave you the best grades. Select teachers who know you the best. Sometimes the teachers of the classes in which you have struggled the most are the ones who have the richest knowledge of you as a student. If you can, meet with your teachers before they write your recommendations, share your long term goals with them and your reasons for applying. Ask them to help you in making your case by including this information in your letter of recommendation. Also, definitely have an interview, preferably with a member of the Admission staff. Note that you aren't a straight A student and talk about why WITHOUT turning the explanation into a round of 'everyone else is to blame except me'. Talk about the trade-offs you've made and the reasons for them. Be specific in your reasons for being interested in the college, highlighting the traits and skills that you will bring and those you hope to develop. Write thank you notes to your interviewers and use this as another opportunity to highlight the reasons you, your goals and your learning style fit with the school."

Coppin State University

Baltimore, MD

Address: 2500 W. North Ave., Baltimore, MD 21216-3698
Phone: 410-951-3600
Admissions email: Contact the college through its website
Website: www.coppin.edu

Admissions Stats

Percentage of applicants admitted: open admission policy
SAT range: NA
ACT range: NA

Size

Number of undergraduates: 3,451

Costs

Tuition and fees: $4,910 in state; $11,934 out of state
Books and supplies: $800
On campus room and board and other expenses: $9,812
Off campus room and board and other expenses: $10,184

Academics

Favorite majors: security and protective services, psychology, liberal arts and sciences, general studies and humanities, business, management, marketing and related support services and public administration and social service professions

---

The B Features

Coppin offers a variety of Student Support Services with one-on-one help. They also require that each new student take a one-semester Freshman Seminar course. Students may receive help at the Academic Resource Center, which features four labs with basic, intermediate and advanced levels of instruction and tutoring at no cost.

Cornell College

. . . .

Mount Vernon, IA

Address: 600 First St. West, Mount Vernon, IA 52314-1098
Phone: 319-895-4477
Admissions email: admissions@cornellcollege.edu
Website: www.cornellcollege.edu

Admissions Stats

Percentage of applicants admitted: 66%
SAT range: 560-680 critical reading, 550-680 math
ACT range: 23-20 composite

Size

Number of undergraduates: 1,160

Costs

Tuition and fees: $24,800
Books and supplies: $7,200
On campus room and board and other expenses: $8,220
Off campus room and board and other expenses: NA

Academics

Favorite majors: art, biology, education, English, philosophy, psychology, politics and theatre

---

The B Features

Cornell has a first-year-only course that helps new students acclimate to doing college-level work. It includes a writing emphasis course, student mentors and a full advising system. Instructors help students develop skills in writing, reading comprehension, oral communication, information literacy, creativity, research and mathematics. They also show students how to build independent work habits.

Cornell is known for its "one-course-at-a-time model" and because of its small size, there is a lot of personal attention given to help students be successful in a rather intense program.

Dean College

Franklin, MA

Address: 99 Main St., Franklin, MA 02038-1994
Phone: 877-TRY-DEAN (877-879-3326)
Admissions email: admission@dean.edu
Admissions contact: Jay Leiendecker, vice president of enrollment services

---

Admissions Stats

Percentage of applicants admitted: 73%
Average GPA range: 2.3-2.75
Average SAT range: 390-490 critical reading, 380-490 math
Average ACT range: 15-20 composite

Size

Number of undergraduates: 975

Costs

Tuition and fees: $25,420 in state and out of state
Books and supplies: $1,500
On campus room and board and other expenses: $10,960
Off campus room and board and other expenses: NA

Academics

Majors offered: Bachelor of arts in dance and bachelor of arts in arts management, associate degree programs in business administration, business technology, communications, criminal justice, dance, early childhood education, English, health sciences, history, math/science, philosophy, psychology, sociology, sports and fitness studies and theatre arts.

Favorite majors: business administration, sports and fitness studies, criminal justice and dance

---

The B Features

A quote from Dean College offers these words regarding their staff and programs: "Dean College provides a level of academic support that goes above and beyond the norm found in higher education today. Our full-time academic advisors are completely dedicated to helping students through their time at Dean and thus do not have any faculty responsibilities. Faculty, meanwhile, are required to submit progress reports on every student periodically during the semester. In addition, Dean offers a comprehensive learning center that provides students with opportunities for personalized, drop-in or peer-tutoring services according to their academic needs."

Insight

"Dean College is more focused on a student's future than we are on his/her past. While we are not about open enrollment, we are about providing students with opportunity and helping them to reposition their academic profile in the hopes of transferring to the school of choice. Applicants need to show us academic potential in the admissions process. If we can identify academic potential (be it through improving grades, SAT scores, recommendations, etc.) we feel that Dean's supportive learning environment and structure can help harness that potential and position students for what is near in their academic lives.

"Dean College helps students get into four-year schools and more often than not, we help them get into four-year schools that academically are at least one level higher than what their profile would have allowed them to get into as incoming freshmen. Dean College is made for the B or C student who aspires to transfer to a higher level school as we foster the type of initial accomplishment, growth and confidence necessary for them to ultimately pursue and complete a bachelor's degree at a four-year institution."

Depaul University

Chicago, IL

Address: 55 E. Jackson, Chicago, IL 60604
Phone: 312-362-8300
Admissions email: admssion@depaul.edu
Website: www.depaul.edu

Admissions Stats

Percentage of applicants admitted: 70%
SAT range: 510-610 critical reading, 500-610 math
ACT range: 22-26 composite, 21-27 English, 20-26 math

Size

Number of undergraduates: 14,893

Costs

Tuition and fees: $22,365
Books and supplies: $1,000
On campus room and board and other expenses: $10,727
Off campus room and board and other expenses: NA

Academics

Favorite majors: accounting, computer science, finance, music, theatre, communication and psychology

---
The B Features

Student Support Services at Depaul is a program that is open to students who demonstrate a need for academic support and meet one of the following three requirements: 1) a low income as defined by the U.S. Department of Education, 2) from a family from which neither parent has a bachelor's degree or 3) has a documented physical or learning disability.

SSS provides advising, academic assistance and mentoring to undergrads meeting the above requirements. Students are assigned an advisor who will help develop an educational plan, select courses and find resources to help with financing the student's education. SSS also offers individual tutoring and group study opportunities in a variety of subjects. Workshops are offered each quarter to help with learning on topics such as memory, active learning, note taking and test preparation.

Drew University

Madison, NJ

Address: 36 Madison Ave., Madison, NJ 07940
Phone: 973-408-3739
Admissions email: cadm@drew.edu
Website: www.drew.edu

Admissions Stats

Percentage of applicants admitted: 95%
SAT range: 550-660 critical reading, 540-650 math
ACT range: 24-27 composite, 22-31 English, 23-28 math

Size

Number of undergraduates: 1,561

Costs

Tuition and fees: $33,608
Books and supplies: $1,090
On campus room and board and other expenses: $11,438
Off campus room and board and other expenses: $13,054

Academics

Favorite majors: psychology, English, political science, biology, and theatre

The B Features

Peer tutors are available for all courses taught in any given semester at Drew University. The campus also features a Writing Center where students can learn more about the writing process and bring reports, papers and other written material to receive feedback in the form of impartial and helpful responses. At the Center, students can find out more about organizing papers, the process of revisions, grammar techniques, writing speeches and resumes and looking at proper word choice.

Drexel University

Philadelphia, PA

Address: 3141 Chestnut St., Philadelphia, PA 19104
Phone: 215-895-2400
Admissions email: enroll@drexel.edu
Website: www.drexel.edu

Admissions Stats

Percentage of applicants admitted: 82%
SAT range: 530-630 critical reading, 550-660 math
ACT range: Not available

Size

Number of undergraduates: 10,158

Costs

Tuition and fees: $25,500
Books and supplies: $1,655
On campus room and board and other expenses: $14,040
Off campus room and board and other expenses: $14,565

Academics

Favorite majors: graphic design, architecture, film and video

---

The B Features

Free tutoring is available to all students of the College of Nursing and Health Professions, the School of Public Health and non-medical students of the College of Medicine. Some tutoring is individualized, while other situations include group settings.

The Student Counseling Center helps students with personal issues, including making the adjustment to university life. At different times throughout the year, workshops on study skills, stress management, assertiveness training and sexual health are offered. The center provides academic skills testing, and counselors can help students to establish an individualized time-management system to improve study skills and test taking abilities and to reduce test anxiety.

Duquesne University

Pittsburgh, PA

Address: Administration Building, 600 Forbes Ave., Pittsburgh, PA 15282
Phone: 412-396-6222
Admissions email: admissions@duq.edu
Website: www.duq.edu

Admissions Stats

Percentage of applicants admitted: 72.5%
SAT range: 510-660 critical reading, 520-620 math
ACT range: 21-26 composite, 20-26 English, 20-26 math

Size

Number of undergraduates: 5,650

Costs

Tuition and fees: $22,665
Books and supplies: $600
On campus room and board and other expenses: $9,446
Off campus room and board and other expenses: $9,446

Academics

Favorite majors: psychology, business, management, marketing and related support services, communication, journalism and related programs, education and health professions and related clinical sciences, biological and biomedical sciences

The B Features

At Duquesne's Michael P. Weber Learning Skills Center, students will find three programs that are designed to help them achieve academic success: Individualized Study Skills Assistance, College Success Credit Courses and tutoring.

Individualized Study Skills Assistance teaches students about reading, note taking, organizing information, listening, test taking and more. The program is designed to assist students in understanding how to learn more effectively and efficiently. Tutoring is done on a one-to-one basis on in small-group settings and is free for all students. Study skills classes can also be taken for college course credit.

Earlham College

Richmond, IN

Address: 801 National Rd. West, Richmond, IN 47374-4095
Phone: 765-983-1600
Admissions email: admissions@earlham.edu
Website: www.earlham.edu

Admissions Stats

Percentage of applicants admitted: 70%
SAT range: 570-700 reading, 530-650 math
ACT range: 23-29 composite

Size

Number of undergraduates: 1,226

Costs

Tuition and fees: $29,320
Books and supplies: $850
On campus room and board and other expenses: $7,200
Off campus room and board and other expenses: $7,200

Academics

Favorite majors: biology, English, psychology, politics, sociology/
anthropology and art

The B Features

Based on Quaker traditions and orientation, Earlham College
is considered a high-level liberal arts school. Class discussions
are more common than lectures here. Their Center for Academic
Enrichment offers free peer tutoring to all students and has regular
information on study skills. A Writing Lab is available for those having trouble with any aspect of the writing process, from brainstorm-
ing the initial idea to making the final edits.

Eckerd College

St. Petersburg, FL

Address: 4200 54th Ave. South, St. Petersburg, FL 33711-4700
Phone: 727-864-8331
Admissions email: admissions@eckerd.edu
Website: www.eckerd.edu

Admissions Stats

Percentage of applicants admitted: 72%
SAT range: 510-630 critical reading, 500-620 math
ACT range: 22-27 composite, 21-28 English, 20-26 math

Size

Number of undergraduates: 1,845

Costs

Tuition and fees: $27,618
Books and supplies: $1,000
On campus room and board and other expenses: $10,918
Off campus room and board and other expenses: $10,918

Academics

Favorite majors: psychology, marine science, biology, international relations and international business, creative writing and literature, management and environmental studies

The B Features

Eckerd does a number of things differently than other colleges, including support for struggling students. Faculty advisors are like mentors and provide continuing support and counsel through the student's years. Freshmen choose a mentor from a list of professionals who lead what is called Autumn Term at Eckerd. First-year students report to the school three weeks before returning students and take part in a course (for credit) that provides a thorough introduction to the campus and its resources as well as academic requirements and policies. Following the freshman year, students can choose a new mentor who specializes in their area of academic interest.

Graduates receive more than the official academic transcript. They also get a co-curricular transcript that includes all of the out-of-class activities in which the student has been involved, including volunteer work, sports, leadership positions and club involvement. This transcript can be used to supplement applications for jobs, graduate work or other postgraduate plans.

Elmira College

Elmira, NY

Address: One Park Place, Elmira, NY 14901
Phone: 607-735-1724
Admissions email: admissions@elmira.edu
Website: www.elmira.edu

Admissions Stats

Percentage of applicants admitted: 76.5%
SAT range: 510-620 critical reading, 500-600 math
ACT range: 23-27 composite, 21-28 English, 23-28 math

Size

Number of undergraduates: 1,489

Costs

Tuition and fees: $30,050
Books and supplies: $450
On campus room and board and other expenses: $9,650
Off campus room and board and other expenses: NA

Academics

Favorite majors: education, business, management, marketing and related support services, English language and literature/letters, health professions and related services, social sciences and psychology

---
The B Features

In addition to small class sizes (12 or less usually), Elmira also offers a special writing class during the fall term of a student's first year. It is held on Saturdays and comes with a tutor. Elmira states that the class is designed to "hone one of the most important skills you will ever develop in your life: the ability to communicate clearly in writing." The college holds that this special program will help students develop good academic habits by making studying a part of weekend plans. Their final comment says it all: "And finally, we care enough about your academic development to get up and teach on Saturday."

Endicott College

Beverly, MA

Address: 376 Hale St., Beverly, MA 01915
Phone: 978-921-1000
Admissions email: admissio@endicott.edu
Website: www.endicott.edu

Admissions Stats

Percentage of applicants admitted: 44.3%
SAT range: 450-540 critical reading, 480-560 math
ACT range: 20-24 composite, 20-24 English, 19-23 math

Size

Number of undergraduates: 1,886

Costs

Tuition and fees: $21,374
Books and supplies: $1,000
On campus room and board and other expenses: $12,254
Off campus room and board and other expenses: $9,740

Academics

Favorite majors: business, marketing, management and related support services, education, visual and performing arts, communication, journalism and related services, health professions and related clinical services, psychology, parks and recreation, leisure and fitness studies

---

The B Features

Endicott offers students access to an extensive computer lab, plus the availability of the Scangas Center for Media and Learning where workshops and training sessions are taught throughout the year. The Academic Technology Workshops provide tips on common software packages.

The college also offers FYE 101 (first year experience), which is a one-credit class taught by faculty and staff, addressing the challenges incoming students face and strategies on how to meet them. This course helps students to learn and use social skills, to find academic resources, to become familiar with college policies and to follow procedures. According to the website, "The program is designed to promote student learning and development, improve student satisfaction and success and encourage engagement in the life of the college which is fostered by connections with the Endicott community. Ultimately, we expect that by the end of the first year, students will have increased self-confidence, stronger academic and professional skills, and will be involved and committed to the 'Endicott Experience'."

Evergreen State College

Olympia, WA

Address: 2700 Evergreen Parkway Northwest, Olympia, WA 98505
Phone: 360-867-6170
Admissions email: admissions@evergreen.edu
Website: www.evergreen.edu

Admissions Stats

SAT range: 530-650 critical reading, 480-600 math
ACT range: 21-27 composite

Size

Number of undergraduates: 3,637

Costs

Tuition and fees: $4,861 in state; $15,048 out of state
Books and supplies: $924
On campus room and board and other expenses: $10,326
Off campus room and board and other expenses: $10,326

Academics

Favorite majors: liberal arts and sciences, general studies and humanities, environmental science, media arts, physical and biological sciences, social sciences, computer science

The B Features

Evergreen has a unique style of teaching that will appeal to students that do not excel in traditional classrooms that are facilitated by the typical lecture/listen methods. This college designs classes so that there is a balance between seminars, hands-on learning and off-campus exploration. Weeklong field trips are not uncommon here. The college also offers a program called Individual Learning Contracts. This allows students to do advanced academic study in an area they already have a background in, working independently and meeting weekly with a sponsor. Evergreen also has an extensive study abroad program for students.

Fairmont State College

Fairmont, WV

Address: 1201 Locust Ave., Fairmont, WV 26554
Phone: 304-367-4173
Admissions email: admit@fairmontstate.edu
Website: www.fscwv.edu

Admissions Stats

Percentage of applicants admitted: 77.2%
SAT range: 420-510 critical reading, 400-530 math
ACT range: 14-25 composite, 18-26 English, 17-25 math

Size

Number of undergraduates: 4,058

Costs

Tuition and fees: $3,640 in state; $7,874 out of state
Books and supplies: $1,200
On campus room and board and other expenses: $8,554
including transportation and personal expenses
Off campus room and board and other expenses: $10,154
including transportation and personal expenses

Academics

Favorite majors: education, business, management, marketing
and related support services, security and protective services,
liberal arts and sciences, humanities and general studies,
engineering technology and technicians

The B Features

Fairmont is two schools in one. Here you can earn an associate degree
through Fairmont State Community and Technical College; then get
a bachelor's degree at the University. The student-to-faculty ratio at
Fairmont is about 17:1, and average class size is 22 students.

Tutoring is free for all students through the Tutorial Services Program,
although the majority of students are limited to 10 hours per semester.
(Students with documented learning disabilities may get additional
sessions.) Virtually all subject areas are covered.

Fairmont also offers a cutting-edge program called Supplemental
Instruction. It is based on the experience of past students and is
designed to help enrollees with courses that have been historically
proven to be the most difficult. The course is free and is taught by
faculty-recommended students.

Fisk University

Nashville, TN

Address: 1000 17th Ave. North, Nashville, TN 37208-4501
Phone: 615-329-8665
Admissions email: admit@fisk.edu
Website: www.fisk.edu

Admissions Stats

Percentage of applicants admitted: 67.7%
SAT range: 410-540 critical reading, 440-540 math
ACT range: 19-23 composite, 16-21 English, 16-20 math

Size

Number of undergraduates: 864

Costs

Tuition and fees: $13,970
Books and supplies: $1,400
On campus room and board and other expenses: $10,362
Off campus room and board and other expenses: $10,362

Academics

Favorite majors: psychology, business, management, marketing and related support services, visual and performing arts, biological and biomedical sciences, social sciences

The B Features

The Core Curriculum is really the heart of Fisk's education program. It centers around eight multicultural and interdisciplinary courses and is designed to help students grasp oral and written communication skills, logical and critical thinking, knowledge of the arts, history and literature and the processes and methods of science.

Flagler College

St. Augustine, FL

Address: 74 King St., St. Augustine, FL 32084
Phone: 904-829-6481
Admissions email: admiss@flagler.edu
Website: www.flagler.edu

Admissions Stats

Percentage of applicants admitted: 26.2%
SAT range: 520-610 reading, 520-600 reading, 510-590 math
ACT range: 22-26 composite, 22-28 English, 22-26 math

Size

Number of undergraduates: 2,158

Costs

Tuition and fees: $9,450
Books and supplies: $900
On campus room and board and other expenses: $9,660
Off campus room and board and other expenses: NA

Academics

Favorite majors: business, management, marketing and related
support services, communication, journalism and related services,
visual and performing arts, education, social services and
psychology

The B Features

Flagler College was established as a memorial to Henry M. Flagler,
and in accordance with his high standards, the college adheres to
strict requirements on values. They have a strong attendance policy,
prohibit alcohol and inter-dorm visitation and put a heavy emphasis
on social justice and service. According to their web site, "The
objectives of the student life program at Flagler are to establish
appropriate standards of conduct and to promote activities that
will contribute to the development of self-discipline, integrity, and
leadership."

Florida Agricultural and Mechanical University

Tallahassee, FL

Address: Office of Admissions, Foote Hilyer Administration Center, Suite G9, Tallahassee, FL 32307
Phone: 850-599-3796
Admissions email: amd@famu.edu
Website: www.famu.edu

Admissions Stats

Percentage of applicants admitted: 61%
SAT range: 400-510 critical reading, 400-510 math
ACT range: 17-21 composite, 17-21 English, 20-22 math

Size

Number of undergraduates: 10,552

Costs

Tuition and fees: $3,224 in state; $15,196 out of state
Books and supplies: $1,400
On campus room and board and other expenses: $8,004
Off campus room and board and other expenses: NA

Academics

Favorite majors: business, management, marketing and related support services, health professions and related clinical sciences, education, social sciences, security and protective services, psychology, education

The B Features

While academics are very important at Florida A&M, the school also seeks students with diverse backgrounds, believing that other skills and talents students may possess can benefit the university. Applicants may demonstrate their strengths through the admission essay.

Florida State University

Tallahassee, FL

Address: 211 Westcott Bldg, Tallahassee, FL 32306-1037
Phone: 850-644-6200
Admissions email: admissions@admin.fsu.edu
Website: www.fsu.edu

Admissions Stats

Percentage of applicants admitted: 59.2%
SAT range: 530-620 critical reading, 540-630 math
ACT range: 23-27 composite, 22-28 English, 22-26 math

Size

Number of undergraduates: 39,146

Costs

Tuition and fees: $3,307 in state; $16,439 out of state
Books and supplies: $1,000
On campus room and board and other expenses: $9,938
Off campus room and board and other expenses: $10,208

Academics

Favorite majors: business, management, marketing and related support services, social sciences, visual and performing arts, family and consumer sciences, human sciences, security and protective services, psychology and English, literature/letters. Some of the most unusual majors include entrepreneurship, geophysical fluid dynamics, meteorology, professional golf management and Russian and East European studies. The campus also includes the only student-run circus in the country.

The B Features

Although this is a rather large college, its staff and faculty care about the students and their success. FSU's Center for Academic Retention and Enhancement provides preparation, orientation and academic support programming for students who may be facing unique challenges because of cultural, economic of educational circumstances. A program called SSMO, or Student Supporting Students Mentoring Organization, offers mentors that help students in becoming acclimated to the school. They also act as role models in academic areas and in leadership.

Fort Lewis College

Durango, CO

Address: 1000 Rim Dr., Durango, CO 81301-3999
Phone: 970-247-7184
Admissions email: admission@fortlewis.edu
Website: www.fortlewis.edu

Admissions Stats

Percentage of applicants admitted: 73.3%
SAT range: 450-570 reading, 420-530 writing, 450-560 math
ACT range: 18-23 composite, 17-23 English, 17-23 math

Size

Number of undergraduates: 3,946

Costs

Tuition and fees: $5,973
Books and supplies: $1,698
On campus room and board and other expenses: $10,346
Off campus room and board and other expenses: NA

Academics

Favorite majors: business, marketing, management and related support services, liberal arts and science, general studies and sciences and humanities, social sciences, visual and performing arts, psychology, parks, recreation, leisure and fitness studies

---

The B Features

The Academic Success Program at Fort Lewis is free to all college students. It allows students to network with other learning support programs on campus and offers fall and winter symposiums to help first-year students acclimate to college life. An Early Alert System is available for students who are struggling and small study groups are set up across campus. The Algebra Alcove helps students in their math classes, including the provision of problem-solving classes and supplemental instruction. A Writing Center is offered for "building better writers."

Full Sail Real World Education

Winter Park, FL

Address: 3300 University Blvd., Winter Park, FL 32792-7429
Phone: 407-679-6333
Website: www.fullsail.com

Admissions Stats

Percentage of applicants admitted: open admission policy
SAT range: Not required
ACT range: Not required

Size

Number of undergraduates: 4,511

Costs

Tuition and fees: $43,995
Books and supplies: $168
On campus room and board: No on-campus housing
Off campus room and board and other expenses: $14,257

Academics

Favorite majors: computer and information sciences and support services, business, management, marketing and related support services, visual and performing arts

The B Features

Full Sail's curriculum is designed for those who are passionate about film, computer animation and design. It has open admissions, meaning all that is required is a high school diploma or GED for admittance. Full Sail specializes in job placement after graduation. There is no on-campus housing, but a department helps place students in available housing throughout the area. Programs start year round. Students attend classes five or six days a week for a total of 35 to 40 hours per week. With this schedule, students finish school much faster than the traditional four-year program. It is one of the only (if not the only) colleges that features a Guitar Hall of Fame in its buildings.

Goucher College

Baltimore, MD

Address: 1021 Dulaney Valley Rd., Baltimore, MD 21204-2794
Phone: 410-337-6100
Admissions email: admissions@goucher.edu
Website: www.goucher.edu

Admissions Stats

Percentage of applicants admitted: 67%
SAT range: 560-670 critical reading, 540-640 math
ACT range: 23-27 composite, 23-29 English, 21-24 math

Size

Number of undergraduates: 1,303

Costs

Tuition and fees: $29,325
Books and supplies: $800
On campus room and board and other expenses: $10,726
Off campus room and board and other expenses: $7,302

Academics

Favorite majors: dance, creative writing, biology, political science, and international relations

---

The B Features

Goucher's Academic Center for Excellence (ACE) is for all students and is based on the premise that each student has the ability to learn and successfully complete all college course work. Individual help in study skills is provided by mentors who are successful students that have been trained in peer counseling. They meet with students one or two times a week. Others work with students on issues like time management, procrastination prevention, organizational skills, memory and concentration, note and test taking strategies and test preparation. Study Skills Workshops are offered repeatedly on these same subjects.

In addition to these services, Goucher offers supplemental instruction in the sciences and humanities. Study groups meet regularly with an instructor and work together as a team to better understand the material. A drop-in Math Lab is offered on campus Sunday through Thursday, and a Writing Center, although not part of ACE, is available to help students at all stages of the writing process.

Grand Canyon University

Phoenix, AZ

Address: 3300 W. Camelback Rd., Phoenix, AZ 85017
Phone: 602-589-2855
Website: www.gcu.edu

Admissions Stats

Percentage of applicants admitted: 61%
SAT range: Open admissions
ACT range: Open admissions

Size

Number of undergraduates: 2,091

Costs

Tuition and fees: $12,000
Books and supplies: $1,560
On campus room and board and other expenses: $12,650
Off campus room and board and other expenses: $12,650

Academics

Favorite majors: health professions and related clinical services, business, management, marketing and related support services, education, biological and biomedical services, visual and performing arts

The B Features

While the college features open admissions, it has some minimal standards. A minimum GPA of 2.25, a combined SAT score of 920 or above or a composite ACT score of 19 or above are required. The school does have a strong Christian focus and bills itself as the "University with a Heart" because of its strong commitment to the student-teacher relationship.

Granite State College

Concord, NH

Address: 125 N. State St., Concord, NH 03301
Phone: 603-228-3000 x320
Website: www.granite.edu

Admissions Stats

Percentage of applicants admitted: 93.2%
SAT range: Open admissions
ACT range: Open admissions

Size

Number of undergraduates: 1,732

Costs

Tuition and fees: $4,563 in state; $5,043 out of state
Books and supplies: $600
On campus room and board: No on-campus housing
Off campus room and board and other expenses: $9,399

Academics

Favorite majors: liberal arts and sciences, general studies and humanities, business, management, marketing and related support services, multi/interdisciplinary studies, security and protective services and computer and information sciences and support services

The B Features

At this college, recently renamed Granite State, students can design their own bachelor's degree programs. Orientation sessions are offered year round, and academic advisors focus on helping enrollees prepare for tests, study and take notes. Academic Resource Coordinators provide additional academic services.

Guilford College

Greensboro, NC

Address: 5800 W. Friendly Ave., Greensboro, NC 27410
Phone: 336-316-2100
Admissions email: admission@guilford.edu
Website: www.guilford.edu/admission

Admissions Stats

Percentage of applicants admitted: 58%
Average GPA range: 3.4
SAT range: 1020-1240 critical reading and math
ACT range: 23.6 average

Size

Number of undergraduates: 2,742 (traditional students 1,405; adult students 1,242 and early college students 95)

Costs

Tuition and fees: $24,540
Books and supplies: $700-$800
On campus room and board and other expenses: $6,860
Off campus room and board and other expenses: Varies
Degrees offered: bachelor's degrees

Academics

Favorite majors: business management, English, biology and psychology; unusual majors include forensic biology, peace and conflict studies

Student Life

The campus: This campus is in Greensboro, population 250,000. It has recently added a new community center and residence halls. Guilford was founded by the Religious Society of Friends (Quakers).

The students: 53% women, 48% men. 10% African American, 2% Hispanic, 1% American Indian/Alaskan Native, 2% Asian/Pacific Islander

The B Features

At Guilford, the SAT is optional. Writing samples and an interview are required when a student does not submit standardized test scores. It is home to a high school preparation school with 100 students. In a required first-year class, students are taken on campus tours, shown various resources and helped to transition to college life.

Insight

Here are some thoughts from staff at Guilford: "We have a multi-layer approach to student success. The First Year Program addresses the needs of First Year Guilford students from the time they are admitted to the college until they declare their major. To assist the students in their transition into college life, the First Year Program coordinates all contact with the students during the summer prior to their first year. Through CHAOS (Guilford College's Orientation Program), First Year Experience classes and the FYE lab, the First Year Program steers students to target issues of diversity, academic success and the new student experience.

"The Learning Commons is ready to help students become more efficient and self-directed learners. The LC offers faculty tutors and peer tutors, in group or individual sessions. Faculty tutors help students with quantitative skills, writing, reading, study skills, test-taking and time management. Students are active in our three peer tutoring groups: Writing Studio peer tutors (students can help brainstorm a paper, discuss the focus and support in a paper a student has written, or give feedback on a draft); Chemistry 911 (students can get help with intro-level chemistry courses); and a large Student Tutoring Service (tutoring in specific courses across the curriculum).

"In addition, Guilford is proud of its support services for students with learning differences. Although we have no special program, we do have a broad system of services that many students find useful and encouraging. At Guilford, many students do well academically in spite of frustrating 'glitches'. Their retention rate is about that of the college in general. Students who do best are generally those who work hard, consult with advisors to carefully plan/balance classes and schedules, and who are good self-advocates (or learn to be while they are students here!). In fact, students with learning differences often know themselves well as learners and so they regularly offer us new ideas and strategies, and fresh insights into methods that work.

"We are looking for students who have challenged themselves academically, who have been involved in their high school and home communities, who have shown leadership and the potential to be successful in our rigorous academic environment. Students can show a desire to be successful in college. Drive to succeed goes a long way to making us feel that a student can make a difference in our environment. Grades are relative to the school environment. We want to see that a student has given a strong effort in a challenging course setting. The grade alone does not tell the whole story. We look at the school setting, the course title and level. We want hard-working students who have the desire to be successful at Guilford and to graduate.

"Guilford College's mission is to provide a transformative, practical and excellent liberal arts education that produces critical thinkers in an inclusive, diverse environment, guided by Quaker testimonies of community, equality, integrity, peace and simplicity and empha-sizing the creative problem-solving skills, experience, enthusiasm and international perspectives necessary to promote change in the world. The purpose of the campus life office is to support Guilford College's mission and core values through its programs, policies and personnel, preparing students for citizenship in an increas-ingly complex world by encouraging them to develop responsibility, accountability for oneself (both as individuals and as members of a community) and to obtain and develop the pragmatic life skills necessary to balance their academic and co-curricular involvement at the college. Campus life at Guilford is charged with a current of activity, the product of many interests represented in a diverse student body. Guilford students pursue variety with a passion; they rock climb, read to homeless children, play Ultimate Frisbee and jazz music, run a newspaper, yearbook and radio station, cycle and recycle, debate issues and question speakers, and come together for worship and fellowship in many religious traditions. The diversity of interests and activities not only creates opportunities for students to try new things but also gives shape and texture to friendships on campus."

Gustavus Adolphus

St. Peter, MN

Address: 800 W. College Ave., St. Peter, MN 56082
Phone: 507-933-7676
Admissions email: admissions@gustavus.edu
Website: www.gustavus.edu

Admissions Stats

Percentage of applicants admitted: 79%
SAT range: 570-670 critical reading, 565-675 math
ACT range: 23-28 composite

Size

Number of undergraduates: 2,546

Costs

Tuition and fees: $26,310
Books and supplies: $800
On campus room and board and other expenses: $7,400
Off campus room and board and other expenses: NA

Academics

Favorite majors: biology and biochemistry, education, music, physics, psychology and political science

The B Features

Gustavus Adolphus offers a Writing Center for one-on-one consultation and help with reading and interpreting assignments. The Advising Center helps coordinate meetings between students, advisors and professors to make the most of career help.

Hampton University

Hampton, VA

Address: Hampton, VA 23668-0099
Phone: 757-727-5328
Admissions email: admit@hamptonu.edu
Website: www.hamptonu.edu

Admissions Stats

Percentage of applicants admitted: 51.3%
SAT range: 481-629 critical reading, 484-606 math
ACT range: 17-26 composite, 17-27 English, 18-25 math

Size

Number of undergraduates: 5,325

Costs

Tuition and fees: $14,818
Books and supplies: $904
On campus room and board and other expenses: $9,671
Off campus room and board and other expenses: $12,162

Academics

Favorite majors: psychology, business, management, marketing and related support services, communication, journalism and related programs, health professions and related clinical services, social sciences, biological and biomedical sciences

The B Features

This is a primarily African American college (95.5%). Student Support Services is a federally funded program that, like many others, helps to support students as long as they meet one or more of three criteria: 1) come from a family where neither parent has a college degree, 2) come from a low-income family or 3) have a documented learning or physical disability. This program provides educational support service through counseling, tutoring and educational and career seminars. The overall goal is to "develop and implement educational services and activities that will motivate and assist students toward the achievement of their academic, career, social and personal goals."

Harcum College

Bryn Mawr, PA

Address: 750 Montgomery Ave., Bryn Mawr, PA 19010-3417
Phone: 610-526-6050
Admissions email: Email the college through its website.
Website: www.harcum.edu

Admissions Stats

Percentage of applicants admitted: 63.9%
SAT range: 380-470 critical reading, 350-440 math
ACT range: NA

Size

Number of undergraduates: 787

Costs

Tuition and fees: $16,450
Books and supplies: $1,200
On campus room and board and other expenses: $10,038
Off campus room and board and other expenses: $10,862

Academics

Favorite majors: health professions and related clinical services

Harrisburg University of Science and Technology

Harrisburg, PA

Address: 215 Market St., Harrisburg, PA 17101-2116
Phone: 717-901-5101
Admissions email: admissions@harrisburgu.net
Website: www.harrisburgu.net

Admissions Stats

Percentage of applicants admitted: 53.9%
SAT range: scores recommended
ACT range: scores recommended

Size

Number of undergraduates: 112

Costs

Tuition and fees: $14,000
Books and supplies: $2,100
On campus room and board and other expenses: NA
Off campus room and board and other expenses: $9,800

Academics

Favorite majors: biotechnology and biosciences, computer and information sciences, e-business and management, geography and geospatial imaging and integrative science

---

The B Features

Harrisburg University offers a small-school setting, which makes it is easy to get one-on-one attention for any academic needs. The school emphasizes connecting school with work through their Business Mentor Program. During the first semester, students are paired with a business mentor in their field of study. They also offer internships and projects and a corporate faculty.

University of Hartford

West Hartford, CT

Address: 200 Bloomfield Ave., West Hartford, CT 06117-1599
Phone: 860-768-4296
Admissions email: admission@mail.hartford.edu
Website: www.hartford.edu

Admissions Stats

Percentage of applicants admitted: 60.3%
SAT range: 480-580 critical reading, 480-580 math
ACT range: 20-24 composite

Size

Number of undergraduates: 5,592

Costs

Tuition and fees: $25,776
Books and supplies: $860
On campus room and board and other expenses: $11,272
Off campus room and board and other expenses: $12,530

Academics

Favorite majors: visual and performing arts, business, management, marketing and related support services, communication, journalism and related programs, health professions and related clinical services, education

The B Features

The Center for Reading and Writing (CRW) at Hartford provides writing tutors that work one on one with students in all phases of writing, from start to finish. Hartford also has a math and physics tutoring lab, chemistry tutors, computer science tutoring labs and an on-campus tutoring service that matches new students with trained and experienced student tutors.

The All University Curriculum covers 11 categories of learning, from arts and culture to responsibility for civic life and values identification. These classes are taught through a variety of methods including simulations, debates, field trips, interviews, surveys, discussions, oral reports and skits or dramatic scenes. Students are required to take at least four of these courses over a four-year period.

Hartwick College

Oneonta, NY

Address: One Hartwick Dr., Oneonta, NY 13820-4020
Phone: 607-431-4150
Admissions email: admissions@hartwick.edu
Website: www.hartwick.edu

Admissions Stats

Percentage of applicants admitted: 87%
SAT range: 520-620 critical reading, 500-620 math
ACT range: 21-27 composite

Size

Number of undergraduates: 1,463

Costs

Tuition and fees: $28,030
Books and supplies: $700
On campus room and board and other expenses: $8,910
Off campus room and board and other expenses: $5,700

Academics

Favorite majors: psychology, business, management, marketing and related support services, visual and performing arts, biological and biomedical sciences, social sciences, health professions and related clinical services

The B Features

Hartwick's Academic Center for Excellence assigns each incoming student to a professional advisor. Together they discuss academic progress and course selection. Other ACE staff members are available to advise students in related areas such as schedule changes and degree planning.

Tutoring is available in most subject areas simply by filling out a request form. Supplemental instructors also help with courses that are considered especially challenging. They organize group tutoring sessions and work one on one inside the classroom.

If a student's overall GPA falls below 2.0, he/she must sign a probationary agreement. All students on probation are to be involved in one of three programs: Close Scrutiny (a weekly one on one with a professional staff member); College Success (a small group weekly meeting to discuss issues of concern and develop strategies for academic success); or regular meetings with professional staff (to ensure students are staying on track).

University of Hawaii at Manoa

Honolulu, HI

Address: 2530 Dole St., Room C, Honolulu, HI 96822
Phone: 808-956-8975
Admissions email: ar-info@hawaii.edu
Website: www.manoa.hawaii.edu

Admissions Stats

Percentage of applicants admitted: 68%
SAT range: 480-580 critical reading, 520-620 math
ACT range: 21-25 composite, 19-24 English, 20-25 math

Size

Number of undergraduates: 11,525

Costs

Tuition and fees: $4,522 in state; $12,394 out of state
Books and supplies: $1,145
On campus room and board and other expenses: $8,789
Off campus room and board and other expenses: $12,804

Academics

Favorite majors: Asian and Pacific area studies, astronomy, languages, travel, ethnomusicology, tropical agriculture and geosciences

The B Features

The Learning Center at UH has a variety of services including testing, tutoring, study skills information and computer services. Practical skills are taught in areas like speed reading, test taking and time management. Tutoring in math, English, foreign language and other subjects is available by appointment or walk-in. The university also has two computer labs that provide extra assistance to students.

High Point University

High Point, NC

Address: 833 Montlieu Ave., High Point, NC 27262-3598
Phone: 336-841-9216
Admissions email: admiss@highpoint.edu
Website: www.highpoint.edu

Admissions Stats

Percentage of applicants admitted: 71.1%
SAT range: 450-560 critical reading, 450-560 math
ACT range: 18-23 composite

Size

Number of undergraduates: 2,524

Costs

Tuition and fees: $18,130
Books and supplies: $1,000
On campus room and board and other expenses: $10,090
Off campus room and board and other expenses: $9,800

Academics

Favorite majors: business, management, marketing and related support services, computer and information sciences and support services, psychology, education, parks, recreation, leisure and fitness studies

The B Features

The Academic Services Center at High Point "strives to foster the academic growth and development" of its students, according to its website. Tutoring is available at no charge year round. Walk-in tutoring promotes group tutoring, while individual tutoring can be scheduled with a simple request form. In addition, supplemental instruction puts a tutor in classrooms to listen and take notes and then help students with those classes. For communication classes, Writing Fellows review students' essays to help them improve their work.

Hiram College

Hiram, OH

Address: Hinsdale Hall, Third floor, Hiram, OH 44234
Phone: 330-569-5169 or 800-362-5280
Admissions email: admission@hiram.edu
Website: www.hiram.edu

Admissions Stats

Percentage of applicants admitted: 88%
SAT range: 490-610 critical reading, 490-600 math
ACT range: 20-25 composite, 20-26 English, 19-26 math

Size

Number of undergraduates: 1,205

Costs

Tuition and fees: $24,180
Books and supplies: $700
On campus room and board and other expenses: $9,875
Off campus room and board and other expenses: $11,522

Academics

Favorite majors: biology, chemistry, English, history, psychology, environmental studies, communication

The B Features

Hiram offers hands-on experiences in academics as well as off-campus study programs. Student Academic Services provides a variety of assistance programs including online time management tips and free peer tutoring with fellow students who excel in the class the student finds to be a challenge.

The Writing Center offers information, services and programs to help students write more efficiently and effectively, as well as to foster a love and respect for language. Trained writing assistants are available by appointment. Along with these services, the college provides test-taking tips.

Hollins University

Roanoke, VA

Address: 7916 Williamson Rd., P.O. Box 9707, Roanoke, VA 24020
Phone: 540-362-6401 or 800-465-9595
Admissions email: huadm@hollins.edu
Website: www.hollins.edu

Admissions Stats

Percentage of applicants admitted: 86%
SAT range: 530-640 critical reading, 490-590 math
ACT range: 22-27 composite

Size

Number of undergraduates: 848

Costs

Tuition and fees: $23,800
Books and supplies: $800
On campus room and board and other expenses: $10,300
Off campus room and board and other expenses: $10,300

Academics

Favorite majors: psychology, visual and performing arts, English/creative writing, communication studies, biology and political science

The B Features

While Hollins is listed as an all women college, men do account for 4 percent of the student body. Help for students is available through the Center for Learning Excellence, which is made up of a Writing Center and a Quantitative Reasoning Center.

The Writing Center is there to advise and guide students to understanding the writing process. Students learn about developing thesis statements, finding source materials and doing revisions.

The Quantitative Reasoning Center was originally established in 2002. It is focused on assisting students to improve their reasoning skills. Tutors answer questions about Math 100.

Hood College

Frederick, MD

Address: 401 Rosemont Ave., Frederick, MD 21701
Phone: 301-696-3400
Admissions email: admissions@hood.edu
Website: www.hood.edu

Admissions Stats

Percentage of applicants admitted: 51%
SAT range: 490-600 critical reading, 490-600 math
ACT range: 20-25 composite

Size

Number of undergraduates: 1,274

Costs

Tuition and fees: $23,655
Books and supplies: $800
On campus room and board and other expenses: $9,335
Off campus room and board and other expenses: $8,300

Academics

Favorite majors: psychology, management, biology, education, communication, arts

The B Features

Student-to-faculty ratios are an impressive 10:1 for undergrads. Class sizes are also smaller than the average.

Academic Services focuses on helping students who are having trouble in specific courses as well as those who just want to be more effective learners. Freshmen and sophomores are advised by a special group of faculty. Once a major is declared they are reassigned to an advisor in that subject.

Assessment of skills and knowledge is available through a Basic Skills Inventory. The results are studied so that students can be encouraged to take remedial courses before entering the college classroom. For example, should a student find that he/she would benefit from a review of math foundations before enrolling in a college math course, algebra review classes are available. In addition, classroom teaching, tutoring, videos, computer software and printed materials are provided. Individualized programs are also sometimes offered.

University of Houston at University Park

Houston, TX

Address: University Park, East Cullen, Suite 212, Houston, TX 77024
Phone: 713-743-1010
Admissions email: admissions@uh.edu
Website: www.uh.edu

Admissions Stats

Percentage of applicants admitted: 80.6%
SAT range: 450-570 critical reading, 490-600 math
ACT range: 19-23 composite, 17-23 English, 18-25 math

Size

Number of undergraduates: 27,048

Costs

Tuition and fees: $4,082 in state; $10,274 out of state
Books and supplies: $1,150
On campus room and board and other expenses: $10,130
Off campus room and board and other expenses: $13,850

Academics

Favorite majors: business, management, marketing and related support services, psychology, social sciences, engineering, communication, journalism and related programs

---

The B Features

Learning and Assessment Services at UH offers workshops covering topics such as improving memory power, overcoming procrastination, reducing test anxiety, preparing for exams and time management. Tutoring is available for no cost on both a walk-in and appointment basis. Multimedia Resources can help students who learn best on the computer, and math, science and business majors can find supplemental instruction study groups that meet on a regular basis. The Texas Success Initiative Program provides non-course, non-credit developmental instruction in reading, writing, math and test preparation.

Howard University

. . . .

Washington, DC

Address: 2400 Sixth St. NW, Washington, DC 20059-0001
Phone: 202-806-2763
Admissions email: admission@howard.edu
Website: www.howard.edu

Admissions Stats

Percentage of applicants admitted: 56%
SAT range: 440-680 critical reading, 420-600 math
ACT range: 20-29 composite

Size

Number of undergraduates: 6,982

Costs

Tuition and fees: $12,985
Books and supplies: $1,200
On campus room and board and other expenses: $8,322
Off campus room and board and other expenses: $14,044

Academics

Favorite majors: business, management, marketing and related support services, biology, psychology and history

---
The B Features

A predominantly African American college (68.7%), Howard assigns undergraduates an academic advisor during their first week of school.

The Center for Academic Reinforcement assists students with academic difficulties, conducts pre-orientation programs for entering freshmen, offers three-credit-hour courses in mathematics, verbal, study skills and reading and recently provided 2,000 tutoring and laboratory assistance sessions.

University of Idaho

Moscow, ID

Address: 875 Perimeter Dr., Moscow, ID 83844-2282
Phone: 208-885-6326
Admissions email: admappl@uidaho.edu
Website: www.uidaho.edu

Admissions Stats

Percentage of applicants admitted: 80%
SAT range: 480-610 critical reading, 490-620 math
ACT range: 20-26 composite

Size

Number of undergraduates: 9,503

Costs

Tuition and fees: $4,200 in state; $13,800 out of state
Books and supplies: $1,388
On campus room and board and other expenses: $9,932
Off campus room and board and other expenses: $9,932

Academics

Favorite majors: business, management, marketing and related support services, communication, journalism and related programs, education, natural resources and conservation, psychology and engineering

---

The B Features

The University of Idaho offers three academic assistance programs, each with its own focus. Tutoring and Learning Services provides one-on-one tutoring as well as a series of workshops called The College Success Series. These workshops cover such areas as note taking, active learning, college textbook reading and time management. Freshmen are also offered a one-credit study skills course, and there is an online learning center as well. Students in accounting, computer science and chemistry have their own learning labs and study groups and there is a separate Math Lab. The English Writing Center helps with all facets of written communication.

Student Support Services is designed to provide academic support and assistance to students who meet the TRIO eligibility standards: 1) neither parent has a college degree, 2) they come from a low-income family or 3) they are physically/learning disabled. The Disability Support Services is geared to assist students that are physically challenged as defined by the American Disabilities Act.

Indiana State University

Terre Haute, IN

Address: 210 N. 7th St., Terre Haute, IN 47809
Phone: 812-237-2121
Website: www.indstate.edu

Admissions Stats

Percentage of applicants admitted: 80%
SAT range: 420-520 critical reading, 420-530 math
ACT range: 16-22 composite, 16-22 English, 17-23 math

Size

Number of undergraduates: 8,670

Costs

Tuition and fees: $6,436 in state; $13,852 out of state
Books and supplies: $1,140
On campus room and board and other expenses: $8,976
Off campus room and board and other expenses: $10,084

Academics

Favorite majors: business, management, marketing and related support services, education, social sciences, engineering technologies/technicians, communication, journalism and related programs

---

The B Features

The Student Academic Services Center at Indiana State helps in several ways. The Mentoring Program's primary goal, according to the college, is to "assist first-year students so that they may benefit from additional support, encouragement and services." Staff members are updated weekly on each student's progress and adjustment to college life. Students sign a Mentoring Contract at the beginning of the process.

A professional advisement staff is always available for help or advice. The school offers a tutoring program for all general studies classes on either a drop-in or appointment basis. Additionally, students are invited to take University 101-Learning in the University Community, a two-credit hour elective that helps with the transition to the college. Students can learn study strategies, critical thinking and writing skills while being introduced to campus resources and services. The course also discusses the history of the school and the community around it.

Indiana University at Bloomington

Bloomington, IN

Address: 107 S. Indiana Ave., Bloomington, IN 47405-7000
Phone: 812-855-0661
Admissions email: iuadmit@indiana.edu
Website: www.iub.edu

Admissions Stats

Percentage of applicants admitted: 78.3%
SAT range: 490-610 critical reading, 510-630 math
ACT range: 22-27 composite, 22-28 English, 22-27 math

Size

Number of undergraduates: 29,562

Costs

Tuition and fees: $7,460 in state; $20,472 out of state
Books and supplies: $740
On campus room and board and other expenses: $9,890
Off campus room and board and other expenses: $9,890

Academics

Favorite majors: business, management, marketing and related support services, biological and biomedical sciences, communication, journalism and related programs, education, public administration and social service professions

The B Features

The Student Academic Center of Indiana University is focused on helping with any problems students might have. According to the college, its philosophy is "student support, student respect and student success."

Study Smarter Workshops cover a wide field of topics, including learning from returned exams, improving reading speed and catching up in a course when all hope seems gone.

Supplemental Instruction offers small group study sessions guided by fellow students who have already taken the same course and have been recommended by the professor. Here, students can review content, ask questions, discuss issues and learn effective reading and study strategies.

The Phoenix Program serves students who have been put on academic probation. It offers several courses to help these individuals get back on track. Those that do are later offered the chance to serve as peer mentors to others.

Individualized Academic Assessment and Assistance is offered to students who are not sure about their strengths and weaknesses or exactly what kind of help they need. This free assessment program is done on a walk-in or appointment basis.

Outreach Services is a program of mini-workshops or presentations that are offered in the residence halls, fraternity houses, classes or organizations on topics such as test taking and time management.

Non-Credit Programs and Services is an hour-long, individual session that can help students identify and target areas causing academic stress.

The Right Start Program is for freshmen who are not familiar with campus/college life (first-generation students, or students from small towns or high schools, etc.). It offers an orientation to the college life and culture of IU through resources in small seminar groups. This is a full semester course that earns the student two credit hours and teaches lessons about the campus, college lifestyles and study skills.

Indiana University of Pennsylvania

Indiana, PA

Address: 1011 South Dr., 201 Sutton Hall, Indiana, PA 15705-1098
Phone: 724-357-2230
Admissions email: admissions-inquiry@iup.edu
Website: www.iup.edu

Admissions Stats

Percentage of applicants admitted: 55.3%
SAT range: 480-570 critical reading, 470-570 math
ACT range: Not available

Size

Number of undergraduates: 12,047

Costs

Tuition and fees: $6,390 in state; $14,013 out of state
Books and supplies: $1,000
On campus room and board and other expenses: $8,236
Off campus room and board and other expenses: $8,236

Academics

Favorite majors: business, management, marketing and related support services, social sciences, education, visual and performing arts, communication, journalism and related programs

---

The B Features

IU offers credit courses that help students cope with the demands of college. Through the Learning Enhancement Center, a student can take classes on such topics as learning strategies, vocabulary expansion, reading skills for college study and introduction to college math. The center provides tutoring, supplemental instruction, workshops and a campus-wide academic support program to help all levels of students.

The Writing Center offers tutoring by other students on a drop-in basis. The center also sponsors writing workshops with subjects such Internet use in research and resume writing.

If a student's GPA falls below 2.0, he/she is placed on academic probation and must implement an Academic Recovery Plan, which is designed to help students make progress toward academic good standing.

Lake Forest College

Lake Forest, IL

Address: 555 N. Sheridan Rd., Lake Forest, IL 60045
Phone: 847-735-5000 or 800-828-4751
Admissions email: admissions@lakeforest.edu
Website: www.lakeforest.edu

Admissions Stats

Percentage of applicants admitted: 61%
SAT range: 1140-1230 composite
ACT range: 24-28 composite
Lake Forest is a test optional institution. Students may choose to include test scores for consideration of admission.

Size

Number of undergraduates: 1,400

Costs

Tuition and fees: $30,964
Books and supplies: NA
On campus room and board and other expenses: $7,326
Off campus room and board and other expenses: NA

Academics

Favorite majors: communications, business/economics, psychology, education, pre-med, pre-law, English, international relations, politics, art, chemistry, biology, history and Asian studies. Also includes Independent Scholar with Advertising in the Arts, The Theology and Philosophy of Niko Kazantzakis, Trade Liberalization in Poorer Latin America and Psychoneuroimmunology

The B Features

Insight from Lake Forest College includes the following: "We offer a comprehensive Academic Resource Center, which provides tutorial support open to all students. The program is coordinated by a Learning Resource Specialist. The college also supports a strong Writing Center, seminars in time management and study skills development. Lake Forest College maintains a 12:1 student-faculty ratio, providing personal access to professors and their mentorship. As stated in our mission statement, 'We know our students by name.'

"The personal interview is strongly recommended and is the best re-source for assessing a student's potential to flourish at Lake Forest. We value students who are committed to community and campus involvement, who have a clear understanding of why they have applied to Lake Forest and whose needs are well matched with the college. In addition to the interview, students should strive to take a challenging high school curriculum, including honors or advanced placement courses when possible.

"We consider the rigor of a student's high school curriculum in con-test to the grade point average and we read transcripts carefully. In this regard, we can appreciate strengths and weaknesses of each individual student, including a consideration of B or even C grades. There is a 'story' behind each transcript and we seek to understand a student's academic journey through the personal interview.

"Lake Forest College offers students a rare combination: an excep-tionally beautiful residential campus where they are challenged by a rigorous curriculum, an outstanding faculty, and the resources of Chicago just 30 miles away, where they step outside the classroom to enhance learning in powerful ways."

Longwood College

Farmville, VA

Address: 201 High St., Farmville, VA 23909
Phone: 434-395-2060
Admissions email: admit@longwood.edu
Website: www.longwood.edu

Admissions Stats

Percentage of applicants admitted: 67.2%
SAT range: 490-570 critical reading, 490-570 math
ACT range: NA

Size

Number of undergraduates: 4,374

Costs

Tuition and fees: $7,589 in state; $15,259 out of state
Books and supplies: $800
On campus room and board and other expenses: $8,673
Off campus room and board and other expenses: NA

Academics

Favorite majors: Íbusiness, marketing, management and related support services, liberal arts and sciences, general studies and humanities, social services, psychology, history and visual and performing arts

---

The B Features

Longwood College offers a Learning Center that is located in the Greenwood Library. It features a speaking center, as well as a writing center and open labs. There is no charge for any of the services offered and sessions are on a drop-in basis.

University of Louisiana at Lafayette

Lafayette, LA

Address: 104 University Circle, Lafayette, LA 70503
Phone: 377-482-6467
Admissions email: admissions@louisiana.edu
Website: www.louisiana.edu

Admissions Stats

Percentage of applicants admitted: 73.1%
SAT range: Not available
ACT range: 19-25 composite, 18-25 English, 17-24 math

Size

Number of undergraduates: 14,585

Costs

Tuition and fees: $3,382 in state; $9,562 out of state
Books and supplies: $1,000
On campus room and board and other expenses: $6,341
Off campus room and board and other expenses: $10,679

Academics

Favorite majors: business, management, marketing and related services, education, engineering, health professions and related clinical services, liberal arts and sciences, general studies and humanities

The B Features

Students may be admitted through the University of Louisiana's Guaranteed Admission requirements, which are these:

Completion of the Louisiana Board of Regents' high school core curriculum and a mathematics ACT score of at least 18 (430 math SAT) or an English ACT score of at least 18 (450 critical reading SAT) and one of the following:

■ high school GPA of 2.5 or higher using an unweighted 4.0 scale

■ ACT composite score of at least 23 (SAT 1060) with at least a 2.0 GPA or

■ rank in the top 25% of the high school graduating class and at least a 2.0 GPA

Students who don't meet the Guaranteed Admission requirements may apply for Admission by Committee by submitting a completed application.

Once students are accepted and enrolled at the University of Louisiana, they can find help for succeeding in their studies. The Learning Center offers walk-in tutoring, although appointments are sometimes recommended. The Writing Center helps students with all stages of the writing process. Free online tutoring is another service offered through Smart Thinking. With it, students can access live tutorials in writing, math, accounting, statistics and economics. They can also consult writing manuals, sample problems, research tools and study skills manuals.

Study groups are available on campus so that several students can get help on a weekly basis. They are student led, and sessions cover problems and questions from weekly class material.

Study skills and time management helps are found on the college website, including information on reading, note taking, studying, test anxiety, test taking and general study skills.

The college also offers a Career Counseling Center that can provide help to a student in deciding a major. A career counselor is there to guide students to resources and informational material. Along with this, a half-semester, one-credit course on career decision-making assists students who want an in-depth career analysis.

Luther College

· ·

Decorah, IA

Address: 700 College Dr., Decorah, IA 52101-1045
Phone: 563-387-1287
Admissions email: admissions@luther.edu
Website: www.luther.edu

Admissions Stats

Percentage of applicants admitted: 81.4%
SAT range: 500-660 critical reading, 540-650 math
ACT range: 22-27 composite, 21-28 English, 21-27 math

Size

Number of undergraduates: 2,545

Costs

Tuition and fees: $26,380
Books and supplies: $830
On campus room and board and other expenses: $6,850
Off campus room and board and other expenses: NA

Academics

Favorite majors: business, management, marketing and related support services, visual and performing arts, biological and biomedical sciences, social sciences, education, foreign language and literatures and linguistics

The B Features

This Lutheran college has a Student Academic Support Center. The goals of the Center include assisting students in becoming self confident critical thinkers and learners, helping with peer tutoring, linking students to helpful resources and meeting the needs of all students who need any kind of academic assistance. Luther offers a class called Critical Reading and Learning Strategies (GS110) that helps students become better readers through the description, interpretation and evaluation of different texts. Additionally, they offer the Learning and Study Skills Inventory (LASSI) which is a diagnostic measure to help students discover the areas in which they need help. This assessment measures everything from attitude and motivation to test anxiety and information processing. The college's Academic Support Services includes independent tutoring and group sessions, as well as learning skills workshops, academic advising and access to a series of helpful hand-outs.

Lycoming College

Williamsport, PA

Address: 700 Cottage Place, Williamsport, PA 17701-5192
Phone: 570-321-4026
Admissions email: admissions@lycoming.edu
Website: www.lycoming.edu

Admissions Stats

Percentage of applicants admitted: 76.1%
SAT range: 460-560 reading, 460-550 writing, 470-580 math
ACT range: 20-24 composite

Size

Number of undergraduates: 1,485

Costs

Tuition and fees: $25,120
Books and supplies: $800
On campus room and board and other expenses: $9,677
Off campus room and board and other expenses: NA

Academics

Favorite majors: business, management, marketing and related support services, biological and biomedical sciences, psychology, social sciences, visual and performing arts, communication, journalism and related programs

---

The B Features

Lycoming has an Academic Resource Center that offers subject tutors, writing consultants, study groups, study skills workshops and support services for learning disabilities. In addition, the school provides a program called Writing across the Curriculum, which helps students develop their ability to communicate clearly.

Lynn University

Boca Raton, FL

Address: 3601 N. Military Trail, Boca Raton, FL 33431-5598
Phone: 561-237-7900
Admissions email: admission@lynn.edu
Website: www.lynn.edu

Admissions Stats

Percentage of applicants admitted: 70.8%
SAT range: 400-500 critical reading, 430-510 math
ACT range: Not available

Size

Number of undergraduates: 2,348

Costs

Tuition and fees: $26,200
Books and supplies: $1,050
On campus room and board and other expenses: $13,450
Off campus room and board and other expenses: $13,450

Academics

Favorite majors: business, management, marketing and related support services, psychology, communication, journalism and related programs, education, security and protective services

The B Features

Lynn's Institute for Achievement and Learning focuses on personalized education. The college states that the institute "embraces, empowers and engages its students to offer opportunities for greater accomplishments in higher education and career realization." Programs include First Year Experience, the Tutoring Center, Discovery Writing Center, Metamorphosis Coaching, Probationary Support and Academic Status Support.

First Year Experience is required of all freshmen. This two-semester academic program connects new students with peers, campus resources and faculty. In the first class (FYE-1), students focus on the nature of education, including units on time management, test taking, communication skills, study techniques, university policies and procedures, resources and services, health and wellness issues and personal issues. FYE-1 also includes a pre-orientation to Academic Adventure, a faculty-led program in which the entire freshman class spends five days in the Caribbean on a ship studying the region's cultures and people. In FYE-2, students explore multicultural and diversity awareness, educational planning, career development, leadership, community service and learning potential—plus reflect upon their Academic Adventure!

The Discovery Writing Center offers one-on-one tutoring for all levels of writing skills. The Hannifan Center for Career Development and Internships provides personalized career counseling, group career workshops, internships and job-placement assistance.

Academic Status Support assists students who are on academic probation. This no-cost program includes advising and learning strategy suggestions to help students improve their grades. Probationary Support is similar and offers free advising, group tutoring, social activities, counseling sessions and workshops.

Metamorphosis Coaching is geared to students who learn best from hands-on experience rather than traditional classroom methods. It takes students out of the classroom and into such settings as the campus butterfly garden or a local nature center as they learn observation skills logged into journals. According to the college, this program is not just about studying nature, but it also is "a study of life and the nature of our own selves. The 'lessons' learned through this reflective process will provide valuable insights about the way you learn best—and yourself." The program also includes group dinners and guest lecturers as well as private tutoring and field trips. (There is a charge for this program.)

McDaniel College

Westminster, MD

Address: 2 College Hill, Westminster, MD 21157
Phone: 800-638-5005
Admissions email: admissions@mcdaniel.edu
Website: www.mcdaniel.edu

Admissions Stats

Percentage of applicants admitted: 73.5%
SAT range: 490-610 critical reading, 500-620 math
ACT range: 20-25 composite, 24-20 English, 21-28 math

Size

Number of undergraduates: 3,524

Costs

Tuition and fees: $26,980
Books and supplies: $900
On campus room and board and other expenses: $6,970
Off campus room and board and other expenses: $4,850

Academics

Favorite majors: business, management, marketing and related support services, social sciences, visual and performing arts, psychology, communication, journalism and related programs, biological and biomedical sciences

The B Features

The Academic Support Services at McDaniel include tutoring, expert faculty advising, help with writing through the Writing Center and computer resources.

McKendree College

Lebanon, IL

Address: 701 College Rd., Lebanon, IL 62254
Phone: 618-537-4481 ext. 6831
Admissions email: inquiry@mckendree.edu
Admissions contact: Mark Campbell, vice president for enrollment management
Website: www.mckendree.edu

Admissions Stats

Percentage of applicants admitted: 68.5%
Average GPA range: 3.6
SAT range: 420-530 critical reading, 430-600 math
ACT range: 21-25 composite, 19-26 English, 19-26 math

Size

Number of undergraduates: 2,257

Costs

Tuition and fees: $18,900
Books and supplies: $1,200
On campus room and board and other expenses: $9,000
Off campus room and board and other expenses: $8,300

Academics

Favorite majors: business, management, marketing and related support services, health professions and related clinical services, education, social sciences, computer and information sciences and support services

Student Life

The campus: McKendree has a main campus and three satellite campuses which include one at Scott Air Force Base and two in Kentucky. It is the oldest college in Illinois and was founded in 1828 by "circuit-riding Methodists." Twenty-five minutes east of the St. Louis Arch, the campus integrates the old and new with buildings that range from 1820 to the new $10 million arts center.

The students: Women are in the majority (55%); about 80% of the student body is white/non-Hispanic.

The B Features

The college features small classes, is eager to accept students who are really trying and is dedicated to not letting any of them "slip through the cracks."

Insight

"McKendree is the only place in southern Illinois where you have an average class size of 15 and all classes are under 50," explains Mark Campbell vice president for enrollment management." The more intimate classes help students to feel less anonymous.

"We do not evaluate students with multiple-choice tests," he adds. "Instead, we want to see how they write. There is a real gray area between students who are easy to admit and those who are easy to deny. The key is in the students' strength in English. How do they read, write and comprehend?" All students who are admitted must submit a writing sample before they are placed in an English class.

"All potential students are invited to write an essay for us," explains Campbell. "We even allow graded papers from school. In the end, we are obligated to not admit students who will not do well. We simply focus on a student's determination to succeed."

University of Maine—Orono

Orono, ME

Address: 5713 Chadbourne, Orono, ME 04469
Phone: 207-581-1561
Admissions email: um-admit@umaine.edu
Website: www.umaine.edu

Admissions Stats

Percentage of applicants admitted: 80%
SAT range: 480-590 critical reading, 490-600 math
ACT range: 20-25 composite

Size

Number of undergraduates: 7,617

Costs

Tuition and fees: $7,464 in state; $18,414 out of state
Books and supplies: $700
On campus room and board and other expenses: $8,974
Off campus room and board and other expenses: $8,012

Academics

Favorite majors: marine science, environmental science, forestry, new media, biological science, physics and psychology

---

The B Features

The Tutor Program at the University of Maine is designed to meet with students in small group settings who need help in their 100- and 200-level, non-web-based courses. Peer tutors meet with students two or three times a week throughout the semester. One student is quoted on the website as saying, "I was not grasping the problems in lecture and I was often confused on which technique to apply. Having students explain ideas and concepts to each other has been very helpful. I have had to be prepared for each session, which keeps me on task." This no-cost service is open to any student who has registered for at least six credit hours as well as students who need help in math classes.

For those needing help with writing, the college's Writing Center staff is there to give advice as well.

Marietta College

Marietta, GA

Address: Irvine Building, Marietta, GA 45750
Phone: 740-376-4600
Admissions email: admit@marietta.edu
Website: www.marietta.edu

Admissions Stats

Percentage of applicants admitted: 78.9%
SAT range: 490-600 critical reading, 490-590 math
ACT range: 20-26 composite, 20-26 English, 19-26 math

Size

Number of undergraduates: 1,466

Costs

Tuition and fees: $23,815
Books and supplies: $660
On campus room and board and other expenses: $8,180
Off campus room and board and other expenses: NA

Academics

Favorite majors: business, management, marketing and related support services, communication, journalism and related program, visual and performing arts, education, health professions and related clinical services

The B Features

At Marietta, the Academic Resource Center offers individualized academic support for students by means of several different avenues. Students are advised early on when their performance assessment may be dangerously low through the use of the college's early warning system. Help is available to struggling students through individual and small group tutoring and study skills assistance. Additionally, students have access to computers and educational technology, personal development workshops on topics like study skills and time management, a resource library and referral to additional resources.

University of Maryland—Eastern Shore

Princess Ann, MD

Address: J.T. Williams Hall, Princess Ann, MD 21853-1299
Phone: 410-651-6410
Admissions email: umesadmissions@umes.edu
Website: www.umes.edu

Admissions Stats

Percentage of applicants admitted: 66.2%
SAT range: 370-460 critical reading, 360-460 math
ACT range: 14-17 composite, 12-18 English, 14-17 math

Size

Number of undergraduates: 3,870

Costs

Tuition and fees: $5,908 in state; $12,475 out of state
Books and supplies: $1,600
On campus room and board and other expenses: $9,360
Off campus room and board and other expenses: $8,030

Academics

Favorite majors: business, management, marketing and related support services, security and protection services, biological and biomedical sciences, English language and literature/letters, health professions and related clinical sciences

The B Features

UMES has an extensive Academic Support Center which includes a tutorial program that helps students in all lower-level courses. Both individual and small group tutoring is available and all services are free.

Through the school's Computer Assisted Instruction Program, students can use a system known as Accuplacer to obtain a comprehensive analysis of where they stand in reading, math and English. Developmental skills classes are offered by professional staff specialists. Students who need a stronger background in liberal arts may find help through the General Studies Program.

Additionally, students who are 1) from families with low income, 2) first generation college enrollees, or 3) disabled (learning or physical) can take part in the federally funded Student Support Services Program.

Marymount Manhattan College

New York, NY

Address: 221 E. 71st St., New York, NY 10021-4597
Phone: 800-MARYMOUNT or 212-517-0430
Admissions email: admissions@mmm.edu
Website: www.mmm.edu

Admissions Stats

Percentage of applicants admitted: 75.8%
Average GPA range: 3.2
SAT range: 490-600 critical reading, 460-570 math
ACT range: 20-25 composite, 20-26 English, 22-26 math

Size

Number of undergraduates: 2,007

Costs

Tuition and fees: $19,638
Books and supplies: $1,000
On campus room and board and other expenses: $14,190
Off campus room and board and other expenses: $13,620

Academics

Favorite majors: visual and performing arts, communication, journalism and related programs, business, management, marketing and related support services, psychology, social sciences

The B Features

Marymount's students may find assistance with coursework at a tutoring center that provides full support to walk-ins through student tutors as well as trained staff. The Center for Academic Advancement (formerly known as College Skills) has courses for students who need to reinforce their skills in reading comprehension, vocabulary, grammar and basic writing. According to the college, "It is our mission to provide these services in any reasonable manner in order to secure student futures. Our main objective is to assure each student who passes through our doors that they can and will succeed in college."

George Mason University

Fairfax, VA

Address: 4400 University Dr., Fairfax, VA 22030-4444
Phone: 703-993-2400
Admissions email: admissions@gmu.edu
Website: www.gmu.edu

Admissions Stats

Percentage of applicants admitted: 61%
SAT range: 490-600 critical reading, 510-610 math
ACT range: Not available

Size

Number of undergraduates: 18,091

Costs

Tuition and fees: $6,408 in state; $18,552 out of state
Books and supplies: $1,011
On campus room and board and other expenses: $8,246
Off campus room and board and other expenses: $13,090

Academics

Favorite majors: business, management, marketing and related support services, English language and literature/letters, social sciences, psychology, health professions and related clinical services

---
The B Features

Learning Services at George Mason encompasses many different methods to help support students who are struggling academically. Study skills workshops are offered on topics such as concentration, procrastination, academic skills, motivation and goal setting. Tutor Referral matches students with peer tutors (which charge varying fees). Services are confidential, and use of these services does not become part of the student's academic record.

The college also offers a Certificate in Academic Skills to help students study more effectively, improve test-taking skills, decrease anxiety about performance and improve grades. Through this process, students go to workshops, listen to audiotapes, watch videotapes, use interactive computer programs and get books from the Self-Help Resource library.

Manhattanville College

Purchase, NY

Address: 2900 Purchase St., Purchase, NY 10577
Phone: 800-328-4553
Admissions email: admissions@mville.edu
Website: www.manhattanville.edu

Admissions Stats

Percentage of applicants admitted: 52.8%
SAT range: 480-610 critical reading, 500-610 math
ACT range: 20-25 composite

Size

Number of undergraduates: 1,800

Costs

Tuition and fees: $28,000
Books and supplies: $800
On campus room and board and other expenses: $12,650
Off campus room and board and other expenses: $12,650

Academics

Favorite majors: business, management, marketing and related support services, social sciences, visual and performing arts, psychology, history

---

The B Features

Manhattanville's Academic Resource Center offers individual tutoring, group supplemental instruction and a variety of workshops. ARC has full-time professional instructors in writing, math and study strategies and part-time tutors in subjects that include accounting, foreign languages, math, music theory, statistics for social sciences and economic statistics. Special credit-bearing courses are offered to help students learn science, math and the humanities.

According to the college, the philosophy of the ARC is one of "fostering independence in the students who seek help. We are equipped to deal with many types of academic difficulties and to offer personal assistance in a relaxed and supportive atmosphere."

University of Memphis

Memphis, TN

Address: 101 Wilder Tower, Memphis, TN 38152
Phone: 901-678-2101
Admissions email: recruitment@memphis.edu
Website: www.memphis.edu

Admissions Stats

Percentage of applicants admitted: 71.1%
SAT range: 450-619 critical reading, 440-590 writing, 470-590 math
ACT range: 19-24 composite, 19-25 English, 17-24 math

Size

Number of undergraduates: 20,465

Costs

Tuition and fees: $5,256 in state; $15,722 out of state
Books and supplies: $1,000
On campus room and board and other expenses: $10,406
Off campus room and board and other expenses: $10,406

Academics

Favorite majors: business, management, marketing and related support services, multi/interdisciplinary studies, education, communication, journalism and related programs, liberal arts and sciences, general studies and humanities, psychology and social sciences

The B Features

The University of Memphis offers its students help through its Advanced Learning Center. A Learning Lab provides consultations, open forum learning, special topics training and educational seminars.

Menlo College

Atherton, CA

Address: 1000 El Camino Real, Atherton, CA 94027-4301
Phone: 650-543-3753
Website: www.menlo.edu

Admissions Stats

Percentage of applicants admitted: 57.4%
SAT range: 410-510 critical reading, 420-560 math
ACT range: 15-22 composite, 13-22 English, 16-22 math

Size

Number of undergraduates: 769

Costs

Tuition and fees: $26,220
Books and supplies: $1,212
On campus room and board and other expenses: $12,564
Off campus room and board and other expenses: NA

Academics

Favorite majors: business, management, marketing and related support services, liberal arts and sciences, general studies and humanities, communication, journalism and related programs

The B Features

Menlo's Academic Success Center provides support to students through peer tutoring. Areas of help include time management, test taking strategies, exam preparation and note taking. The college offers students assistance through its Writing Lab as well.

Michigan State University

· ·

East Lansing, MI

Address: 250 Hannah Administration Building, East Lansing, MI 48824-1046
Phone: 517-355-8332
Admissions email: admis@msu.edu
Website: www.msu.edu

Admissions Stats

Percentage of applicants admitted: 73%
SAT range: 1040-1270 composite
ACT range: 22-27 composite

Size

Number of undergraduates: 35,678

Costs

Tuition and fees: $8,893 in state; $21,538 out of state
Books and supplies: $889
On campus room and board and other expenses: $7,776
Off campus room and board and other expenses: $7,776

Academics

Favorite majors: no preference, psychology, finance, accounting, marketing, communication, advertising, education and English. Unusual majors include veterinary medicine, music therapy, political theory and constitutional democracy

---
The B Features

MSU's Learning Resource Center offers help to students who are looking to improve their grades, to develop study strategies and to boost their overall scholastic performance. The Center features a professional staff, interactive learning lab and tutoring services in the residence halls. Daytime tutoring is offered in one-hour individual sessions at no cost, and evening tutoring is available for math groups twice a week. Seminars and workshops are also offered on topics such as test taking and preparing for finals.

Insight from the school includes this quote: "Great, dynamic learning environment highlighted by extremely helpful and accessible professors and great on campus resources, including the Learning Resource Center, the English Language Center and the Office of Supportive Services.

"Apply before November 1. Complete a challenging curriculum in high school. Complete a well written personal statement, required as part of the application. Use it to show how well rounded you are as a student and person. Be involved in activities."

Mills College

Oakland, CA

Address: 5000 MacArthur Blvd., Oakland, CA 94613
Phone: 800-876-4557
Admissions email: admissions@mills.edu
Website: www.mills.edu

Admissions Stats

Percentage of applicants admitted: 74%
SAT range: 500-640 critical reading, 470-590 math
ACT range: 21-27 composite

Size

Number of undergraduates: 927

Costs

Tuition and fees: $33,024
Books and supplies: $1,100
On campus room and board and other expenses: $12,290
Off campus room and board and other expenses: $12,410

Academics

Favorite majors: English, psychology, studio art, chemistry, economics, biology, anthropology and sociology

The B Features

The Writing Center at Mills College provides assistance for students who need help in developing communication skills. It is staffed by graduate students from the English Department, and one-on-one tutoring is available. In addition, workshops on writing are offered throughout the entire school year. Classes are commonly 20 students or less, and the student-to-faculty ratio is 10:1.

University of Mississippi

University, MS

Address: 145 Martindale, University, MS 38677
Phone: 662-915-7226
Admissions email: admissions@olemiss.edu
Website: www.olemiss.edu

Admissions Stats

Percentage of applicants admitted: 73.1%
SAT range: 480-580 critical reading, 490-600 math
ACT range: 20-26 composite, 20-28 English, 18-25 math

Size

Number of undergraduates: 12,197

Costs

Tuition and fees: $4,602 in state; $10,566 out of state
Books and supplies: $1,000
On campus room and board and other expenses: $9,232
Off campus room and board and other expenses: $9,232

Academics

Favorite majors: business, management, marketing and related support services, education, social sciences, psychology, health professions and related clinical services, family and consumer sciences

---
The B Features

The Academic Support Center at the University of Mississippi aids struggling students and those who have not yet declared a major. It helps with scheduling classes, exploring possible majors and fulfilling core requirements for a bachelor's degree. In addition, the Center assists with questions or problems with student schedules, explanations of university policies and procedures as well as providing referrals to other offices as needed.

Mitchell College

New London, CT

Address: 437 Pequot Ave., New London, CT 06320
Phone: 800-243-2811
Admissions email: hodges_k@mitchell.edu
Admissions contact: Kevin Mayne, vice president for enrollment
management and marketing
Website: www.mitchell.edu

Admissions Stats

Percentage of applicants admitted: 67%
Average GPA: 2.75
SAT range: does not require the SAT
ACT range: does not require the ACT

Size

Number of undergraduates: 800

Costs

Tuition and fees: $23,093
Books and supplies: $1,000
On campus room and board and other expenses: $10,406
Off campus room and board and other expenses: $10,406

Academics

Favorite majors: criminal justice, early childhood education,
sports management, hospitality and tourism, communications and
environmental studies, homeland security, human development and
family studies, transitional program (Thames Academy)

Student Life

The campus: Located on 65 acres along the Connecticut shoreline,
Mitchell has two beaches, athletic fields and wooded trails. Of the
seven residence halls, four of them are waterfront Victorian homes.
The college was founded in 1938 and is two hours from Boston and
New York City.

The students: The population of the college includes students from
22 states and 18 countries with a ratio is 49.2% men and 50.8%
women. A little over one-third of the total student body is comprised
of students of color.

The B Features

This statement from Mitchell College gives insight into its facilities and programs: "Mitchell College prides itself on the fact that its greatest success and satisfaction comes from working with students who have yet to realize their full academic potential. The College embraces student differences and provides the following resources and strategies that can help B students achieve success:

- Free professional content tutoring
- Learning and writing specialists
- Nationally recognized LD support program
- STEP—5 week summer transition enrichment program
- Thames Academy—Post Grad Transitional Year Certificate Program
- FIG—Freshman Interest Groups
- Mentoring program
- Discovery program for undecided students"

Insight

"You are more than just your grade point average. While admission to Mitchell College is based on a comprehensive appraisal of your entire academic record, a huge part of that is also your personal character, aptitude, motivation and above all, your potential for academic success. We welcome the B student who recognizes his/her strengths and weaknesses and wants to be in an environment that will challenge him/her to improve and succeed.

"We would encourage B students to showcase their talents—those within the classroom and outside the classroom. Community and club involvement, volunteer and work experience, as well as hobbies and leadership opportunities, are a great way to show that a student has more to offer than just grades alone.

"Mitchell College has always been a college that focuses on asset development rather than deficit management. Our mission says it well when it states that we 'support individual learning differences and nurture untapped academic potential.' We welcome B and C students and find it very rewarding to have the privilege to be able to work with them to realize their full potential.

"Mitchell College's educational philosophy is one that is based on five distinctive values called C.A.R.E.S.—Character, Achievement, Respect, Engagement and Self-Discovery. It is a learning experience that provides students with the foundation and knowledge base they need for the education and life they wish to pursue. This partnership enables students to take their classroom instruction and apply it directly to the real world through a variety of unique internship and service learning opportunities—experiences that enable students to make a difference locally, nationally and globally."

Montana Tech of the University of Montana

Butte, MT

Address: 1300 W. Park St., Butte, MT 59701
Phone: 406-496-4178 or 800-445-TECH
Admissions email: admissions@mtech.edu
Website: www.mtech.edu

Admissions Stats

Percentage of applicants admitted: 96%
SAT range: 940-1180 composite
ACT range: 19-24 composite

Size

Number of undergraduates: 2,214

Costs

Tuition and fees: $4,946 in state; $14,718 out of state
Books and supplies: $800
On campus room and board and other expenses: $5,178
Off campus room and board and other expenses: $5,000

Academics

Favorite majors: petroleum engineering, general engineering, nursing, business, health care information

---
The B Features

A quote about Montana Tech explains the services that the college provides to its students: "Montana Tech has a great learning center. This is a place where all students can get help with any of their courses. Tech also has very attentive professors that are always available for personal help.

"Montana Tech admits students that are in the top half of their graduating class or who have a 2.5 or higher. You do not need to have straight A's to get admitted or to get scholarships here. All B students are accepted to Montana Tech! Any student above a 2.5 is accepted in good academic standing. Students with lower GPAs than 2.5 are accepted on academic probation. They will be in college success courses and monitored carefully."

Morehouse College

Atlanta, GA

Address: 830 Westview Dr. Southwest, Atlanta, GA 30314
Phone: 404-215-2632 or 800-851-1254
Admissions email: admissions@morehouse.edu
Website: www.morehouse.edu

Admissions Stats

Percentage of applicants admitted: 75%
SAT range: 440-680 critical reading, 470-680 math
ACT range: 19-32 composite, 17-24 English, 18-25 math

Size

Number of undergraduates: 2,970

Costs

Tuition and fees: $17,536
Books and supplies: $850
On campus room and board and other expenses: $13,254
Off campus room and board and other expenses: NA

Academics

Favorite majors: psychology, business, economics, biology, political science

---

The B Features

Morehouse is an African American (93%) college for men. The Wellness Resource Center offers personal counseling to help students "resolve personal difficulties and acquire the skills, attitudes and knowledge that will enable them to take full advantage of their experiences at Morehouse College."

Muskingum College

New Concord, OH

Address: 163 Stormont St., New Concord, OH 43762
Phone: 740-826-8137
Admissions email: adminfo@muskingum.edu
Website: www.muskingum.edu

Admissions Stats

Percentage of applicants admitted: 78.5%
SAT range: 450-610 critical reading, 450-610 writing, 450-610 math
ACT range: 19-24 composite, 19-24 English, 19-24 math

Size

Number of undergraduates: 2,396

Costs

Tuition and fees: $17,035
Books and supplies: $1,000
On campus room and board and other expenses: $8,300
Off campus room and board and other expenses: NA

Academics

Favorite majors: education, business, management, marketing and related support services, biological and biomedical sciences, psychology, communication, journalism and related programs

The B Features

The Center for Advancement of Learning at Muskingum provides assistance to students in a number of different ways. Their PLUS program is a complex system for students with significant learning disabilities. There is also a Learning Strategies and Resources Program that helps at-risk students through weekly workshops, weekly strategy sessions, and more. In addition, their First Step Transition Program provides an intensive and comprehensive summer orientation for students before they begin their undergraduate studies.

University of Nevada-Las Vegas

Las Vegas, NV

Address: 4505 S. Maryland Parkway, Las Vegas, NV 89154
Phone: 702-895-3443
Admissions email: undergraduate.recruitment@ccmail.nevada.edu
Website: www.unlv.edu

Admissions Stats

Percentage of applicants admitted: 81.5%
SAT range: 450-560 critical reading, 450-570 math
ACT range: 18-24 composite, 17-23 English, 17-24 math

Size

Number of undergraduates: 22,112

Costs

Tuition and fees: $3,822 in state; $13,733 out of state
Books and supplies: $850
On campus room and board and other expenses: $11,357
Off campus room and board and other expenses: $11,357

Academics

Favorite majors: psychology, business, management, marketing and related support services, social science, communication, journalism and related programs, education

The B Features

Student Support Services at UNLV helps students "overcome personal concerns, academic deficiencies and financial difficulties that could impair their chances of succeeding in college." It focuses on the development of good study habits and decision-making skills through tutoring and workshops on subjects such as study skills, time management, note taking, listening skills, reading and outlining textbooks, test-taking strategies, motivation, concentration and stress reduction. These services are free.

An academic enrichment program for high school students called Upward Bound offers academic counseling, career exploration, tutoring, college admission testing workshops, motivation, personal development and concentration in computer literacy, English, foreign language, history, government, math and science. Upward Bound students are often involved in weekend or after-school instruction. During the summer, they can participate in daily classes emphasizing academic skills, study techniques and test preparation.

University of New Haven

West Haven, CT

Address: 300 Boston Post Rd., West Haven, CT 06516
Phone: 203-932-7319
Admissions email: adminfo@newhaven.edu
Website: www.newhaven.edu

Admissions Stats

Percentage of applicants admitted: 73.2%
SAT range: 460-570 critical reading, 470-580 math
ACT range: NA

Size

Number of undergraduates: 4,466

Costs

Tuition and fees: $24,000
Books and supplies: $750
On campus room and board and other expenses: $11,430
Off campus room and board and other expenses: $4,000

Academics

Favorite majors: security and protective services, business, management, marketing and related support services, engineering, visual and performing arts, biological and biomedical sciences

---
The B Features

The Center for Learning Resources at UNH offers students support for writing assignments, plus sophomore-level core courses. It is made up of three labs: 1) Mathematics, Science and Business, 2) Writing and 3) Computer.

In addition, the Office of Academic Services has many different programs to help. The Freshman Year Program is a one-credit seminar required for graduation. It helps to make the transition from high school to college. Academic Skills Counseling is offered individually and in small groups. The focus is on study and time management skills. Developmental mentoring assists students with developing the skills needed for college-level math and/or English.

University of New Mexico

Albuquerque, NM

Address: Office of Recruitment Services, Student Services Center, Room 180, Albuquerque, NM 87131
Phone: 505-277-2446
Admissions email: apply@unm.edu
Website: www.unm.edu

Admissions Stats

Percentage of applicants admitted: 74%
SAT range: 490-600 critical reading, 470-600 math
ACT range: 19-24 composite, 18-25 English, 17-24 math

Size

Number of undergraduates: 14,269

Costs

Tuition and fees: $4,336 in state; $14,177 out of state
Books and supplies: $856
On campus room and board and other expenses: $9,782
Off campus room and board and other expenses: $10,584

Academics

Favorite majors: Southwest Hispanic studies, photography, lithography, geology, environmental studies, laser optical, Latin American affairs

The B Features

UNM's Center for Academic Program Support offers free educational assistance through individualized peer tutoring (done by upper division undergraduates and graduate students) for courses numbered 100-499 as well as library and study strategies (by appointment only). Drop-in tutoring labs are available for biology, chemistry, physics, astronomy, writing, pre-calculus, statistics, calculus and engineering. In a new program called CAPS Across Campus, tutoring will be offered in the theater, library and student resident center commons room.

University of New Orleans

New Orleans, LA

Address: Lakefront Campus, 2000 Lakeshore Dr., New Orleans, LA 70148
Phone: 504-280-6595
Admissions email: admissions@uno.edu
Website: www.uno.edu

Admissions Stats

Percentage of applicants admitted: 63.4%
SAT range: 450-590 critical reading, 450-580 math
ACT range: 18-23

Size

Number of undergraduates: 4,651

Costs

Tuition and fees: $3,292 in state; $10,336 out of state
Books and supplies: $1,150
On campus room and board and other expenses: $7,150
Off campus room and board and other expenses: $10,037

Academics

Favorite majors: business, management, marketing and related support services, communication, journalism and related programs, education, liberal arts and sciences, psychology, general studies and humanities, engineering

---

The B Features

UNO's Learning Resource Center offers free writing and math tutoring on both an individual and group basis. The computer lab has 24 workstations, and tutors are available for biology, business, chemistry, foreign language, psychology and physics. Much of the tutoring is performed by upperclassmen. Classes on time management, test taking, note taking and communication are offered, as are short workshops on test taking and note taking. A media library supplies videotapes and CD ROMs in math, science and liberal arts.

The college's Writing Center guides students through their papers, while the Math Tutor Center and Study Hall assists students in math requirements to "maximize their math potential."

University of North Carolina at Greensboro

Greensboro, NC

Address: 1000 Spring Garden St., Greensboro, NC 27412
Phone: 336-334-5243
Admissions email: admissions@uncg.edu
Website: www.uncg.edu

Admissions Stats

Percentage of applicants admitted: 60%
SAT range: 470-580 critical reading, 470-580 math
ACT range: 18-23 composite, 17-23 English, 17-23 math

Size

Number of undergraduates: 10,569

Costs

Tuition and fees: $3,813 in state; $15,081 out of state
Books and supplies: $1,575
On campus room and board and other expenses: $7,958
Off campus room and board and other expenses: $11,425

Academics

Favorite majors: business, management, marketing and related support services, social sciences, education, visual and performing arts, health professions and related clinical services, art, dance and music

---

The B Features

The Student Success Center at Greensboro's University of North Carolina has three divisions to help students succeed academically: the Learning Assistance Center, Resource Lab and Special Support Services.

The Learning Assistance Center (LAC) provides tutoring, academic skills assessment and counseling, academic workshops and a resource lab with computers, academic software and handouts. Tutoring is done on an individual basis for at least one hour a week or through small groups of no more than three students in sessions that last one and one-half to two hours a week. Walk-in tutoring is available also.

The Resource Lab gives students a peaceful place to study and to receive tutoring. Students have access to computers, a text book library, academic-skills assessment, as well as computer tutorials in math and foreign languages and handouts on academic skills like time management, note taking, textbook reading and test taking. In addition to this, the LAC works to help students increase their understanding of course content, enhance self-confidence and encourage positive attitudes toward learning.

Special Support Services provides aid to students who are 1) first-generation college enrollees, 2) from low-income families or 3) have a documented disability. This program offers counseling, tutoring and a learning lab.

A program known as Supplemental Instruction provides a series of weekly discussion/review sessions for students taking notoriously difficult courses. Each class is led by students who have success-fully completed the course. According to the college, students who attend these supplemental classes attain grades that are one-third to one whole grade higher than the grades of those who do not participate.

Norwich University

Northfield, VT

Address: 158 Harmon Dr., Northfield, VT 05663-1035
Phone: 802-485-2001
Admissions email: nuadm@norwich.edu
Website: www.norwich.edu

Admissions Stats

Percentage of applicants admitted: 73%
SAT range: 470-570 critical reading, 470-590 math
ACT range: 18-23 composite, 17-24 English, 17-22 math

Size

Number of undergraduates: 2,486

Costs

Tuition and fees: $22,506
Books and supplies: $1,000
On campus room and board and other expenses: $8,764
Off campus room and board and other expenses: NA

Academics

Favorite majors: security and protection services, health professions and related clinical sciences, architecture and related services, business, management, marketing and related support services, history

The B Features

Norwich's Learning Support Services (LSC) offers assistance to those students who need it. LSC provides support for students who need help in planning, organizing and managing their responsibilities as well as assessing best ways of learning in different environments. Support services are also available in areas of reading, writing, note taking and exam-taking strategies. Additionally, students are afforded opportunities to receive tutoring and to participate in review sessions in selected course subject areas. Students may request counseling and coaching for specific academic problems such as probation status and learning disorders.

College of Notre Dame

Baltimore, MD

Address: 4701 N. Charles. St., Baltimore, MD 21210-2476
Phone: 410-532-5330
Website: www.ndm.edu

Admissions Stats

Percentage of applicants admitted: 74.1%
SAT range: 470-590 critical reading, 440-550 math
ACT range: NA

Size

Number of undergraduates: 3,358

Costs

Tuition and fees: $22,400
Books and supplies: $1,000
On campus room and board and other expenses: $9,610
Off campus room and board and other expenses: $6,460

Academics

Favorite majors: health professions and related clinical services, business, management, marketing and related support services, liberal arts and sciences, general studies and humanities

---

The B Features

College of Notre Dame's campus-wide peer tutoring program is known as "Each One, Teach One." It is designed to achieve "increases in the success rate of students in courses that have historically proved to be extremely challenging." A Writing Center is also available to all students either by appointment or on a drop-in basis.

Ohio University

Athens, OH

Address: Undergraduate Admissions, 120 Chubb Hall, Athens, OH 45701-2979
Phone: 740-593-4100
Admissions email: admissions.freshmen@ohiou.edu
Website: www.ohiou.edu

Admissions Stats

Percentage of applicants admitted: 89%
SAT range: 490-600 critical reading, 490-600 math
ACT range: 21-25 composite, 19-25 English, 19-25 math

Size

Number of undergraduates: 17,207

Costs

Tuition and fees: $8,727 in state; $17,691 out of state
Books and supplies: $870
On campus room and board and other expenses: $11,316
Off campus room and board and other expenses: $11,316

Academics

Favorite majors: business, management, marketing and related support services, social sciences, communications, journalism and related programs, arts and sciences, general studies and humanities, art history, home economics, engineering and film

The B Features

Ohio University's Academic Advancement Center helps prepare students for college-level work through a variety of student services that focus on computer, writing, reading, and study skills. A brief overview of areas in which help is offered follows:

Computer Skills: The computer lab offers equipment such as digital cameras, zip drives, scanners and more. A one-credit hour course for freshmen is available that provides detailed instruction in basic computer skills needed for college work.

Writing Support: The Writing Center gives free assistance to all undergrad and graduate students through peer tutoring. Help is given at all steps of the process from writing an outline to final revisions. Tutoring is available on a walk-in and appointment basis.

Reading Skills: Reading instructors help students develop comprehension and vocabulary skills. They also explain how to draw conclusions, make inferences and recognize tone. A two-credit course called College Reading Skills is offered.

Study Skills: A two-credit course called Learning Strategies teaches note taking, time management, exam preparation and other study habits. Private tutoring is available (at a cost) for students, and the college has a referral service to match tutors with students.

Supplemental Instruction: Extra sessions in which students review lecture notes outside of class, clarify text materials, discuss ideas, organize material, evaluate and improve study skills are available for certain courses. These are free and led by students who have already completed the course.

College Adjustment Program: Ohio University also offers assistance to students who are struggling with the adjustment to college life. Services include free tutoring, academic advising and study skills instruction.

Ohio Northern University

Ada, OH

Address: 525 S. Main St., Ada, OH 45810
Phone: 419-772-2260
Admissions email: admissions-ug@onu.edu
Admissions contact: Karen Condeni, vice president and dean of enrollment
Website: www.onu.edu

Admissions Stats

Percentage of applicants admitted: 87.1%
Average GPA range: 3.4-3.5
SAT range: 520-620 critical reading, 540-650 math
ACT range: 23-29 composite, 21-29 English, 24-29 math

Size

Number of undergraduates: 2,597

Costs

Tuition and fees: $28,260
Books and supplies: $1,200
On campus room and board and other expenses: $8,880
Off campus room and board and other expenses: $8,880

Academics

Majors offered: engineering, business, management, marketing and related support services, education, health professions and related clinical sciences, biological and biomedical sciences, arts and sciences, pharmacy, business administration and law

Favorite majors: engineering, business, management, marketing and related support services, education, health professions and related clinical sciences, biological and biomedical sciences

Student Life

The campus: ONU covers 285 acres but is located in a city of only 5,000 people, which lends itself to a small-town atmosphere.

The students: The student population is 53% men and 47% women.

The B Features

Admission to Ohio Northern is based on class rank and SAT or ACT scores, but there is a strong willingness to look beyond the numbers. Letters of recommendation are not required but will be read if submitted. Extracurricular activities are considered, as well as recent academic trends. A special program helps with college transition.

Insight

This private liberal arts school is affiliated with the United Methodists. According to Karen Condeni, vice president and dean of enrollment, the school makes a real effort to look past the standard statistics to the student behind them. "A strong number of students show potential but not number-wise," she says. "We look at their high school records overall as a whole picture and we look at trends." According to Condeni, the school also considers personal information that might affect grades. "We look to see if students were working while going to school or if they had a single parent they had to help. We are looking for students who show determination.

"Ohio Northern University has a support program called College Transition that is not remedial work but helps students that need extra attention," says Condeni. For example, students in this program do not take a full load of classes (17 to 18 hours) but average 12 to 14 hours or three classes. "These students are monitored more closely and meet regularly with an advisor. Tutors are also available," she adds.

Ohio Wesleyan University

Delaware, OH

Address: 61 S. Sandusky St., Delaware, OH 43015-2370
Phone: 740-368-3020
Admissions email: awadmit@cc.owu.edu
Website: www.owu.edu

Admissions Stats

Percentage of applicants admitted: 73.7%
SAT range: 550-660 critical reading, 570-660 math
ACT range: 23-28 composite, 23-29 English, 23-28 math

Size

Number of undergraduates: 1,941

Costs

Tuition and fees: $30,290
Books and supplies: $1,000
On campus room and board and other expenses: $8,840
Off campus room and board and other expenses: $6,750

Academics

Favorite majors: business, management, marketing and related support services, psychology, zoology, economics, sociology, anthropology, English, history, politics, government and biology

---
The B Features

Students who need additional attention or academic help at Ohio Wesleyan will find the assistance they need at the Academic Skills Center where the motto is "Improving the Student Inside You." The Center offers individual counseling that helps students assess their strengths and weaknesses and gives support in areas like time management, note taking, reading from texts, test taking and overcoming procrastination and anxiety. Group presentations are available on the same topics and may be given in fraternity houses, residence halls and other spots across the campus.

A Lending Library gives students access to books on a variety of topics, including coping with learning disabilities and developing study skills. Computerized assessments help identify individual specific study skill deficits. In addition, the college offers a Quantitative Skills Center that helps students gain confidence in their ability to do math and related subjects like astronomy, chemistry and economics.

Old Dominion University

Norfolk, VA

Address: 5115 Hampton Blvd., Norfolk, VA 23529
Phone: 800-348-7926
Admissions email: admit@odu.edu
Website: www.odu.edu

Admissions Stats

Percentage of applicants admitted: 69.2%
SAT range: 480-570 reading, 450-540 writing, 490-580 math
ACT range: 19-22 composite, 18-22 English, 17-23 math

Size

Number of undergraduates: 21,274

Costs

Tuition and fees: $4,916 in state; $13,364 out of state
Books and supplies: $900
On campus room and board and other expenses: $9,180
Off campus room and board and other expenses: $9,180

Academics

Favorite majors: business, management, marketing and related support services, health professions and related clinical services, social sciences, English language and literature/letters, multi/inter-disciplinary studies, engineering technologies and technicians

---

The B Features

Old Dominion's Student Support Services provides academic support to increase the retention and graduation rates of eligible students. It includes tutorials, academic skills workshops, career exploration, advising services and cultural enrichment.

At the end of each semester, the Office of Continuance reviews the records of all students who do not maintain a 2.0 GPA. They are placed on academic warning and have one semester to bring their grades up or to be placed on suspension.

University of Oregon

Eugene, OR

Address: Box 1226, 110 Johnson Hall, Eugene, OR 97403-01226
Phone: 800-BE-A-DUCK or 541-346-3201
Admissions email: uoadmit@uoregon.edu
Website: www.uoregon.edu

Admissions Stats

Percentage of applicants admitted: 90%
SAT range: 498-617 critical reading, 503-615 math
ACT range: NA

Size

Number of undergraduates: 15,985

Costs

Tuition and fees: $5,838 in state; $18,252 out of state
Books and supplies: $900
On campus room and board and other expenses: $9,901
Off campus room and board and other expenses: $9,901

Academics

Favorite majors: architecture, music, creative writing, business, chemistry, journalism and communication

---

The B Features

UO's Academic Learning Services offers a number of one-credit and multiple-credit courses each quarter to help with test taking, time management, communication skills and group dynamics. In the fall, the college offers "Get Savvy: Focus on Academic Success," a get-together geared to help students improve their study approaches, meet new people and even win prizes! Other workshops include "Active Learning," "Grammar Hour" and "Statistics." Math and Writing Labs are available, as is tutoring in small group or private settings. Workshops to help prepare for standardized test preparation (GRE, GMAT, SAT, MCAT, etc.) are also offered.

Oregon State University

Corvallis, OR

Address: Office of Admissions, 104 Kerr Administration Building, Corvallis, OR 97331
Phone: 541-737-4411
Admissions email: osuadmit@oregonstate.edu
Website: www.oregonstate.edu

Admissions Stats

Percentage of applicants admitted: 93%
SAT range: 470-590 critical reading, 490-610 math
ACT range: 20-26 composite, 18-25 English, 19-26 math

Size

Number of undergraduates: 15,106

Costs

Tuition and fees: $5,643 in state; $17,559 out of state
Books and supplies: $1,443
On campus room and board and other expenses: $9,672
Off campus room and board and other expenses: $9,672

Academics

Favorite majors: business, management, marketing and related support services, engineering, agriculture, biotechnology, forestry

The B Features

OSU's College of Business Beta Alpha Psi is a co-ed professional accounting fraternity that sponsors an accounting library, provides resource materials and whose members tutor accounting students.

The Center for Writing and Learning gives instructions and advice to students and provides a study skills program. Basic writing skills such as organizing and revising are offered, and short grammar questions can be emailed for assistance.

A student chapter offers tutoring in chemical engineering, and the chemistry department has a tutor list for an hourly fee. A general chemistry tutorial room known as the Mole Hole is available during certain weeks of each term.

Free tutoring is available for undergrads in lower division core economics courses and for students of electrical engineering and computer science. Other departments offer assistance as well. The department of ethnic studies offers mentoring for students of color or anyone else interested in changing social patterns of race, gender, ethnic, class and other issues. Students taking French, German and Spanish can find tutorial support through the Department of Foreign Languages and Literatures. The College of Forestry offers tutoring to students in forestry or related classes. The Math Learning Center is available for drop-in tutoring from undergrads and volunteers and multiple resources, while the Microbiology Student Association tutors students in that subject, and physics grad students offer help to students in introductory physics courses. For students who have not yet declared a major, Exploratory Studies gives information, resources and other important materials to help.

Pace University

New York, NY

Address: 1 Place Plaza, New York, NY 10038-1598
Phone: 212-346-1323
Admissions email: infoctr@pace.edu
Website: www.pace.edu

Admissions Stats

Percentage of applicants admitted: 72.6%
SAT range: 470-570 critical reading, 470-590 math
ACT range: 21-26 composite

Size

Number of undergraduates: 14,177

Costs

Tuition and fees: $30,086
Books and supplies: $800
On campus room and board and other expenses: $11,670
Off campus room and board and other expenses: $19,130

Academics

Favorite majors: business, management, marketing and related support services, health professions and related clinical sciences, computer and informational sciences and support services, communication, journalism and related programs, psychology

The B Features

Pace's Center for Academic Excellence is a comprehensive academic support network that helps students find their ideal path and make the transition from home to college life. It offers the following programs:

The Office of First Year Programs: This one-credit, Pass/Fail course helps all freshmen with the transition through academic advisement, and the UNV 101 program. It provides students with an in-depth look at the University's academic and cultural life, its support network and the services it provides for students. It meets for 13 weeks during fall semester and covers topics such as time management, study skills, critical thinking, health and wellness and campus diversity.

Academic Resources: The services of this program include meeting with an advisor, learning about different major and minors and choosing a course of study.

The Tutoring Center: Students can find assistance with classes that they find difficult by calling the Tutoring Center. It offers individualized and small group tutoring in upper and lower division courses.

University of the Pacific

Stockton, CA

Address: 3601 Pacific Ave., Stockton, CA 95211
Phone: 209-946-2211
Admissions email: admissions@pacific.edu
Website: www.pacific.edu

Admissions Stats

Percentage of applicants admitted: 56%
SAT range: 530-630 critical reading, 550-670 math
ACT range: 22-27 composite

Size

Number of undergraduates: 3,457

Costs

Tuition and fees: $27,350
Books and supplies: $1,314
On campus room and board and other expenses: $9,788
Off campus room and board and other expenses: NA

Academics

Favorite majors: business, pharmacy, engineering

The B Features

University of the Pacific's Retention Services offers tutoring, study skills sessions, peer mentoring, career counseling and academic counseling. Their student-to-student advising program has 40 undergrads that are there to help with time management, preparing for tests, choosing a major, meeting general education requirements and even dealing with homesickness.

Pacific Lutheran University

Tacoma, WA

Address: 101 122nd St., South, Tacoma, WA 98447-0003
Phone: 253-535-7151
Admissions email: admission@plu.edu
Website: www.plu.edu

Admissions Stats

Percentage of applicants admitted: 74.4%
SAT range: 480-610 critical reading, 490-610 math
ACT range: 21-28 composite, 21-28 English, 20-27 math

Size

Number of undergraduates: 3,680

Costs

Tuition and fees: $23,450
Books and supplies: $924
On campus room and board and other expenses: $9,063
Off campus room and board and other expenses: $10,110

Academics

Favorite majors: business, management, marketing and related support services, social sciences, health professions and related clinical sciences, communication, journalism, and related programs, biological and biomedical sciences and psychology

The B Features

PLU's Academic Assistance Center offers tutors, foreign language conversation groups, independent study strategies, group review sessions and even free flashcards—and a treat: they provide hand-outs on issues like critical reading, time management, note taking and test taking. There is a math lab, a computer science lab, a biology/chemistry lab and even a geo-science lab. All services are free of charge.

Pine Manor College*

Chestnut Hill, MA

Address: 400 Heath St., Chestnut Hill, MA 02467
Phone: 617-731-7104 or 800-PMC-1357
Admissions email: admissions@pmc.edu
Website: www.pmc.edu/admission

Admissions Stats

Percentage of applicants admitted: 74.9%
SAT range: 360-480 critical reading, 340-450 math
ACT range: 15-20 composite, 14-22 English, 14-19 math

Size

Number of undergraduates: less than 500

Costs

Tuition and fees: $14,544
Books and supplies: $300-500
On campus room and board and other expenses: $10,500
Off campus room and board and other expenses: $6,500

Academics

Favorite majors: biology, psychology, economic and financial systems, social and political systems, organizational change and management, communications, nursing, articulation agreement with Boston College

---

The B Features

Freshmen at Pine Manor are required to take a First Year Experience Seminar that is led by faculty members, student life professionals and peer mentors. During their second year, they take a Portfolio Learning Seminar. Its purpose is to "encourage students to become reflective, self-directed learners, as well as to help them understand and fulfill degree requirements through development of a personalized learning portfolio." Presentation of this portfolio is one of the requirements for graduation.

Many students use the Brown Learning Resource Center, staffed by professional, full-time tutors. Assistance is offered in writing, math, reading, study skills and time management. According to the college, students who use the Resource Center are "able to discover previously untapped strengths, adjust to new demands of the college environment, fill gaps in prior learning and most of all, learn how to take charge of their own learning."

Other advice from the college includes these statements: "Students can tell us about themselves and their accomplishments and their goals in their personal essay. Recommendation letters and personal interviews also give us great insights to the young women we counsel. There are many talented and deserving young women with B and C level grades that would grow and be successful at Pine Manor.

"Young women who attend PMC develop self confidence and leadership skills. You can really see these women transform themselves over the years."

* All women college

University of Portland

Portland, OR

Address: 5000 N. Willamette Blvd., Portland OR 97203-5798
Phone: 503-943-7147
Admissions email: admissio@up.edu
Website: www.up.edu

Admissions Stats

Percentage of applicants admitted: 64.7%
SAT range: 530-640 critical reading, 540-640 math
ACT range: NA

Size

Number of undergraduates: 3,415

Costs

Tuition and fees: $27,210
Books and supplies: $1,000
On campus room and board and other expenses: $9,650
Off campus room and board and other expenses: $9,650

Academics

Favorite majors: health professions and clinical sciences, business, management, marketing and related support services, engineering, biological and biomedical sciences and education

---
The B Features

The University of Portland's Academic Resources offers services that are extensive. An Integrated Writing Center, Speech Resource Center and Math Resource Center give information and advice for academic skills. The Shepard Freshman Resource Center is a one-stop place for first year students who want to know more about the campus and college life. The Learning Assistance program is geared to teach students various learning strategies and skills. Counselors help guide students to improving learning skills like time management and prioritizing assignments, plus how to deal with overdue assignments, text anxiety, study overload and difficulty with reading and note taking.

Prescott College

Prescott, AZ

Address: 220 Grove Ave., Prescott, AZ 86301
Phone: 877-350-2100
Admissions email: admissions@prescott.edu
Admissions contact: Natalie Canfield, admissions counselor
Website: www.prescott.edu

Admissions Stats

Percentage of applicants admitted: 80%
Average GPA range: 3.0
SAT range: 1010-1270 composite
ACT range: 21-27 composite

Size

Number of undergraduates: 450

Costs

Tuition and fees: $20,230
Books and supplies: $1,800
On campus room and board and other expenses: $6,400
Off campus room and board and other expenses: $6,400

Academics

Favorite majors: environmental studies, creative writing, cultural and regional studies, and adventure education, outdoor education and recreation

---
Student Life

The campus: This campus has a small, urban atmosphere and is close to the city of Prescott. It has a dozen buildings, including a library, café, classrooms and a community Cross Roads Center. All buildings are within walking distance.

The students: 52% are women.

The B Features

According to the college, "Prescott is an ideal environment for both A and B students. Our programs are academically rigorous and experientially-based. We are able to accommodate a variety of learning styles. Qualified applicants demonstrate solid, consistent academic performance, well written college essays and a high level of personal motivation. We use holistic evaluation that looks at our applicant's overall prospects for success in the college."

Insight

"We welcome students from a variety of backgrounds," says Natalie Canfield, admissions counselor. "We look at each person as a whole, not just numbers and essays. We look at bad grades and try to see how we can fix them." At Prescott, the essay is particularly evaluative for both writing level and content. The school requires two kinds of essays: one that is autobiographical ("To get to know the student") and one that is an academic autobiography ("To learn the student's writing style"). "Interviews are optional," continues Canfield. "They are relaxed and we talk about past education and different situations. We also give students a chance to ask us questions to see if we are a fit."

Prescott College focuses on degrees having to do with the environment. According to Canfield, it has more 15-passenger vans for field trips than it does buildings on campus. "Many courses are field based and most courses involve weekend-long trips," she explains.

In an article entitled, "Every Student is an Honor Student," K.L. Cook writes, "While theoretically every student journey is unique, all students must deal with common issues. It's important that they understand that Prescott College is foremost, 'for the liberal arts, the environment and social responsibility.' Everything we do and plan and dream is embodied in that phrase. We are not a vocational school. We believe that the best stewards of the Earth and the most effective agents of change are liberally educated citizens. We expect students to have some experience with and appreciation for various modes of understanding the world: historical, literary, artistic, scientific, social, physical and spiritual. We expect them to cultivate political cultural and ecological awareness, as well as communication and mathematical skills. We also believe that a liberal arts education emphasizes process as much as content. At its best, experiential learning animates theory and engages the whole person."

Purchase College— SUNY

Purchase, NY

Address: 735 Anderson Hill Rd., Purchase, NY 10577-1400
Phone: 914-251-6300
Admissions email: admission@purchase.edu
Website: www.purchase.edu

Admissions Stats

Percentage of applicants admitted: 31%
SAT range: 510-620 critical reading, 480-580 math
ACT range: 20-25 composite

Size

Number of undergraduates: 3,163

Costs

Tuition and fees: $5,709 in state; $11,969 out of state
Books and supplies: $1,500
On campus room and board and other expenses: $10,228
Off campus room and board and other expenses: $10,700

Academics

Favorite majors: visual and performing arts, liberal arts and sciences, women's studies, art history, film and music

The B Features

Struggling students at Suny can go to the Learning Center for free tutoring services in writing, math and foreign languages. Sessions with tutors in additional subjects can be arranged.

The Center also offers students study skills help and printed materials in areas such as time management, making outlines, taking notes and studying. There are multimedia stations for computer assisted learning. Students interested in forming a study group can organize it through the Learning Center, and those with learning disabilities or other special needs can get help using a reading machine and other software.

Quinnipiac University

Hamden, CT

Address: Mt. Carmel Ave., Hamden, CT 06518
Phone: 203-582-8600
Admissions email: admissions@quinnipiac.edu
Website: quinnipiac.edu

Admissions Stats

Percentage of applicants admitted: 57.9%
SAT range: 500-580 reading, 510-590 writing, 530-610 math
ACT range: 21-25 composite, 20-25 English, 20-26 math

Size

Number of undergraduates: 7,293

Costs

Tuition and fees: $26,280
Books and supplies: $800
On campus room and board and other expenses: $11,900
Off campus room and board and other expenses: $12,150

Academics

Favorite majors: health professions and related clinical services, business, management, marketing and related support services, communication, journalism, and related programs, psychology and social sciences

The B Features

Quinnipiac students have three special courses open to them to help introduce them to major topics in university life: QU 101, 201 and 301.

The first course is QU 101, entitled "The Individual in the Community." It explores the relationship between individual and community identities, the rights and responsibilities of citizenship, ethics of community life and so on. In QU 201, "National Community," students explore the structure of the pluralistic American community and in QU 301, "Global Community," students find out about the political, social, cultural, ecological and economic systems that shape global communities.

The college also offers a program called Writing across the Curriculum where students are engaged in hands-on learning experiences to become better writers, strong critical thinkers and innovative scholars.

Radford University

Radford, VA

Address: E. Main St., Radford, VA 24141-0672
Phone: 540-831-5371
Admissions email: ruadmiss@radford.edu
Website: www.radford.edu

Admissions Stats

Percentage of applicants admitted: 78.3%
SAT range: 450-540 critical reading, 450-540 math
ACT range: 19-23 composite

Size

Number of undergraduates: 9,552

Costs

Tuition and fees: $5,746 in state; $13,494 out of state
Books and supplies: $800
On campus room and board and other expenses: $8,604
Off campus room and board and other expenses: NA

Academics

Favorite majors: business, management, marketing and related support services, multi/interdisciplinary studies, security and protection services, visual and performing arts, communication, journalism and related programs, social sciences

---
The B Features

Radford University's Learning Assistance and Resource Center provides test prep tutoring and workshops. It also offers a study skills survey that shows ways to improve study habits.

Randolph College

. . . .

Lynchburg, VA

Address: 2500 Rivermont Ave., Lynchburg, VA 24503
Phone: 800-745-7692
Admissions email: admissions@rmvc.edu
Website: www.randolphcollege.edu

Admissions Stats

Percentage of applicants admitted: 87%
SAT range: 540-670 critical reading, 510-630 math
ACT range: 23-29 composite

Size

Number of undergraduates: 665

Costs

Tuition and fees: $24,500
Books and supplies: $800
On campus room and board and other expenses: $9,800
Off campus room and board and other expenses: NA

Academics

Favorite majors: English language, literature/letters, psychology, biological and biomedical services, environmental studies, global studies, chemistry, fine arts and classics

---

The B Features

Randolph College offers a number of academic services to students. First year students are assigned faculty advisors to help guide them in making course selections and career decisions. A Career Development Center focuses on helping students to "develop self knowledge related to their career choice and work performance by identifying, assessing, and understanding competencies, interests, values and personal characteristics."

The Ethyl Science and Mathematics Center provides tutoring to science and math students. The Learning Resources Center has interactive workshops, a Learning Strategies Program to help develop study strategies and clarify academic goals, tutors for every subject, and printed and computerized materials.

University of Redlands

Redlands, CA

Address: 1200 E. Colton Ave., P.O. Box 3080, Redlands, CA 92373-0999
Phone: 800-455-5064
Admissions email: admissions@redlands.edu
Website: www.redlands.edu

Admissions Stats

Percentage of applicants admitted: 63%
SAT range: 540-630 critical reading, 540-630 math
ACT range: 22-26 composite

Size

Number of undergraduates: 2,313

Costs

Tuition and fees: $28,476
Books and supplies: $1,300
On campus room and board and other expenses: $12,222
Off campus room and board and other expenses: $11,862

Academics

Favorite majors: business, management, marketing and related support services, government, English, creative writing, biology, chemistry and environmental studies

The B Features

The University of Redlands' Academic Support Services helps students develop and strengthen the skills they will need most for academic success, accomplishing this through academic counseling, subject tutoring, writing tutoring and a learning skills course. With academic counseling, students are encouraged to talk to their advisors when choosing a major, planning for possible study abroad and learning time management and study skills. The tutoring center provides time management calendars, study skills handouts and other materials.

A learning skills course is offered each semester and covers time management, improving memory, understanding learning styles and developing positive attitudes and motivation. Time is spent discussing goal setting, career planning, test taking and note taking. Redlands also offers up to two hours a week of free peer tutoring. Students with documented learning disabilities may receive more.

Writing tutors can be accessed on a drop-in basis. Students are able to receive help at all stages of their writing assignments from outlining to footnoting.

University of Rhode Island

. . . . .

Kingston, RI

Address: Undergraduate Admissions Office, 14 Upper College Rd., Kingston, RI 02881
Phone: 401-874-7100
Admissions email: uriadmit@etal.uri.edu
Website: www.uri.edu

Admissions Stats

Percentage of applicants admitted: 77%
SAT range: 510-600 critical reading, 520-610 math
ACT range: Not available

Size

Number of undergraduates: 11,546

Costs

Tuition and fees: $7,724 in state; $21,424 out of state
Books and supplies: $1,000
On campus room and board and other expenses: $9,984
Off campus room and board and other expenses: $10,982

Academics

Favorite majors: business, management, marketing and related support services, pharmacy, textiles, fashion merchandising and design, oceanography, marine and environmental science and international engineering

---

The B Features

URI's Academic Enhancement Center's motto is "Teaching Is Learning." This phrase reflects its belief that "learning happens best when the learner is engaged in teaching subject matter to others." Thus, students are helped through peer tutoring and study groups that focus both on general study skills topics as well as specific courses. The college advocates study groups that get together once a week and share responsibility for the material they are all learning. Students are encouraged to discuss class materials, work together to solve problems, compare notes and help each other to succeed.

The URI Writing Center is free to all students who need help with all levels of writing. Additionally, the online assistance center has excellent materials to be read and/or downloaded.

Rider University

. . . .

Lawrenceville, NJ

Address: 2083 Lawrence Rd., Lawrenceville, NJ 08648-3099
Phone: 609-896-5042
Admissions email: admissions@rider.edu
Website: www.rider.edu

Admissions Stats

Percentage of applicants admitted: 79%
SAT range: 470-570 critical reading, 480-590 math
ACT range: 18-21 composite

Size

Number of undergraduates: 4,375

Costs

Tuition and fees: $24,790
Books and supplies: $1,400
On campus room and board and other expenses: $11,280
Off campus room and board and other expenses: $11,280

Academics

Favorite majors: psychology, business, management, marketing and related support services, English language, literature/letters, education, computer and information sciences and support services

---
The B Features

Tutoring services are available through the Rider Learning Center. Students struggling with academics can meet with peer tutors who have received excellent grades in their courses and are recommended by professors. Tutors work on both a drop-in and appointment basis. The Center also offers a math skills lab. In addition to peer tutoring, Rider offers supplemental instruction for the most difficult classes. Students meet together to review notes, go over readings and learn test-taking strategies.

Rider has two core classes for first-year students who have not met the criteria for college-level reading. These are "Introduction to Academic Reading" and "College Reading." In the first class, which is required, reading and learning strategies are taught to help students increase their reading comprehension. This class earns two credits. In the second (elective) course, students may earn three credits by developing and improving reading comprehension skills and study strategies.

Ripon College

Ripon, WI

Address: 300 Seward St., P.O. Box 248, Ripon, WI 54971
Phone: 920-748-8114
Admissions email: adminfo@ripon.edu
Website: www.ripon.edu

Admissions Stats

Percentage of applicants admitted: 81%
SAT range: 480-650 critical reading, 500-620 math
ACT range: 21-27 composite

Size

Number of undergraduates: 934

Costs

Tuition and fees: $22,437
Books and supplies: $750
On campus room and board and other expenses: $7,310
Off campus room and board and other expenses: NA

Academics

Favorite majors: sciences, education, history

The B Features

Ripon offers new college students an extensive program called "Communicating Plus" that emphasizes the core basics of written and oral communication. The course focuses on communication, as well as critical thinking and problem solving skills. It involves student peer mentoring and outreach programming.

Roanoke College

Salem, VA

Address: 221 College Lane, Salem, VA 24153-3794
Phone: 540-375-2270
Admissions email: admissions@roanoake.edu
Website: www.roanoke.edu

Admissions Stats

Percentage of applicants admitted: 74.4%
SAT range: 490-600 reading, 470-560 reading, 490-590 math
ACT range: NA

Size

Number of undergraduates: 1,936

Costs

Tuition and fees: $24,653
Books and supplies: $850
On campus room and board and other expenses: $9,902
Off campus room and board and other expenses: $9,902

Academics

Favorite majors: business, management, marketing and related support services, social sciences, psychology, biological and biomedical sciences and history

---

The B Features

Roanoke College's Center for Learning and Teaching offers a number of special services to help the B student. It is located in the Fintel Library and all students are welcomed on a drop-in or appointment basis.

A Writing Center provides students with assistance for creating papers for class, while peer mentoring is also available as is subject tutoring.

A program called Success Skills Forum offers students access to workshops that deal with the transitional issues of college life. Workshop titles include these: "Getting Started, Getting Organized," "Time Management," "Reading Textbooks and Taking Notes," "Study Skills" and "Test Preparation."

Roger Williams University

Bristol, RI

Address: One Old Ferry Rd., Bristol, RI 02809-2923
Phone: 401-254-3500
Admissions email: admit@rwu.edu
Website: www.rwu.edu

Admissions Stats

Percentage of applicants admitted: 67.6%
SAT range: 490-570 critical reading, 510-600 math
ACT range: 21-25 composite

Size

Number of undergraduates: 4,605

Costs

Tuition and fees: $23,040
Books and supplies: $900
On campus room and board and other expenses: $11,932
Off campus room and board and other expenses: NA

Academics

Favorite majors: business, marketing, management and related support services, security and protection services, architecture and related services, psychology and biological and biomedical sciences

---

The B Features

Roger Williams University provides a number of helpful tools for the B student, including three university libraries on site. The school's Center for Academic Development offers workshops, seminars and individual tutorial sessions. Topics such as time management, organization, note taking, textbook strategies, test preparation, learning styles, classroom technology and academic success are all covered. A Writing Center helps with the development of papers from beginning to end, while a Math Center helps with homework in a number of math courses. Finally, a Core Tutoring Center provides peer tutors for the school's five-course interdisciplinary Core Curriculum.

Rust College

Holly Springs, MO

Address: 150 Rust Ave., Holly Springs, MO 38535
Phone: 662-252-8000 ext. 4059
Website: www.rustcollege.edu

Admissions Stats

Percentage of applicants admitted: 40.9%
SAT range: Open admissions
ACT range: 14-17 composite

Size

Number of undergraduates: 970 total enrollment

Costs

Tuition and fees: $6,550
Books and supplies: $250
On campus room and board and other expenses: $6,050
Off campus room and board and other expenses: $5,100

Academics

Favorite majors: computer and information sciences and support services, business, management, marketing and related support services, social sciences, biological and biomedical services and English language and literature/letters

---

The B Features

With its open admissions system, Rust College considers students whose "educational goals, career objectives and intellectual abilities match the institution's academic and non-academic programs." The Academic Counseling Program helps students plan their courses and careers based on needs and interests. Freshmen are assigned faculty advisors. After the first year, a major is declared, and each student is given an academic counselor from the faculty to help with any problems or questions that might follow.

Saint John's University and College of St. Benedict

Collegeville, MN

Address: P.O. Box 7155, Collegeville, MN 56321
Phone: 320-363-2196 or 800-544-1489
Admissions email: admissions@csbsju.edu
Website: www.csbsju.edu

Admissions Stats

Percentage of applicants admitted: 87%
SAT range: 530-650 critical reading, 530-650 math
ACT range: 23-28 composite, 22-27 English, 23-28 math

Size

Number of undergraduates: 1,940

Costs

Tuition and fees: $22,148
Books and supplies: $800
On campus room and board and other expenses: $7,017
Off campus room and board and other expenses: $7,017

Academics

Favorite majors: business, management, marketing and related support services, social sciences, psychology, English language and literature/letters and biological and biomedical sciences

---

The B Features

Saint John's University offers help to its students through several programs and facilities. The Writing Center provides tutoring on both a drop-in and appointment basis. The Math Skills Center helps students with all 100-level math classes as well as preparation for the math proficiency exam. Tutors help students review algebra, geometry, trigonometry and pre-calculus as they work on assignments for math classes and prepare for the math portions of standardized tests. In addition, the college offers an Academic Skills Center Reading Lab.

St. Lawrence University

Canton, NY

Address: 23 Romoda Dr., Canton, NY 13617
Phone: 800-285-1856
Admissions email: admissions@stlawu.edu
Website: www.stlawu.edu

Admissions Stats

Percentage of applicants admitted: 43.7%
SAT range: 1150-1310 composite
ACT range: NA

Size

Number of undergraduates: 2,182

Costs

Tuition and fees: $35,590
Books and supplies: $1,450
On campus room and board and other expenses: $4,890
Off campus room and board and other expenses: NA

Academics

Favorite majors: psychology, English, economics, government, biology, history, global studies and multi-field major

The B Features

According to St. Lawrence, it "is a student-centered institution which focuses on active learning. With a student to faculty ratio of 11:1, students are expected to be fully engaged in their academic coursework. Small seminar courses are common at St. Lawrence, allowing students to interact easily with faculty and other students. Professors are very accessible to students who need/want extra assistance. Our Academic Resources department also offers students peer tutors as needed. We have writing and quantitative labs available to students who seek extra assistance with their communication and mathematical skills.

"St. Lawrence uses a holistic review process, which is to say that we look at all components of an applicant's record. We will be looking most closely at a student's transcript. We want to see that a student has challenged him/herself as much as possible within the context of the high school's curriculum. We also like to see an upward trend in grades. If there are any significant weak spots on a student's transcripts, the student should definitely seek to explain those to the Admissions Committee in the application.

"Students should take the most challenging courses that are available and appropriate for them. They should also work as hard as possible to make sure that the junior and senior year grades are as strong as they can be. Students should also choose carefully when selecting teachers to write their recommendations. They want to pick teachers who have seen them in challenging courses and can speak to a student's progress, achievement and potential.

"St. Lawrence has become increasingly selective over the last several years. It is more difficult to gain admission with a B record than it has been in the past, and a student with a C record would need to present exceptional extenuating circumstances to be considered competitive for admission. We do, however, offer admission to particularly compelling students whom we believe will contribute to life on our campus in spite of their modest high school performance. As noted above, we evaluate the whole student—if we are convinced that a student has the potential to succeed at St. Lawrence and would be a good match for the experience we offer, we may offer the student admission."

College of Saint Mary

Omaha. NE

Address: 700 Mercy Rd., Omaha, NE 68106
Phone: 402-399-2408
Admissions email: enroll@csm.edu
Website: www.csm.edu

Admissions Stats

Percentage of applicants admitted: 57.3%
SAT range: NA
ACT range: 18-24 composite, 17-23 English, 16-24 math

Size

Number of undergraduates: 955

Costs

Tuition and fees: $19,036
Books and supplies: $800
On campus room and board and other expenses: $10,104
Off campus room and board and other expenses: $11,198

Academics

Favorite majors: health professions and related clinical services, business, management, marketing and related support services, education, liberal arts and sciences, general studies and humanities, legal professions and studies

---

The B Features

CSM's Achievement Center offers help to struggling students through individual and group tutoring, content study groups, writing assistance, supplementary materials and academic support workshops.

Saint Thomas University

Miami Gardens, FL

Address: 16401 NW 37th Ave., Miami Gardens, FL 33054-6459
Phone: 305-628-6546
Admissions email: signup@stu.edu
Website: www.stu.edu

Admissions Stats

Percentage of applicants admitted: 68.8%
SAT range: 400-500 critical reading, 380-510 math
ACT range: 16-22 composite, 14-19 English, 15-19 math

Size

Number of undergraduates: 2,692

Costs

Tuition and fees: $18,750
Books and supplies: $1,000
On campus room and board and other expenses: $9,900
Off campus room and board and other expenses: $12,206

Academics

Favorite majors: business, management, marketing and related support services, psychology, education, security and protection services, social sciences, communication, journalism and related programs

The B Features

STU has a university writing center supplied with tutors to help with all aspects of writing papers for a variety of classes.

Salve Regina University

Newport, RI

Address: 100 Ochre Point Ave., Newport, RI 02840
Phone: 401-341-2908
Admissions email: sruadmis@salve.edu
Admissions contact: Amanda (Mandy) Warhurst Webster, senior associate director of admissions
Website: www.salve.edu

Admissions Stats

Percentage of applicants admitted: 55.5%
Average GPA range: 2.7-3.7
SAT range: 500-590 critical reading, 510-580 math
ACT range: 21-25 composite, 20-26 English, 20-25 math

Size

Number of undergraduates: 2,095

Costs

Tuition and fees: $25,175
Books and supplies: $2,950
On campus room and board and other expenses: $11,500
Off campus room and board and other expenses: $11,500
Degrees offered: doctor's, master's, bachelor's and associate's degrees

Academics

Favorite majors: business, management, marketing and related support services, education, security and protective services, English language and literature/letters, psychology

Student Life

The campus: Covering 79 acres, the SRU campus has 44 buildings and is on the oceanfront in the mansion district of Newport, the Sailing Capital of the World. It is 10 minutes from the Newport beaches. Most of the buildings on campus are mansions themselves and considered "architecturally significant." The atmosphere is very New England and a great deal of restoration has been done on the Vanderbilt and other mansions on the grounds. Imported trees from all over the world are found on campus grounds.

The students: Three-quarters of the student body come from New England and the mid-Atlantic states. Although the college was founded in 1934 by the Sisters of Mercy, students do not have to be Catholic to attend the school.

The B Features

Salve Regina looks at a student's high school transcript, and one of the first things it does is recalculate the GPA. All extracurricular classes are eliminated and the average is obtained from the core academic classes only. Students who need academic assistance will find a Writing Center and Student Tutorial Center on campus. Faculty and staff make an extra effort to help first-year students with the transition from high school to college.

Insight

"There is a college for everyone," says Amanda Warhurst Webster, senior associate director of admissions. "Here we look at the profile of the high school itself. Does it offer an honors curriculum? How many academic classes will the student choose to take, including their senior year? Do the students take state tests?" According to Warhurst Webster, emphasis is also put on recommendations. "We want to see the third party perspective," she says. "And we can tell when a letter is a general one or a truly personal one."

The essay is very important at Salve Regina. "It is the only part of the application process that is in the student's own voice," says Warhurst Webster. "The essays bring the kids to life. I always encourage students to think, 'How do I want to appear to the people in admissions?'" The essay topics are open-ended, and officers look at the concepts presented in the essay along with grammar, mechanics and usage issues. One common essay question is 'Tell us something more about yourself that you want us to know.' We certainly give leeway to students who do not have a support system," explains Warhurst Webster.

University of San Francisco

San Francisco, CA

Address: 2130 Fulton St., San Francisco, CA 94117-1080
Phone: 415-422-6563
Admissions email: admission@usfca.edu
Website: www.usfca.edu

Admissions Stats

Percentage of applicants admitted: 72%
SAT range: 510-610 critical reading, 510-610 math
ACT range: 21-26 composite

Size

Number of undergraduates: 4,796

Costs

Tuition and fees: $28,760
Books and supplies: $900
On campus room and board and other expenses: $13,340
Off campus room and board and other expenses: $14,000

Academics

Favorite majors: psychology, business, management, marketing and related support services social sciences, communication, journalism and related programs, computer information sciences and support services

---

The B Features

The Learning Center at USF provides assistance to students through tutors in a variety of academic disciplines. The tutors are undergrads and graduate students that have excelled in certain academic areas and who have had special tutorial training. These students offer help on such topics as math, science, business, languages, computers, arts and general education. Study skills videos, textbooks and reference books are available, and the center also provides students a place to study that is peaceful and supportive.

The Writing Center features tutors that tailor programs of instruction to meet each student's needs. The Center's primary goal is to "guide students in developing their writing skills in rhetoric, style and correctness, through one-on-one interactive conferences with Rhetoric and Composition faculty who have been chosen to work as consultants."

College of Santa Fe

Santa Fe, NM

Address: 1600 St. Michael's Dr., Santa Fe, NM 87505-7634
Phone: 505-473-6133
Admissions email: admissions@csf.edu
Website: www.csf.edu

Admissions Stats

Percentage of applicants admitted: 77.6%
SAT range: 520-640 critical reading, 460-590 math
ACT range: 20-25 composite, 20-26 English, 17-24 math

Size

Number of undergraduates: 1,661

Costs

Tuition and fees: $24,444
Books and supplies: $912
On campus room and board and other expenses: $8,418
Off campus room and board and other expenses: $11,106

Academics

Favorite majors: visual and performing arts, English language, literature/letters, communication, journalism, and related programs, natural resources and conservation, psychology

---

The B Features

CSF has a First year Seminar that is essentially a 9-week introductory course to help ease students into the college life. The class meets for 90 minutes each week during the Fall semester.

TRiO Student Support Services (SSS) and the Center for Academic Excellence (CAE) are available to students who need academic assistance. Workshops are offered that deal with learning strategies such as reading, study skills, note taking, test taking, time management and memory improvement. Tutoring is available through the Center and can be arranged by contacting support personnel. Coordinators help students find the right tutor, sustain motivation, learn stress reduction techniques and "journey wisely through academic and social situations."

Schreiner University

Kerrville, TX

Address: 2100 Memorial Blvd., Kerrville, TX 78028
Phone: 800-343-4919
Admissions email: admissions@schreiner.edu
Admissions contact: Sandra Speed, dean of admission and financial aid
Website: www.schreiner.edu

Admissions Stats

Percentage of applicants admitted: 58.4%
Average GPA range: 3.46
SAT range: 440-545 critical reading, 430-550 math
ACT range: 18-23 composite, 16-23 English, 17-23 math

Size

Number of undergraduates: 770

Costs

Tuition and fees: $15,879
Books and supplies: $1,000
On campus room and board and other expenses: $9,066
Off campus room and board and other expenses: $9,066

Academics

Favorite majors: business administration, life sciences, teacher education, exercise science

Student Life

The campus: About an hour northwest of San Antonio, this small, liberal arts, private college affiliated with the Presbyterian Church (USA) is in Kerrville, a city of 20,000. There are four residence halls and one apartment complex on campus. The campus has wireless hotspots in nearly every area, and a modern activity center where students go to hang out, play pool, listen to music, have a snack, work out in the fitness center or relax by the fireplace. The campus is located on the banks of the Guadalupe River and is home to an abundance of gentle wildlife including a flock of whitetail deer.

The students: Most students live on campus and enjoy the traditional residential lifestyle. Nearly a quarter of Schreiner's undergraduates participate in NCAA Division III athletics. There are slightly more women than men at Schreiner and almost a quarter of the population is minority.

The B Features

Because the student-to-faculty ratio at Schreiner is 13:1, students receive individual attention. In some instances, they can even help to design their own internships. There is also a strong honors program at Schreiner.

Students with learning disabilities can find help through Schreiner's Learning Support Services Program. Tutoring for all classes is free.

Insight

Sandra Speed, dean of admission and financial aid, has important information for anyone thinking about coming to Schreiner. "If you want to fall through the cracks, do not come here," she warns. "If you don't come to class, you will be missed, and someone will try to help you resolve the problem before it becomes a bigger issue. The faculty at Schreiner is very involved with each student's success. They have a real personal commitment to students and will even give you their home phone numbers. At Schreiner, counseling is consistent and ongoing." The school has a faith-based mission and a strong emphasis on extracurricular work within the community, school and church.

A student, Jay Govan III, took time to explain why he chose Schreiner University. "What led me to Schreiner was the ratio of students to professors," he explains. "I knew that would be a great benefit to me because if I were to struggle, the teachers always have their doors open to help students. What also led me to this school was the tutoring they have, which is great."

Govan's freshman and sophomore years of high school were at Trinity Christian Academy, a very small school, and he believes that is where he learned to be responsible in getting his work done on time. His junior and senior years were at Saint Anthony's Catholic High School, an all-boys school. He admits he was not looking forward to attending the school at first, but he says, "after a couple of weeks, things started going well. The good thing about an all-boys school is that you don't have to try to impress anyone but just worry about getting your studies done. While I was a senior there, my grades were good enough to allow me to also take a couple of college courses at the University of the Incarnate Word."

During his first year at Schreiner, Govan's GPA dropped from 3.0 to 2.5, an issue he is keenly aware of. "I have been working hard to continue to increase it to where it was in high school," he says. "The teachers are always persuading me to give it all I have and not hold anything back."

Govan has suggestions for students thinking about attending Schreiner. "This is a great school to come to. Be focused on your books and you won't get sidetracked like if you went to a college in a big city. I would also encourage students to get all the education you can get now because after school is over that's it, it's time to go out and look for a job, and no more thinking about skipping or being late."

He has learned some important things at college already. "You have to make goals for yourself and make studying and class your number one priority," he advises.

Seton Hill University

Greensburg, PA

Address: 1 Seton Hill Dr., Box 991, Greensburg, PA 15601
Phone: 724-838-4255
Admissions email: admit@setonhill.edu
Website: www.setonhill.edu

Admissions Stats

Percentage of applicants admitted: 53.7%
SAT range: open admissions
ACT range: open admissions

Size

Number of undergraduates: 1,863

Costs

Tuition and fees: $23,180
Books and supplies: $1,000
On campus room and board and other expenses: $9,950
Off campus room and board and other expenses: $9,300

Academics

Favorite majors: business, management, marketing and related support services, public administration and social service professions, health professions and related clinical sciences, psychology and social services

---

The B Features

Seton Hill's Academic Support program provides assistance to students through a tutoring center, which offers individual and small group tutoring. There is a Writing Center, which helps with prewriting skills, organizing, drafting, revising and editing.

The college also offers an Opportunity Program, which is a summer experience designed to help students get a head start by living on campus, participating in workshops and mastering the skills they will need for college work. The students who qualify for this program either have low SAT or ACT scores, a low high school GPA, non-academic courses in high school, or grades that simply don't truly reflect the student's potential.

In addition to these services, Seton Hill also offers Academic Counseling on study skills such as taking notes, reading college textbooks, and taking tests. Common topics include time management, test anxiety, critical thinking and identifying personal learning styles.

Shaw University

Raleigh, NC

Address: 118 E. South St., Raleigh, NC 27601
Phone: 919-546-8275
Website: www.shawu.edu

Admissions Stats

Percentage of applicants admitted: 64.6%
SAT range: 330-430 critical reading, 320-430 math
ACT range: 12-16 composite, 9-15 English, 13-16 math

Size

Number of undergraduates: 2,565

Costs

Tuition and fees: $10,020
Books and supplies: $700
On campus room and board and other expenses: $7,910
Off campus room and board and other expenses: $7,910

Academics

Favorite majors: business, management, marketing and related support services, security and protective services, public administration and social service professions, social sciences, philosophy and religious studies

---
The B Features

Shaw's Freshman Year Program is focused on providing the tools students need to reach their academic goals. It features a series of activities and events that help ease the transition as students become more familiar with college life. Every student must take this program as part of graduation requirements. It includes a number of classes, including a cultural and spiritual enrichment seminar.

Note that the college has a dress code, and community worship is mandatory, as is attendance to college events such as Homecoming, Senior Appreciation Day and University Awards Day.

A new, free program called Freshmen Academy earns credit hours. It is an intense summer academic program, and participants receive room, board, books and supplies. They attend workshops, seminars, and presentations and go on field trips.

Shenandoah University

Winchester, VA

Address: 1460 University Dr., Winchester, VA 22601-5195
Phone: 540-665-1481
Admissions email: admit@su.edu
Website: www.su.edu

Admissions Stats

Percentage of applicants admitted: 91.5%
SAT range: 450-580 critical reading, 450-580 math
ACT range: 17-24 composite, 15-24 English, 17-24 math

Size

Number of undergraduates: 2,998

Costs

Tuition and fees: $21,090
Books and supplies: $1,000
On campus room and board and other expenses: $9,750
Off campus room and board and other expenses: NA

Academics

Favorite majors: health professions and related clinical services, visual and performing arts, education, business, management, marketing and related supper services, biological and biomedical sciences, psychology

The B Features

Known as the "Yes You Can" University, Shenandoah offers a Writing Center that stresses "making better writers, not just better papers." The college also has a Center for Lifelong Learning which offers many non-credit courses for personal and professional development.

Shepherd University

. . . .

Shepherdstown, WV

Address: P.O. Box 3210, Shepherdstown, WV 25443-3210
Phone: 304-876-5212
Admissions email: admissions@shepherd.edu
Website: www.shepherd.edu/admin.web

Admissions Stats

Percentage of applicants admitted: 83.1%
SAT range: 940-1098 composite
ACT range: 19-24 composite

Size

Number of undergraduates: 4,091

Costs

Tuition and fees: $4,566 in state; $12,036 out of state
Books and supplies: $1,100
On campus room and board and other expenses: $6,986
Off campus room and board and other expenses: NA

Academics

Favorite majors: business administration, education (elementary and secondary), art, recreation and leisure studies, nursing, environmental science, photography, musical theatre

---

The B Features

Shepherd has quite a bit to offer the B student. First, it has "stretch" model courses, i.e. courses that can be stretched to two semesters. The Academic Support Center offers tutoring and academic counseling and the Writing Center provides help for papers and writing assignments.

"We welcome students without straight A's. The mean incoming GPA for freshmen is 3.07. The mean freshman SAT composite is 1024, and the mean freshman ACT composite is 21.72. SU's admission requirements are 2.0 GPA and 920 SAT or 19 ACT for freshmen. Applicants with a B average are successful at Shepherd University if they are successful on the SAT or ACT.

Tutoring can aid students in their weaker skills. SU's philosophy toward B students and C students is that if they have completed a rigorous high school program, scored adequately on the ACT or

SAT and have a good work ethic, the student will be successful here. We offer a good support system.

"Because of the size of the student body at Shepherd, students are known individually by faculty and staff. Shepherd is a very inclusive school allowing students to be accepted as themselves. Expect the unexpected at SU!"

Simmons College*

Boston, MA

Address: 300 The Fenway, Boston, MA 02115-5898
Phone: 617-521-8468
Admissions email: ugadm@simmons.edu
Website: www.simmons.edu

Admissions Stats

Percentage of applicants admitted: 58.8%
SAT range: 510-610 critical reading, 500-590 math
ACT range: 22-27 composite, 22-28 English, 21-26 math

Size

Number of undergraduates: 1,965

Costs

Tuition and fees: $25,914
Books and supplies: $960
On campus room and board and other expenses: $14,075
Off campus room and board and other expenses: $14,075

Academics

Favorite majors: social sciences, health professions and related clinical services, communication, journalism and related programs, psychology, visual and performing arts

---
The B Features

Simmons' Academic Support Center is focused on providing high-quality assistance to help students succeed academically. According to the college, its goal is to "help students become independent learners and to encourage them to take an active part in their educational and intellectual pursuits." The center achieves this through various methods.

Academic Advising and Counseling assigns advisors to students who are having academic struggles. Placement examinations are given that provide results for math, language and chemistry levels.

Services for Students with Disabilities is a program for those with a documented disability, while Tutorial Services matches students with course tutors in such subjects as biology, chemistry, foreign languages, math and physics. There are also study groups with weekly reviews of course material. Specialists offer one-on-one help by appointment and give instruction on study skills. Writing Assistance provides coaches to help students organize and structure their writing and learn how to self-edit.

* All women college

Paul Smiths College of Arts and Science

Paul Smiths, NY

Address: P.O. Box 265, Paul Smiths, NY 12970-0265
Phone: 518-327-6227
Admissions email: admiss@paulsmiths.edu
Website: www.paulsmiths.edu

Admissions Stats

Percentage of applicants admitted: 82%
SAT range: open admission
ACT range: open admission

Size

Number of undergraduates: 846

Costs

Tuition and fees: $19,410
Books and supplies: $2,000
On campus room and board and other expenses: $10,920
Off campus room and board and other expenses: NA

Academics

Favorite majors: business, management, marketing and related support services, natural resources and conservation, personal and culinary services, parks and recreation, leisure and fitness studies, biological and biomedical sciences

The B Features

The theme at Paul Smith's Academic Center is "Helping Students Achieve their Goals for Academic Success." Here they offer peer tutoring, supplemental instruction, study groups and a Writing Center where experts strive to help students understand the assignment, build confidence, organize ideas, listen carefully, formulate comments and more.

Sonoma State University

Rohnert Park, CA

Address: 1801 E. Cotati Ave., Rohnert Park, CA 94928-3609
Phone: 707-664-2326
Admissions email: admitme@sonoma.edu
Website: www.sonoma.edu

Admissions Stats

Percentage of applicants admitted: 60.9%
SAT range: 470-570 critical reading, math 470-570
ACT range: 19-24 composite, 19-25 English, 18-24 math

Size

Number of undergraduates: 6,674

Costs

Tuition and fees: $3,648 in state; $13,818 out of state
Books and supplies: $1,314
On campus room and board and other expenses: $12,712
Off campus room and board and other expenses: $13,968

Academics

Favorite majors: business, management, marketing and related support services, engineering, computer and informational sciences and support services, health professions and related clinical sciences, visual and performing arts

The B Features

Sonoma's Educational Mentoring Team helps students transition to college life with a Freshman Seminar and a strong advising department. They feel students should be connected to a faculty member, a student services professional and a peer mentor.

The Freshman Seminar is an optional class, but all new students are encouraged to take it. The course focuses on the skills needed to succeed in college classes. Information is provided that teaches students how to be involved in their own education and individualized advising is available as well. Another part of the Freshman seminar is the study of the university culture.

SOAR, or Sonoma Orientation, Advising and Registration, is held each summer for entering freshmen and their parents and is geared to help with the transition to college life.

Free tutoring is available for all undergraduate courses. Students are allowed four hours a week, with a maximum of two hours per subject.

University of South Carolina

Columbia, SC

Address: Columbia, SC 29208
Phone: 803-777-7700
Admissions email: admissions-ugrad@sc.edu
Website: www.sc.edu

Admissions Stats

Percentage of applicants admitted: 67%
SAT range: 520-620 critical reading, 530-630 math
ACT range: 22-27 composite

Size

Number of undergraduates: 17,689

Costs

Tuition and fees: $7,808 in state; $20,236 out of state
Books and supplies: $838
On campus room and board and other expenses: $10,275
Off campus room and board and other expenses: NA

Academics

Favorite majors: biology, English, international business, psychology, criminal justice, nursing, business

The B Features

At the University of South Carolina—the college where students are known as "Gamecocks"—the Academic Center for Excellence provides free writing consultations, math tutoring and other services. Guidance from ACE coaches is offered in areas of time management, procrastination, reading comprehension, note taking, goal setting, test taking, motivation, anxiety management, concentration and information processing. In addition, USC has a site called "My Game Plan" that helps each student design a personal approach for achieving academic success in college. It includes a personal assessment, study strategies and much more.

Southern Oregon University

Ashland, OR

Address: 1250 Syskiyou Blvd., Ashland, OR 97520
Phone: 541-552-6411
Admissions email: admissions@sou.edu
Website: www.sou.edu

Admissions Stats

Percentage of applicants admitted: 80.2%
SAT range: 460-580 critical reading, 460-560 math
ACT range: 20-25 composite, 19-25 English, 18-24 math

Size

Number of undergraduates: 4,986

Costs

Tuition and fees: $5,233 in state; $16,918 out of state
Books and supplies: $1,200
On campus room and board and other expenses: $10,704
Off campus room and board and other expenses: NA

Academics

Favorite majors: business, management, marketing and related support services, communication, journalism, and related programs, psychology, visual and performing arts and social sciences

The B Features

Southern Oregon University offers students help through its AC-CESS Center, an acronym for Academic Advising, Counseling, Career Services, and Educational Support Services. Their programs include a Writing Center and Math tutoring. Academic advisors help students understand and organize the University Studies Requirements, i.e. General Studies.

Spelman College*

Atlanta, GA

Address: 350 Spelman Lane Southwest, Atlanta, GA 30314-4399
Phone: 404-270-5193 or 800-982-2411
Admissions email: admissions@spelman.edu
Website: www.spelman.edu

Admissions Stats

Percentage of applicants admitted: 39%
SAT range: 510-600 critical reading, 500-580 math
ACT range: 21-25 composite

Size

Number of undergraduates: 2,134

Costs

Tuition and fees: $17,005
Books and supplies: $1,700
On campus room and board and other expenses: $12,250
Off campus room and board and other expenses: $12,250

Academics

Favorite majors: English language and literature/letters, psychology, biological and biomedical sciences, social sciences, computer and information sciences and support services

---

The B Features

Spelman's Learning Resources Center provides extra help to all students and offers services such as lab instruction, academic advisement, peer tutoring, workshops and instruction in study techniques and learning strategies. According to the college, the center's major objective is to "EMPOWER students who will become creative, independent learners and problem solvers capable of processing and handling volumes of information."

Peer tutors are available on both a drop-in and appointment basis throughout the year. Students can get help in study techniques, reading, note taking, test-taking strategies, problem-solving and communication skills. Academic advising is also offered through the Learning Resources Center.

* Historically Black college for women

Springfield College

Springfield, MA

Address: 263 Alden St., Springfield, MA 01109-3797
Phone: 413-748-3136
Admissions email: admissions@spfldcol.edu
Website: www.spfldcol.edu

Admissions Stats

Percentage of applicants admitted: 66.3%
SAT range: 460-550 critical reading, 470-570 math
ACT range: NA

Size

Number of undergraduates: 5,025

Costs

Tuition and fees: $22,715
Books and supplies: $900
On campus room and board and other expenses: $11,280
Off campus room and board and other expenses: NA

Academics

Favorite majors: public administrations and social services professions, health professions and related clinical services, education, parks, recreation, leisure and fitness studies and business, management, marketing and related support services

---

The B Features

Springfield's Academic Support Services includes access to one-on-one academic coaching. Qualified tutors help students in areas that include a variety of topics, including the following: taking and using class notes, preparing for exams, managing time, testing taking and alleviating test anxiety, actively reading and learning from your textbooks, concentrating during study sessions, organizing and outlining papers, avoiding procrastination and organizing study groups.

Suffolk University

Boston, MA

Address: 8 Ashburton Place, Beacon Hill, Boston, MA 02108
Phone: 617-573-8460
Admissions email: admissions@suffolk.edu
Website: www.suffolk.edu

Admissions Stats

Percentage of applicants admitted: 82.7%
SAT range: 450-560 critical reading, 450-550 math
ACT range: NA

Size

Number of undergraduates: 4,784

Costs

Tuition and fees: $22,610
Books and supplies: $1,000
On campus room and board and other expenses: $15,373
Off campus room and board and other expenses: $14,967

Academics

Favorite majors: psychology, business, management, marketing and related support services, visual and performing arts, social sciences, communication, and journalism and related programs

---

The B Features

Suffolk has many different methods of helping students who are feeling a little lost or falling behind. At the Ballotti Learning Center, a Tutor Program matches students with peer tutors who can help students in two ways: 1) by providing extra support for students who are taking a course that is proving difficult for them or 2) through teaching general academic strategies like note taking, exam prep, time management, etc. The service is free, and tutors and students meet up to twice a week for one-hour sessions. In a survey done by the Learning Center, 97 percent of the students tutored reported that tutoring helped them to become more independent learners. Study groups are also offered at the center. They focus on the traditionally high-risk courses and give students the time to review notes and prepare questions for class. Staff consultants at Ballotti are doctoral students in the field of psychology. Their job is to assist students with personal concerns and challenges. (Sessions are private and confidential.)

The AHANA (African Hispanic Asian Native American) International Program is an outreach program for students of color. Peer liaisons help with issues like second language, stereotypes and cultural differences that may occur.

Suffolk recognizes that some students may face academic challenges that could result in low grades. To help provide support for these struggling students, Suffolk has put two programs into place: High Profile and The Roster Project.

The school's High Profile Program is for students who are in "academic jeopardy." A team of counselors and technicians connect these students with services that can provide academic support.

The Roster Project identifies students who are heading for "academic risk" by mid-semester (at risk of failing because of missing class, poor study habits or communication skills, second language issues, etc.). Letters or calls are made as a warning and then students are encouraged to seek the help they need.

Educational consultants are on campus to address issues that affect a student's academic life. This often includes matching student with tutor and then monitoring the relationship to make sure it is successful and effective.

Sweet Briar College*

Sweet Briar, VA

Address: 134 Chapel Dr., Box B, Sweet Briar, VA 24595-9998
Phone: 434-381-6142
Admissions email: admissions@sbc.edu
Website: www.sbc.edu

Admissions Stats

Percentage of applicants admitted: 80%
Average GPA range: 27% in top 10% of high school class
SAT range: 530-640 critical reading, 500-590 math
ACT range: 22-27 composite, 22-28 English, 19-26 math

Size

Number of undergraduates: 538

Costs

Tuition and fees: $23,340
Books and supplies: $600
On campus room and board and other expenses: $10,830

Academics

Favorite majors: English language, literature/letters, psychology, biology, chemistry, government, history, international affairs and business

The B Features

The Academic Resource Center (ARC) at Sweet Briar College provides many different opportunities for student support, including ways to help make college life and courses easier. The Center is available to all students and is staffed by trained student assistants. ARC offers information on time management, writing, reading, study skills, stress management, peer tutoring and mentoring. ARC staff also offers assistance for students with learning differences, intent on "encouraging a higher standard of academic performance."

The writing tutoring service is ARC's main focus. The staff works with students on all stages of their papers' preparation, from forming a thesis to perfecting punctuation. Experienced student mentors help freshmen adjust to college academics.

ARC also offers online and printed resources on topics like weekly time management and course preparation. In addition, ARC assists with the social aspects of college life and the potential stress this can bring.

* All women college

Temple University

· ·

Philadelphia, PA

Address: Temple University, 1801 N. Broad. St., Philadelphia, PA 19122-6096
Phone: 888-340-2222
Admissions email: tuadm@mail.temple.edu
Website: www.temple.edu

Admissions Stats

Percentage of applicants admitted: 60.4%
SAT range: 490-590 critical reading, 500-600 math
ACT range: 20-25 composite

Size

Number of undergraduates: 24,194

Costs

Tuition and fees: $10,180 in state; $18,224 out of state
Books and supplies: $800
On campus room and board and other expenses: $12,793
Off campus room and board and other expenses: $12,793

Academics

Favorite majors: psychology, business, management, marketing and related support services, visual and performing arts, communication, journalism and related programs

The B Features

Temple University offers a myriad of support for its students, including computer labs, counseling, and tutoring. The school provides students with the choice of more than 30 computer labs plus a Student Computer Center. Advisors are available to aid students with choosing majors and resolving academic and/or curriculum issues. Counselors are eager to provide "academic counseling for students to develop a meaningful education plan compatible with life goals." In addition, the advising center offers a new student orientation.

The Student Support Services Program is part of the Russell Conwell Educational Service Center. It gives students intensive academic support through free year-round counseling and tutoring activities. In addition, the college offers a required six-week intensive Summer Bridge Program that includes skill building courses in math, computer technology, library usage, reading, writing and study skills as well as workshops on personal development, art appreciation and career choices. Tutoring in selected subjects is part of the tutorial component of the learning center, while academic, career and personal counseling comprise the counseling portion of the program.

University of Tennessee—Knoxville

Knoxville, TN

Address: 320 Student Services Building, Knoxville, TN 37996
Phone: 865-974-1000
Admissions email: admissions@utk.edu
Website: www.admissions.utk.edu

Admissions Stats

Percentage of applicants admitted: 72%
SAT range: 1090-1270 composite
ACT range: 24-29 composite

Size

Number of undergraduates: 20,435

Costs

Tuition and fees: $5,864 in state; $17,994 out of state
Books and supplies: $1,288
On campus room and board and other expenses: $6,358
Off campus room and board and other expenses: NA

Academics

Favorite majors: psychology, English, biology and accounting

The B Features

According to its website, UT offers "First Year Studies 101: a one credit course to introduce students to the university and resources, a Student Success Center: one stop shopping for academic referrals and resources, a Math Tutorial Center and Writing Center and a College academic advising center." Students are encouraged to "take a challenging curriculum of academic courses."

UT offers this advice to those wishing to apply for acceptance: "Complete the personal statement with your application—it will be read! Letters of recommendation are not required but if you wish to include them, be sure that they are from teachers of academic subjects. Tell us about your academic challenges and successes. Tell about your special talents and abilities. UT welcomes B students with strong and diverse academic backgrounds.

"UT is strongly dedicated to the success of its students with excellent academic programs, diverse extracurricular activities and a welcoming campus environment. Come for a visit or apply online!"

Tuskegee University

Tuskegee, AL

Address: Kresge Center, 3rd floor, Tuskegee, AL 36008-1920
Phone: 334-727-8500
Admissions email: admi@tuskegee.edu
Website: www.tuskegee.edu

Admissions Stats

Percentage of applicants admitted: 80.6%
SAT range: 390-510 critical reading, 390-510 math
ACT range: 17-21 composite, 18-20 English, 17-20 math

Size

Number of undergraduates: 2,510

Costs

Tuition and fees: $12,865
Books and supplies: $949
On campus room and board and other expenses: $9,977
Off campus room and board and other expenses: $9,977

Academics

Favorite majors: psychology, business, management, marketing and related support services, biological/biomedical sciences, engineering, agriculture, agriculture operations and related sciences

The B Features

A predominantly African American college (76.1%), Tuskegee offers a peer tutoring program for students who are taking first- or second-year courses in gross anatomy, microanatomy, neuroanatomy, physiology, microbiology, parasitology or clinical pathology, anatomic pathology and pharmacology. Peer tutors are available to help the needs of nursing, medical technology and occupational therapy students. These tutors give advice and guidance on information given in lectures; they also monitor more general study skills like questioning and answering and they help to establish study groups.

An Academic Skills Guide discusses the importance of effective study skills. According to the college, the guide "addresses the how-to's of studying" and covers such elements as taking part in effective group study, developing thinking skills, taking tests and notes and managing time.

University of Utah

Salt Lake City, UT

Address: 250 SSB, Salt Lake City, UT 84112-9008
Phone: 801-581-7281
Admissions email: admissions@sa.utah.edu
Website: www.utah.edu

Admissions Stats

Percentage of applicants admitted: 85%
SAT range: 495-630 critical reading, 500-630 math
ACT range: 21-26 composite, 20-26 English, 19-26 math

Size

Number of undergraduates: 15,413

Costs

Tuition and fees: $4,642 in state; $14,272 out of state
Books and supplies: $1,100
On campus room and board and other expenses: $9,900
Off campus room and board and other expenses: $10,300

Academics

Favorite majors: business, management, marketing and related support services, communication, journalism and related programs, engineering, psychology, ballet/dance and chemistry

The B Features

Students at the University of Utah can turn to PASS, or Programs for Academic Support, for help in subject areas. Through PASS, students receive free peer tutoring in physics, chemistry, science, some foreign languages and math. Sessions can be either one on one or in a group. Online tutoring has recently been expanded as well. A Self-Help Learning Lab features audio and videotapes, books and computer software for development of study skills. Subject areas for which assistance is available include reading, algebra, calculus, trigonometry, statistics, differential equations, chemistry and foreign language.

Academic advising covers topics such as study skills and time management, effective listening and note taking, improving reading comprehension, test taking, test anxiety and learning style. Supplemental instruction is provided for the historically difficult entry-level classes.

Valparaiso University

Valparaiso, IN

Address: US Highway 30 and Sturdy Rd., Valparaiso, IN 46383
Phone: 219-464-5011
Admissions email: undergrad.admissions@valpo.edu
Website: www.valpo.edu

Admissions Stats

Percentage of applicants admitted: 89.3%
SAT range: 500-620 critical reading, 520-650 math
ACT range: 22-28 composite, 22-29 English, 22-29 math

Size

Number of undergraduates: 3,863

Costs

Tuition and fees: $24,000
Books and supplies: $1,000
On campus room and board and other expenses: $8,010
Off campus room and board and other expenses: $6,920

Academics

Favorite majors: business, management, marketing and related support services, engineering, education, health professions and related clinical services, social sciences, communication, journalism and related programs

The B Features

Valpo offers a Student Counseling and Development Center that features a large number of outreach and workshop topics, including the following: stress reduction, managing procrastination, student and test preparation skills training, time management, mindfulness training and anxiety reduction.

University of Vermont

Burlington, VT

Address: 194 S. Prospect St., Burlington, VA 05401
Phone: 802-656-3370
Admissions email: admissions@uvm.edu
Website: www.uvm.edu

Admissions Stats

Percentage of applicants admitted: 65%
SAT range: 520-630 critical reading, 520-630 math
ACT range: 22-26 composite

Size

Number of undergraduates: 8,784

Costs

Tuition and fees: $11,324 in state; $26,308 out of state
Books and supplies: $900
On campus room and board and other expenses: $8,767
Off campus room and board and other expenses: NA

Academics

Favorite majors: biology, health sciences, environmental studies and business

---
The B Features

UVM has the Learning Cooperative, a place "where students help students learn." It offers individual tutoring, group study sessions and writing and learning skills conferences. The Learning Skills program is there to help students develop learning skills and study habits that lead to a successful college career. They do this through free tutoring and workshops. Along with individualized tutoring, the Cooperative offers a number of group study sessions for the college's most traditionally difficult courses. A Writing Center helps with any class papers.

Virginia Commonwealth University

Richmond, VA

Address: 910 W. Franklin St., Richmond, VA 23284-2512
Phone: 804-828-1222
Admissions email: ugrad@vcu.edu
Website: www.vcu.edu

Admissions Stats

Percentage of applicants admitted: 65.8%
SAT range: 480-580 reading, 460-570 writing, 480-580 math
ACT range: 19-23 composite

Size

Number of undergraduates: 29,168

Costs

Tuition and fees: $5,886
Books and supplies: $1,760
On campus room and board and other expenses: $10,530
Off campus room and board and other expenses: $10,530

Academics

Favorite majors: business management, marketing and related support services, visual and performing arts, psychology, health professions and related clinical services, security and protective services, engineering, English language and literature/letters

The B Features

VCU has a College Success Program that works to "provide assistance to students that will help them attain their academic potential." Along with academic counseling and tutoring, students who need additional development in some academic areas are involved in a mandatory year-long program during their freshman year. The school also offers UNIV 101, An Introduction to the University, which is a one-credit class that guides students to resources and services, plus promotes the development of intellectual, personal and social skills. It examines learning styles and study skills as well.

Virginia Wesleyan College

Norfolk, VA

Address: 1584 Wesleyan Dr., Norfolk, VA 23502-5599
Phone: 757-455-3208
Admissions email: admissions@vwc.edu
Website: www.vwc.edu

Admissions Stats

Percentage of applicants admitted: 84.1%
SAT range: 440-530 critical reading, 430-540 math
ACT range: 17-21 composite, 16-22 English, 17-22 math

Size

Number of undergraduates: 1,392

Costs

Tuition and fees: $22,976
Books and supplies: $800
On campus room and board and other expenses: $8,650
Off campus room and board and other expenses: $8,100

Academics

Favorite majors: business, management, marketing and related support services, social sciences, security and protection services, multi-interdisciplinary studies, education, parks, recreation, leisure and fitness studies

---

The B Features

The Learning Center at VWC offers tutoring and resource materials as well as study skills workshops. With a 13:1 student/teacher ratio, teachers are often willing to take the time to help students with one-on-one counseling and guidance. Career Services assists students with choosing a major and scheduling courses.

Washington and Jefferson College

Washington, PA

Address: 60 S. Lincoln St., Washington, PA 15301
Phone: 888-926-3529
Admissions email: admissions@washjeff.edu
Website: www.washjeff.edu

Admissions Stats

Percentage of applicants admitted: 39%
SAT range: 520-610 critical reading, 530-620 math
ACT range: 23-26 composite

Size

Number of undergraduates: 1,394

Costs

Tuition and fees: $29,532
Books and supplies: NA
On campus room and board and other expenses: $8,030
Off campus room and board and other expenses: NA

Academics

Favorite majors: premed, prelaw, business administration, biology and English

---

The B Features

The Center for Learning and Teaching supports Washington and Jefferson students by providing peer assisted learning in which study skills are taught by fellow students. In addition, assistance is also provided for areas such as memory and concentration, class participation, how to talk to your instructor, stress management and more. The Associate Director of the Center helps students assess their current academic skills by identifying strengths and weaknesses. Specific feedback is then given so that students know what areas to concentrate on within the Center.

Washington State University

Pullman, WA

Address: French Administration Building, Pullman, WA 99164-1009
Phone: 509-335-5586
Admissions email: admiss2@wsu.edu
Website: www.wsu.edu

Admissions Stats

Percentage of applicants admitted: 77.1%
SAT range: 480-590 critical reading, 500-610 math
ACT range: NA

Size

Number of undergraduates: 19,585

Costs

Tuition and fees: $6,448 in state; $16,088 out of state
Books and supplies: $912
On campus room and board and other expenses: $10,868
Off campus room and board and other expenses: $12,322

Academics

Favorite majors: business, management, marketing and related support services, social sciences, communication, journalism and related programs, education and engineering

---

The B Features

WSU students go to the SALC, or Student Advising and Learning Center, for academic assistance. The staff at SALC provides advising, tutoring and other help. Academic Assistance offers services such as learning-strategies workshops, handouts, videos and a peer tutorial program for one-on-one assistance in a wide range of subjects for an hourly fee.

A two-credit elective class called the Freshman Seminar is designed to "help first-year students enhance critical thinking, research, writing and presentation skills as well as deal with transition issues faced when entering into the university." Students enrolled in this class develop a research project about the lessons learned in the course.

Wells College

Aurora, NY

Address: 170 State Route 90, Aurora, NY 13026-0500
Phone: 315-364-3264 or 800-952-9355
Admissions email: admissions@wells.edu
Website: www.wells.edu

Admissions Stats

Percentage of applicants admitted: 64%
SAT range: 520-630 critical reading, 480-580 math
ACT range: 20-26 composite

Size

Number of undergraduates: 402

Costs

Tuition and fees: $16,780
Books and supplies: $700
On campus room and board and other expenses: $8,500
Off campus room and board and other expenses: NA

Academics

Favorite majors: English language literature/letters, psychology, visual and performing arts, biological/biomedical sciences, education

The B Features

The First Year Experience (WLLS 101) is required for freshman enrolled at Wells. The course is designed to acquaint students with the four divisions of social sciences, humanities, sciences and fine arts and their connection to liberal arts. The class helps students to think, read and write critically, discuss complex issues, communicate effectively, use college resources precisely and learn as a group. It is taught in a combination of discussion and workshop.

Wesleyan College*

Macon, GA

Address: 4760 Forsyth Rd., Macon, GA 31210-4462
Phone: 478-757-5206
Admissions email: admissions@wesleyancollege.edu
Website: www.wesleyancollege.edu

Admissions Stats

Percentage of applicants admitted: 38.6%
SAT range: 490-610 critical reading, 460-570 math
ACT range: 19-25 composite, 19-26 English, 17-24 math

Size

Number of undergraduates: 551

Costs

Tuition and fees: $14,500
Books and supplies: $800
On campus room and board and other expenses: $9,000
Off campus room and board and other expenses: $9,000

Academics

Favorite majors: business, management, marketing and related support services, psychology, communication, journalism and related programs, visual and performing arts, biological and biomedical services

The B Features

Student-to-faculty ratio is 11:1, and class sizes are 19 and under. Wesleyan is billed as the oldest college for women in the world. The school offers an Academic Center that provides free tutoring and counseling for students who may be struggling in their classes. Group and individual sessions are available year round, either by appointment or as on a drop-in basis.

* All women college

Western New England College

Springfield, MA

Address: 1215 Wilbraham Rd., Springfield, MA 01119
Phone: 800-325-1122 ext. 1321
Admissions email: ugradmis@wnec.edu
Website: www.wnec.edu

Admissions Stats

Percentage of applicants admitted: 71%
SAT range: 1053 composite average
ACT range: 22-23 composite

Size

Number of undergraduates: 2,400

Costs

Tuition and fees: $35,940 residents; $25,942 off campus; $37,032 engineering residents; $27,034 engineering commuters
Books and supplies: $1,000
On campus room and board and other expenses: NA
Off campus room and board and other expenses: NA

Academics

Favorite majors: criminal justice, sports management, psychology, engineering business, education, 3 + 3 law program, six-year biomedical engineering, pre-pharmacy program to begin in fall 2009

The B Features

Information from Western New England College explains aspects of the school that are of interest to the B student: "math and science tutoring centers, academic advisors, peer advisors, small classes (average 21-22), all professors are required to hold office hours. First year seminar course for freshmen students."

Advice for prospective students includes these remarks: "Students should challenge themselves academically, show consistency in their grades and get involved in their school and community. When the Admission Office reviews a student's application, we calculate their transcript to obtain an overall GPA. We calculate all college prep courses (full credit) from freshmen to senior year. We look for a consistent performance over four years and we like to see students challenging themselves academically. Western New England College facilitates student learning. The college prepares students to bring multiple perspectives of understanding to help them achieve balance and flexibility as proactive solution seekers in the rapidly changing global environment in which they work and live. "

Westminster College

New Wilmington, PA

Address: 319 S. Market St., New Wilmington, PA 16172
Phone: 724-946-7100
Admissions email: admis@westminster.edu
Website: www.westminster.edu

Admissions Stats

Percentage of applicants admitted: 78.2%
SAT range: 470-590 critical reading, 480-590 math
ACT range: 20-25 composite, 19-26 English, 19-25 math

Size

Number of undergraduates: 1,597

Costs

Tuition and fees: $23,200
Books and supplies: $1,700
On campus room and board and other expenses: $7,570
Off campus room and board and other expenses: $6,690

Academics

Favorite majors: education, business, management, marketing and related support services, social sciences, communication, journalism and related programs and biological and biomedical services

The B Features

The Westminster Plan provides a complete core curriculum in science, humanities, math, computer science and religion (the school is Presbyterian based). All students graduate with two majors. Student-to-faculty ratio is 13:1, and most classes are no more than 19 students. The school emphasizes that it takes education seriously and that this is not a "party school."

West Virginia University

Morgantown, WV

Address: President's Office, P.O. Box 6009, Morgantown,
WV 26506-6009
Phone: 800-322-WVU1
Admissions email: go2wvu@mail.wvu.edu
Website: www.wvu.edu

Admissions Stats

Percentage of applicants admitted: 92%
SAT range: 480-570 critical reading, 470-560 math
ACT range: 20-25 composite, 20-26 English, 18-25 math

Size

Number of undergraduates: 19,510

Costs

Tuition and fees: $4,476 in state; $13,840 out of state
Books and supplies: $900
On campus room and board and other expenses: $9,072
Off campus room and board and other expenses: NA

Academics

Favorite majors: engineering, forensic and investigatory sciences,
biometric systems, political science, pharmacy, psychology allied
health

The B Features

With almost 4,000 freshmen entering WVU each year, the school
has designed a large program that provides students academic
support. University 101 is a class geared to help freshmen adjust
to university life and its demands. A passing grade in this course is
required for graduation. In the fall semester, students also may take
the SSS Orientation Course, which is designed to introduce them to
academic requirements and acquaint them with how student support services can help.

In assigning residence halls, the college places freshmen with similar majors and/or passions in the same dorm, enabling them to form
peer study groups and meet others with the same interests.

Other support systems include a math lab at the Learning Center
and the availability of writing assistance through sessions geared to

help with everything from letters to research papers. Free tutoring is available for most general classes in either one-on-one or study group sessions.

Students who are still not sure about their major can get assistance through the Student Support Services professional staff of advisors.

Whittier College

Whittier, CA

Address: 13406 E. Philadelphia St., P.O. Box 634, Whittier, CA 90608-4413
Phone: 562-907-4238
Admissions email: admissions@whittier.edu
Website: www.whittier.edu

Admissions Stats

Percentage of applicants admitted: 58%
SAT range: 490-590 critical reading, 490-600 math
ACT range: 21-26 composite

Size

Number of undergraduates: 1,317

Costs

Tuition and fees: $29,206
Books and supplies: $720
On campus room and board and other expenses: $10,314
Off campus room and board and other expenses: NA

Academics

Favorite majors: English language, literature/letters, psychology, business, management, marketing and related support services, biological and biomedical sciences, social sciences

The B Features

At Whittier's Center for Academic Success (CAS), tutoring is free and classes that have been identified as historically challenging for most students are supported through supplemental instruction. Students in group sessions review notes, practice quizzes and work to reinforce the knowledge and skills they need for the class.

CAS also offers a class called Succeeding in College that helps students find out how to do well in school, both academically and personally. The class features individual exercises, cooperative learning, reading and lectures and is available each spring. Students that need assistance in the writing process can find all the help they need through the Writing Program.

Wilkes University

Wilkes-Barre, PA

Address: 84 W. South St., Wilkes-Barre, PA 18766
Phone: 800-WILKES-U or 570-408-4400
Admissions email: admissions@wilkes.edu
Admissions contact: Mike Frantz, vice president of enrollment and marketing
Website: www.wilkes.edu

Admissions Stats

Percentage of applicants admitted: 77.1%
Average GPA: 3.3
SAT range: 480-580 critical reading, 480-600 math
ACT range: NA

Size

Number of undergraduates: 2,188

Costs

Tuition and fees: $22,990
Books and supplies: $1,050
On campus room and board and other expenses: $11,360
Off campus room and board and other expenses: $7,400

Academics

Majors offered: The school focuses on pre-professional preparation especially in the health sciences and has the only doctorate in pharmacy in the region through the Nesbitt School of Pharmacy.

The B Features

Wilkes has a deep interest in helping the B student achieve excellence through a dedicated faculty and personal tutoring. Admissions are based on secondary-school record, class rank and results of the SAT or ACT. Interviews are not required but highly recommended. Essays and letters of recommendation are not required but will be accepted and considered if submitted.

Student Life

The campus: The 27-acre campus is nestled within historic Wilkes-Barre, right next to the beautiful Susquehanna River. Each of the 24 resident halls is unique and range from stately mansions, to contemporary dorms, to brick Tudor mansions. The campus is fast becoming pedestrian friendly with eight academic buildings, eight administrative buildings, a library, faculty and alumni house, art gallery, bell tower, an athletic sports complex and much more. A virtual tour can be accessed on the school's website.

The students: The student population is 53.6% women and 46.4% men. While the majority are Pennsylvania residents, many come from nearby New York and New Jersey as well as 20 other states and four foreign nations.

Insight

Wilkes was founded to educate first-generation students. "What sets us apart from other colleges can't be measured by numbers on a page. Students succeed here because of the unique atmosphere and philosophy. At Wilkes you will find someone who believes in you," explains Mike Frantz, vice president of enrollment and marketing. "Our professors do everything they can to help students reach their goals. They even help them figure out what those goals are."

According to Frantz, Wilkes is actively looking for reasons to include B students. "We look for signs of potential," he says. "Our faculty and staff truly take a deep interest in students' dreams and aspirations." For those students struggling with any particular skills, Wilkes offers individual tutoring as well as a staff that assists in career strategies and study skills. "We can take any students if they honestly express the desire to improve," explains Frantz. "This campus is full of passionate faculty who treat students as equals and challenge them to strive towards greater accomplishments."

Woodbury University

Burbank, CA

Address: 7500 Glenoaks Blvd., Burbank, CA 91510-7864
Phone: 818-767-0888
Admissions email: info@woodbury.edu
Website: www.woodbury.edu

Admissions Stats

Percentage of applicants admitted: 76.6%
SAT range: 400-520 critical reading, 400-550 math
ACT range: NA

Size

Number of undergraduates: 1,436

Costs

Tuition and fees: $23,232
Books and supplies: $1,314
On campus room and board and other expenses: $10,866
Off campus room and board and other expenses: $12,438

Academics

Favorite majors: business, management, marketing and related support services, architecture and related services, visual and performing arts and psychology

---
The B Features

Woodbury offers a variety of services to help B students through OASIS (Office of Academic Success and Instructional Services). Services include academic peer mentors, faculty advising, individual and small-group tutoring. The school also provides supplemental instruction for historically challenging courses in weekly study sessions. In addition, each freshman student is assigned a Student Orientation, Advising, and Registration (SOAR) peer advisor who helps students with all aspects of college life.

University of Wyoming

Laramie, WY

Address: Corner of Ninth and Ivinson, Laramie, WY 82071
Phone: 800-342-5996
Admissions email: why-wy@uwyo.edu
Website: www.uwyo.edu

Admissions Stats

Percentage of applicants admitted: 95.3%
SAT range: 480-610 critical reading, 500-610 math
ACT range: 20-26 composite, 19-26 English, 19-26 math

Size

Number of undergraduates: 9,510

Costs

Tuition and fees: $2,951 in state; $8,183 out of state
Books and supplies: $1,200
On campus room and board and other expenses: $9,950
Off campus room and board and other expenses: NA

Academics

Favorite majors: business, management, marketing and related support services, social sciences, engineering, agriculture, agriculture operations and related sciences

The B Features

The University of Wyoming's Academic Services provides support for undergraduates through tutoring and study skills development. It includes a series of study skills workshops and individual advising.

Student Success Services is a program designed for students who meet one of these three criteria: 1) first-generation college student, 2) low-income family or 3) documented disability, learning or physical. This support system offers individual and group tutoring, study skills workshops, individualized math assistance, career exploration and more to eligible students.

Xavier University Louisiana

New Orleans, LA

Address: One Drexel Dr., New Orleans, LA 70125-1098
Phone: 504-520-7388
Admissions email: apply@xula.edu
Website: www.xula.edu

Admissions Stats

Percentage of applicants admitted: 62%
SAT range: 410-540 critical reading, 380-520 math
ACT range: 18-23 composite, 18-24 English, 17-23 math

Size

Number of undergraduates: 2,272

Costs

Tuition and fees: $12,900
Books and supplies: $1,000
On campus room and board and other expenses: $8,131
Off campus room and board and other expenses: $9,263

Academics

Favorite majors: biological and biomedical sciences, chemistry, English, psychology and art

---

The B Features

The Office of Academic Support Programs at Xavier provides academic assistance to students who need extra help. Services include one-on-one tutoring, academic counseling, study techniques, test-taking strategies, enrichment and development, time management skills and referrals to the math, reading and writing labs. Tutoring services are free.

The Math Lab helps student develop their mathematical abilities in an informal manner. The college states that the overall goal of the lab is to "increase each student's understanding of her or his course material. This takes time and active participation on the student's part."

Students may also use the Reading Lab to read and study more effectively. Software can be utilized that helps improve vocabulary and comprehension skills. A Speech Lab is also available, as is a Writing Center website for online tutoring in the different stages of the writing process.

CONTRIBUTORS

Shirley Bloomquist, MA, Ed M, NCC

College and Educational Counselor
sbloomqu@aol.com

Marilyn Emerson

Independent Educational Consultant
www.collplan.com
111 E. 85th Street
New York, NY 10028
212-671-1972 or
84 Old Farm Road North
Chappaqua, NY 10514
914-747-1760

Todd Fothergill

President of Strategies for College
www.strategiesforcollege.com

Marjorie Ann Goode

Educational Consultant/School Counselor
Start Early: College and Career Planning Services
agoode2003@yahoo.com

Laura Jeanne Hammond

Editor in Chief
Next Step Magazine
800-771-3117
www.nextstepmagazine.com
AIM screenname: nsmanswergirl

Todd Johnson

College Admissions Partners
2600 15th Street SW
Willmar, MN 56201
320-262-9955
todd@collegeadmissionspartners.com

Judith Mackenzie

Mackenzie College Consulting
4705 16th Avenue NE
Seattle, WA 98105
206-527-2287

Lynda McGee

College Counselor
Downtown Magnets High School
lmcgee00@aol.com

Maureen McQuaid

College Focus LLC
Independent Counselor
www.collegefocus.com
niep1@aol.com
650-343-3940

David Miller

Director of College Counseling
Stevenson School
www.rlstevenson.org

Laurie Nimmo

Career Center and College Admissions Coordinator/Independent College
Advising
Healesburg, CA 95448
lnimmo@sonic.net

Terry O'Banion

Former president of the League for Innovation in the Community College
www.league.org

Patrick O'Brien

Former admission officer and consultant-ambassador for the ACT

Judi Robinovitz

Judi Robinovitz Associates and Educational Consulting
www.scoreatthetop.com

Jennifer Tabbush, MBA, CEP

Headed for College
17328 Ventura Boulevard, Suite 216
Encino, CA 91316
818-996-9540
jtabbush@headedforcollege.com
www.headedforcollege.com

Sarah Wilburn

Campus Bound
617-769-0400
swilburn@campusbound.com
Campus Bound helps families across the country find the right colleges, fill out
all of the applications and apply for financial aid.

Index of
America's Best Colleges for B Students

Index of Colleges by Location

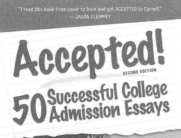

About the Author

Tamra B. Orr is a full-time educational writer and author originally from Indiana and now living in the Pacific Northwest (where she takes a long look at the mountains every single day!). She is the author of more than 50 nonfiction titles for kids, teens and families. Her book, *Violence in Our Schools: Halls of Hope, Halls of Fear* (Scholastic, 2003), won the Best Nonfiction Book of the Year for Teens from the New York Public Library. She is also the author of *Ace the SAT Writing Even If You Hate to Write: Shortcuts and Strategies to Score Higher Regardless of Your Skill Level* (SuperCollege, 2006), *The Purple Cow Guide to Extraordinary Essays* (Scholastic, 2005) and *The Encyclopedia of Notable Hispanic-Americans* (Publications International, 2005).

Orr is involved in education in almost every imaginable way. She writes dozens of nonfiction books each year on a huge variety of topics (from face lifts to fire ants!) and she writes hundreds of stories and items for standardized tests for more than a dozen educational companies. She has a degree in Secondary Education and English from Ball State University in Muncie, Indiana. Orr has been married for more than half of her life to Joseph and together, they have four children ranging in age from 21 to nine. The three that are still living at home are all homeschooled (in between her writing and his messing around with old Volkswagens). Orr has appeared on numerous radio and television shows and has done countless book signings/appearances to promote her books and talk about a variety of issues within education. Since she was once so shy she almost flunked Speech class in high school, this is still an amazing fact to her (and her parents!).

And to think she did all of this…and she was a mere B student!